PRO TOOLS® 10
FOR GAME AUDIO

Greg deBeer

Course Technology PTR

A part of Cengage Learning

COURSE TECHNOLOGY
CENGAGE Learning®

Australia, Brazil, Japan, Korea, Mexico, Singapore, Spain, United Kingdom, United States

COURSE TECHNOLOGY
CENGAGE Learning®

Pro Tools® 10 for Game Audio
Greg deBeer

**Publisher and General Manager,
Course Technology PTR:**
Stacy L. Hiquet

Associate Director of Marketing:
Sarah Panella

Manager of Editorial Services:
Heather Talbot

Marketing Manager:
Mark Hughes

Senior Acquisitions Editor:
Emi Smith

Project and Copy Editor:
Kezia Endsley

Interior Layout:
Shawn Morningstar

Cover Designer:
Avid Technology, Mike Tanamachi

DVD-ROM Producer:
Avid Technology, Brandon Penticuff

Indexer:
Larry Sweazy

Proofreader:
Sam Garvey

For product information and technology assistance, contact us at
Cengage Learning Customer & Sales Support, 1-800-354-9706

For permission to use material from this text or product,
submit all requests online at **cengage.com/permissions**
Further permissions questions can be emailed to
permissionrequest@cengage.com

Avid and Pro Tools are registered trademarks of Avid Technologies, Inc. in the United States. All other trademarks are the property of their respective owners.

This book includes material that was developed in part by the Avid Technical Publications department and the Avid Training department.

All images © Cengage Learning unless otherwise noted.

Library of Congress Control Number: 2011942301

ISBN-13: 978-1-133-78884-3

ISBN-10: 1-133-78884-X

Course Technology, a part of Cengage Learning
20 Channel Center Street
Boston, MA 02210 USA

Cengage Learning is a leading provider of customized learning solutions with office locations around the globe, including Singapore, the United Kingdom, Australia, Mexico, Brazil, and Japan. Locate your local office at:
international.cengage.com/region

Cengage Learning products are represented in Canada by Nelson Education, Ltd.

For your lifelong learning solutions, visit **courseptr.com**.

Visit our corporate Web site at **cengage.com**.

Printed in the
United States of America
1 2 3 4 5 6 7 13 12 11

Acknowledgments

This book includes material that was developed in part by the Avid Technical Publications department and the Avid Training department.

Special thanks to the following individuals: Ric Viers, Douglas Price, Greg Shaw, Frances King, Nick Neutra, Kyle Billingsley, Mary Olson, Jacquie Shriver, Hope Dippel, Jonathan Mayer, Marc Senesac, Joel Yarger, Scott Hanau, Ernest Johnson, Michael Bricker, Paul Lipson, Matt Donner, Mark Altin, Peter Steinbach, and Amy Zimitti.

The media provided with this book is to be used only to complete the exercises contained herein. Rights are not granted to use the footage/sound materials in any commercial or non-commercial production or video.

Sound effects files provided by Blastwave FX (www.blastwavefx.com), The New Wave in Sound Effects.

Vehicle sound files provided by Turn 10 Studios, Microsoft Game Studios.

NetMix Lite provided by Creative Network Design (www.creativenetworkdesign.com).

Foley Image provided by Post Creations.

Vehicle Images provided by Zipper Interactive.

Dialogue and music advice from Sony Computer Entertainment.

Technical consulting provided by Eric Kuehnl.

About the Author

Greg deBeer is a senior sound designer for Sony Computer Entertainment America, where he has also worked as a dialogue manager. He has been with Sony for more than 10 years where he has worked on numerous games including *God of War, SOCOM, Lair, Sly Cooper, Hot Shots Golf: FORE!, Syphon Filter, Infamous,* and *Uncharted 2: Among Thieves.* He holds a Bachelor of Arts from Middlebury College, and a Master of Arts from the California Institute of the Arts.

Contents

Lesson 2
Working with Dialogue   29

Exercise 2
Adding Dialogue to the Game   51

Lesson 3
Working with Foley   61

Exercise 3
Adding/Editing Foley Elements   81

Lesson 4
Working with Sound Effects   89

Exercise 4
Adding/Editing Sound Effects   131

Lesson 5
Working with Backgrounds   139

Exercise 5
Adding/Editing Background Elements   165

Lesson 6
Working with Music   173

Exercise 6
Adding Music to the Game   199

Lesson 7
Working with Vehicle Sounds   207

Exercise 7
Adding Vehicle Sounds to the Game   229

Lesson 8
Working with Cinematics   237

Exercise 8
Adding Cinematics to the Game   269

Index   279

Introduction

Welcome to *Pro Tools 10 for Game Audio* and the Avid Learning Series. Pro Tools is well known for its strength in film post-production and music production, but many people don't realize that it is the main workhorse for many professionals in the game audio business as well. In some sense, Pro Tools' great flexibility is also one of its biggest hurdles—it does so much that it can be difficult for someone just learning the tool to know which parts of the program are best suited for the tasks they are trying to accomplish. One of the primary goals of this book is to introduce you to the Pro Tools features that someone getting started working with game audio may find most helpful.

The other main goal of this book is to provide you with a basic introduction to interactivity in an actual game environment. Although Pro Tools is terrific for creating content, it is strictly a linear editor—it has no capacity to work inside a game. To do this generally requires working directly with a game programmer to set up individual triggers for every sound event in the game. For this book a team of game designers and programmers has built that basic framework for you using the Unity game engine, one of the most robust commercially available game engines around. With this framework in place, you will be able to incorporate the sounds you are building as you work your way through the book into an actual game environment.

Using This Book

This book is broken into eight lessons, each of which should take approximately 90 minutes to work through. Each lesson has a walkthrough on the DVD, which is a Pro Tools session and Unity file that you can work on as you read through the lesson, to help reinforce concepts and techniques as you use them. Additionally, at the end of each lesson (except for Lesson 1) is an exercise, which is a second chance for you to work through the materials learned in the lesson, but in a new game environment. Each exercise is optional, and should take an additional 60 minutes or so to work through. Exercises also have corresponding Pro Tools and Unity files on the included DVD.

The lessons should be read sequentially, as information and concepts from earlier lessons are occasionally referenced in later lessons.

Using the DVD

The DVD-ROM included with this book contains media files for the exercises and hands-on projects. It also contains a collection of sound effects for use in the exercises if you do not have access to your own library.

If you purchased an ebook version of this book, you may download the contents from www.courseptr.com/downloads. Please note that you will be redirected to the Cengage Learning site.

You should create a copy of the entire contents of the DVD to your local drive. Included on the DVD are the following folders:

- **BlastwaveFX:** BlastwaveFX (www.blastwavefx.com) has generously donated a collection of sound effects to allow you to work through the exercises included in this book. You can find them all in the BlastwaveFX folder. If you would like additional sound effects to supplement your work, they have a large collection available for purchase.

- **Completed Projects:** The Completed Projects folder contains Unity projects that have already been fleshed out with sound so you can see what a finished product for each lesson might look like. This folder also contains completed versions of all the sound effects files that you will be creating and editing throughout the book in case you want to compare your results.

- **Netmix Lite Installers:** Netmix Lite is the free version of Netmix Pro, developed by Creative Network Design (http://www.creativenetworkdesign.com/) and is a full-featured sound effects librarian. You are not required to install this to complete the exercises in the book, but it may come in handy, and it is bundled with additional sound effects for you to work with when building out the game.

- **Pro Tools Sessions:** This folder contains all of the Pro Tools session templates that you will need to work through the exercises and labs for each lesson. These are template files, so when you open them, it will build a new session for you, which you will need to name and save to your local drive.

- **Unity Projects:** This folder contains all the Unity projects that you will need to work through the exercises and labs for each lesson. There are a lot of supporting files associated with every Unity project, which can be a little overwhelming at first. The file that opens the project will always end with the .unity extension, and is found in the Assets subdirectory for each project.

- **Video Files:** Each unity project has a video associated with it that you will add sound to in Lesson 8. The videos are found in this folder.

Prerequisites

Completion of the following is required prior to beginning this course:

- Required: Pro Tools 101: Introduction to Pro Tools (See http://www.avid.com/US/support/training/courses/Pro-Tools-101-Introduction-to-Pro-Tools)

- Recommended: Pro Tools 110: Pro Tools Production I (See http://www.avid.com/US/support/training/courses/Pro-Tools-110-Pro-Tools-Production-I)

System Requirements

This book assumes that you have a system configuration suitable to run Pro Tools 10. To verify the most recent system requirements, visit:

http://www.avid.com/US/products/Pro-Tools-Software/support

You also will need to download and install the latest version of Unity 3d, which can be found at http://unity3d.com/unity/download/.

Becoming Avid Certified

Avid certification is a tangible, industry-recognized credential that can help you advance your career and provide measurable benefits to your employer. When you're Avid certified, you not only help to accelerate and validate your professional development, but you can also improve your productivity and project success.

Avid offers programs supporting certification in dedicated focus areas, including Media Composer, Sibelius, Pro Tools, Worksurface Operation, and Live Sound.

In order to become certified in Pro Tools, you must enroll in a program at an Avid Learning Partner, where you can complete additional Pro Tools coursework if needed and take your certification exam. For information about how to locate an Avid Learning Partner, please visit: www.avid.com/training.

Pro Tools Certification

Avid offers three levels of Pro Tools certification:

- Pro Tools User

- Pro Tools Operator

- Pro Tools Expert

The 100-, 200-, and 300-level Pro Tools courses are designed to prepare candidates for each of these certification levels, respectively.

User Certification

User certification prepares individuals to operate a Pro Tools system in an independent production environment. Courses/books associated with *User* certification include:

- Pro Tools 101, *Introduction to Pro Tools 10*
- Pro Tools 110, *Pro Tools Production I*

These core courses can be complemented with Pro Tools 130, *Pro Tools for Game Audio*.

Operator Certification

Operator certification prepares engineers and editors to competently operate a Pro Tools system in a professional environment. Candidates can specialize in Music Production, Post-Production, or both.

Courses/books associated with *Operator* certification include:

- Pro Tools 201, *Pro Tools Production II*
- Pro Tools 210M, *Music Production Techniques*
- Pro Tools 210P, *Post Production Techniques*

Control surface certification options and a live sound certification option are also available at the Operator level.

Expert Certification

The *Expert* curriculum offers professionals the highest level of proficiency with individual or networked Pro Tools systems operating in a professional, fast-paced environment. Candidates can specialize in Music Production, Post-Production, and/or ICON worksurface techniques.

Courses associated with *Expert* certification include:

- Pro Tools 310M, *Advanced Music Production Techniques*
- Pro Tools 310P, *Advanced Post Production Techniques*
- Pro Tools 310I, *Advanced ICON Techniques*

DVD-ROM Downloads

If you purchased an ebook version of this book, and the book had a companion DVD-ROM, you may download the contents from www.courseptr.com/downloads.

If your book has a DVD-ROM, please check our website for any updates or errata files. You may download files from www.courseptr.com/downloads.

Understanding the Game Audio Workflow

Designing game audio requires a broad understanding of tools and techniques. This lesson discusses the equipment requirements for this book. This lesson also reviews some common techniques for creating and implementing game audio.

Media Used: Unity project: PTGA_Walkthrough_Complete
Unity project: PTGA_Exercise_Complete

Duration: 90 Minutes

GOALS

- Understand the players
- Understand the workflow
- Assess your audio requirements
- Acquire sound
- Edit your game audio
- Process your game audio
- Master the use of sounds
- Export game audio
- Implement game audio

Understanding the Players

This book makes use of two primary software tools for the creation and implementation of game audio: Pro Tools 10 and Unity 3.4. You will use Pro Tools for all of your sound design and arranging tasks. After completing each sound design task, you will use Unity to implement the game audio elements and test them in a gaming environment.

Pro Tools Systems

In this book, all recording, editing, and mastering of game audio will be accomplished using a Pro Tools system. The book is designed for Pro Tools 10 systems. The exercises can be completed using any audio interface; however, certain features covered in the text require a larger interface, such as an Mbox Pro.

Pro Tools System Configuration

Generally speaking, a modest Pro Tools system is more than adequate for game audio. Let's take a look at two basic Pro Tools configurations:

- **Mbox configuration (see Figure 1.1).**

   In this configuration, the recording engineer and the talent will both monitor audio through the same output on the Mbox. As with any host-based Pro Tools setup, it's important to remember that the hardware buffer size must remain low in order to route signal through Pro Tools with minimal latency while tracking.

In the Avid Learning Series   For more information on hardware buffer size, see "Optimizing Host Based Pro Tools Performance" in the "Pro Tools 101: An Introduction to Pro Tools 10" book by Avid.

- **Mbox Pro configuration (with discrete cue mix) (see Figure 1.2)**

   In this configuration, the recording engineer and the talent will monitor audio through separate outputs on the Mbox Pro: the regular monitor output will go to the engineer's control room monitors, and a custom cue output will go to the voice actor's headphones. This is easily accomplished on an Mbox Pro by sending the 3-4 outputs from Pro Tools to an additional output on the interface. Once again, it's important to remember that the hardware buffer size must remain low in order to route signal through Pro Tools with minimal latency while tracking.

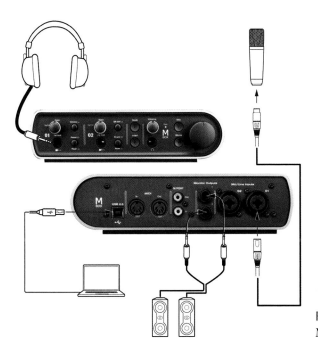

Figure 1.1
Mbox configuration

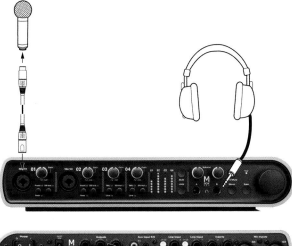

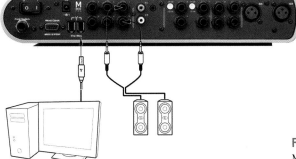

Figure 1.2
Mbox Pro configuration

Unity 3.4

Unity 3.4 is a multi-platform game development tool. It is designed from the ground up to make game application development as easy as possible. Unity 3.4 has an integrated editor, a highly optimized graphics engine, and deployment options that include Mac OS, Windows 2000/XP/Vista/ 7, and web browsers. A single Unity project can be published to all of these platforms. In addition, Unity can be expanded to include iPhone application development.

It should be noted that the Unity 3.4 audio toolset is not as powerful as many proprietary audio engines and audio "middleware" options that are available today. Such audio toolsets offer enhanced features such as sophisticated randomization routines, and dedicated vehicle engine design tools, to name a few. However, for the purposes of this book, the integrated nature of Unity makes it an excellent choice.

Some popular audio middleware solutions include:

- FMOD: www.fmod.org
- Wwise: www.audiokinetic.com

Understanding the Workflow

When developing audio for games, the game development team will usually establish an audio workflow. This workflow will vary depending on schedules and available resources. Let's take a look at a typical workflow.

Example workflow:

1. Assess audio requirements
2. Acquire sound assets
3. Edit sound assets
4. Process sound assets
5. Master sound assets
6. Export sound assets
7. Implement sound assets

It's important to understand that these workflow steps may be repeated multiple times during the game development process. These repetitions (or "iterations") are sometimes due to changes in game audio requirements. More often, multiple iterations are a result of dissatisfaction with an implemented sound. This can result in stepping back several steps in the process depending on the particular aspect of the sound that is unsatisfactory. For example, if the radio processing on a sound asset is not adequate, you would probably return to Step 4 (process sound assets) and make an alteration. The resulting sound asset would then need to be mastered, exported, and implemented again.

Assessing Audio Requirements

The first step in designing sound for a game is to decide where sounds are necessary. This process usually begins with the game producer. The producer will then meet with sound personnel to convey their vision for the sound and music design. This communication is vital for determining not only the placement of sound elements, but also the style that will guide the creative process. It is important to remember that the purpose for game audio is to enhance the playing experience. Occasionally, the best use of sound is no sound at all!

Standard Sound Categories

Sound elements can be grouped into several standard sound categories. Most of these types of sounds appear in a typical game in one form or another.

- **Dialogue**—Spoken dialogue to create context and also to enhance gameplay.
- **Foley**—Foley sounds for footsteps on different materials as well as weapon handling.
- **Sound effects**—High-impact sounds for the weapons and explosions.
- **Backgrounds**—Ambient sounds that reinforce the game location.
- **Music**—Music cues that change to follow the action.
- **Vehicles**—Realistic engine sounds that accompany vehicle gameplay.
- **Cinematic post-production**—Video sections (such as the intro cinematic) that establish the game world in just a few seconds.

It's helpful to keep these categories in mind when assessing audio requirements for a game or any other form of interactive media.

Acquiring Sound

Once audio requirements for the game title have been determined, you'll need to start gathering sound assets. These assets, or "raw" sounds, will become the basis for the final sounds that will be implemented in the game.

Generally, two methods are available for gathering sounds to begin the design process: recording sounds and working with sound libraries.

Recording Sounds

Recording new sound elements is a great way to add something unique to a game title. It's also a good way to get the exact sounds that are needed for a particular game element, such as a special weapon or vehicle. Sound elements are recorded in one of two ways: studio recording and field recording.

Studio Recording

Studio recording refers to the practice of recording new sound elements in a controlled studio environment. This type of recording is discussed in detail in Lesson 3, "Working with Foley," and Lesson 2, "Working with Dialogue."

Field Recording

Field recording refers to the practice of taking portable recorders to a non-studio location to record new sound elements. Some of the most popular uses for field recording are for gathering weapon and vehicle sounds. Feature films have been recording guns, cars, tanks, and planes in their native environment for many years. In recent years, game budgets have grown large enough to take advantage of the same recording techniques.

Many field recorders are available on the market (see Figure 1.3). The newest recorders offer more features at a lower cost than ever before. Features to consider when purchasing a portable recorder include the supported sample rate and bit depth, the number of audio channels, the supported types of storage media, battery life, and synchronization capabilities.

Figure 1.3
An example of a field recorder:
the M-Audio Microtrack II

The field recorder workflow in Pro Tools is elegant and powerful. Pro Tools 7.2 added an entire suite of new tools for working with field recorders.

The supported field recorder metadata includes:

- Scene
- Take
- Channel name
- Duration
- File comment
- Original time stamp
- User time stamp
- And much more...

The Original Time Stamp metadata is of particular importance. This data allows multiple channels of audio to be synchronized in Pro Tools. This feature is especially useful when multiple recorders are used simultaneously (as on some large gun recording sessions) or to find alternate takes after the media have been imported into Pro Tools.

On the Web

For a comprehensive list of field recorder features in Pro Tools, see the "Field Recorder Workflow Guide" at Avid.com.

Working with Sound Libraries

Most sound elements in a game are designed by combining elements that are transferred (or "pulled") from sound libraries. An established sound designer or game audio department usually has a large library of proprietary assets that have been accumulated over many years. In addition, this proprietary library is almost always supplemented with a variety of commercial sound libraries. Commercial libraries are a great starting point for the novice sound designer. Obviously, it can be somewhat difficult (not to mention illegal) to make your own explosion recordings!

Sound Libraries

Many good sound libraries are available for purchase. Most offer a starter collection that includes a broad range of sounds to assist the novice sound designer.

Some sound library manufacturers:

- **BlastwaveFX:** www.blastwavefx.com
- **Hollywood Edge:** www.hollywoodedge.com
- **Sound Ideas:** www.sound-ideas.com

Sound Librarians

When it comes to browsing and searching sound libraries, Pro Tools users have two primary options: DigiBase and third-party applications.

DigiBase is part of the Pro Tools software. It is a powerful tool for searching and cataloging audio files. It is certainly adequate for the novice sound designer or anyone who has a relatively small collection of sounds. However, DigiBase doesn't offer some of the advanced functionality that is found in popular third-party librarians. Such features include clip editing, pitch shifting during audition and import, sophisticated file renaming, enhanced metadata manipulation, and extensive collaboration tools, to name a few. Most game sound professionals invest in a third-party application for sound library browsing.

Some third-party sound effects librarians:

- **NetMix Pro/NetMix Lite (see Figure 1.4):** www.creativenetworkdesign.com

- **SoundMiner:** www.soundminer.com

Figure 1.4
Creative Network Design's NetMix Lite

Editing Game Audio

An overview of all of the editing tools and techniques available in Pro Tools is well beyond the scope of this book. However, certain tools and techniques are vital to the efficient creation of game audio assets.

Note: Additional task specific editing tools and techniques are covered in subsequent lessons of this book.

Creating New Tracks

After you have created a session, the next step is to create new tracks. This is accomplished using the New Tracks dialog box (see Figure 1.5).

Figure 1.5
New Tracks dialog box

To create new tracks:

1. Choose **TRACK > NEW** or press **COMMAND+SHIFT+N** (Mac) or **CTRL+SHIFT+N** (Windows).

2. Choose the number of tracks, track format, track type, and timebase.

3. Click **CREATE**.

Tip: It is also possible to add tracks with different track formats simultaneously.

To add tracks with a different format:

1. Click the **ADD ROW** button (+) at the end of the current row. A new row will appear (see Figure 1.6).

Figure 1.6
Adding multiple tracks with different formats

Whole File Clips vs. Subset Clips

A whole file clip represents a complete audio file on your hard drive. These files may have been recorded in the current Pro Tools session, or they may have been imported from a different session or a sound effects library. Whole file clips are displayed in bold type in the Clip List (see Figure 1.7). These clips are not stored as part of the Pro Tools session file, but are actually separate files that are stored somewhere on your hard drive.

As you begin to edit whole file clips, you create smaller clips called *subset clips* or simply *clips*. Subset clips are displayed in plain type in the Clip List. These subset clips actually point back to the original whole file clip from which they were derived. They only exist in the Pro Tools session file and not as separate files on the hard drive. Therefore, subset clips must be consolidated or exported to create a new whole file clip that can be implemented in a game.

Figure 1.7
Clip List

 For more information, refer to the "Organizing and Recording
In the Avid Audio" section of the Pro Tools 101 book.
Learning Series

Smart Tool

The Smart Tool (see Figure 1.8) is the ultimate tool for editing in Pro Tools. It
allows you to access the Trimmer, Selector, and Grabber tools and create fades and
crossfades without changing tools. Throughout this book, you should use the
Smart Tool whenever possible.

Figure 1.8
Smart Tool selected in the toolbar

To enable the Smart Tool, do one of the following:

■ Click the Smart Tool icon (the bracket above the Trimmer, Selector, and
  Grabber tools) in the Edit window toolbar.

■ Press **F6+F7** or **F7+F8**.

The only drawback to the Smart Tool is that you may find it difficult to switch it
to the desired tool when clips are very small. Fortunately, this is easy to overcome
using Zoom toggle.

 For more information about the Smart Tool, see "Smart Tool" in the
In the Avid Pro Tools 101 book.
Learning Series

Zoom Toggle

The Zoom toggle function is quite useful for editing, especially when used in conjunction with the Smart Tool. When Zoom toggle is enabled, the selection can zoom
both horizontally and vertically based on the Pro Tools preferences. In addition, the
Track view for the selected track(s) can be changed (see Figures 1.9a and 1.9b).

Figure 1.9a
Selection prior
to enabling
Zoom toggle

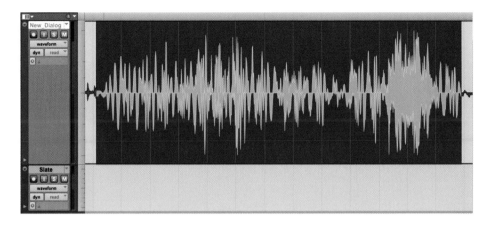

Figure 1.9b
Same selection
after enabling
Zoom toggle

You can access the Zoom toggle preferences by choosing Setup > Preferences and selecting the Editing tab (see Figure 1.10).

Figure 1.10
Zoom toggle preferences

**In the Avid
Learning Series**

For more information about Zoom toggle, see "Zoom Toggle Button" in the book *Pro Tools 101: An Introduction to Pro Tools 10.*

To enable and disable Zoom toggle:

■ Click the **ZOOM TOGGLE** button in the Edit window toolbar (see Figure 1.11).

Figure 1.11
Zoom toggle button in the toolbar

Or

1. Enable Commands Keyboard Focus by clicking the **COMMANDS KEYBOARD FOCUS (A-Z)** button in the Edit window (see Figure 1.12) or pressing **OPTION+COMMAND+1** (Mac) or **CTRL+ALT+1** (Windows).

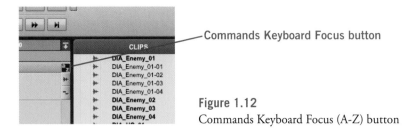

Commands Keyboard Focus button

Figure 1.12
Commands Keyboard Focus (A-Z) button

2. Press the **E KEY** on the computer keyboard.

Tab To Transients

In Pro Tools, standard Tab key functionality moves the cursor between clip boundaries (and sync points). Adding Option (Mac) or Alt (Windows) when pressing Tab moves the cursor backwards between clip boundaries.

When Tab To Transients mode is enabled, the Tab key moves between clip boundaries, but also stops on waveform transients. This is particularly useful when editing a clip that contains a series of sound effects. Pressing Tab repeatedly will move the cursor through the clip, automatically stopping on each transient. You can use a variety of edit commands along with Tab To Transients to quickly isolate the desired portion of the clip.

To toggle Tab To Transients, do one of the following:

■ Click the **TAB TO TRANSIENTS** button in the toolbar (see Figure 1.13).

Figure 1.13
Tab to Transients button in the toolbar

■ Press **OPTION+COMMAND+TAB** (Mac) or **CTRL+ALT+TAB** (Windows).

In the Avid Learning Series

For more information on Tab To Transients, see "Tabbing to Transient Points" in the book *Pro Tools 101: An Introduction to Pro Tools 10.*

Consolidate

The Consolidate command is one of the most used commands during the creation of game audio assets. Consolidate creates a single, whole file clip from any selection (see Figures 1.14a and 1.14b). The selection may include whole file clips, subset clips, fades and crossfades, and silence. This is a critical step in the game audio workflow because the resulting clip will then be ready to be exported using the Export Clips as Files command. If a clip with fades is not consolidated before using Export Clips as Files, the fades will not be applied to the resulting file.

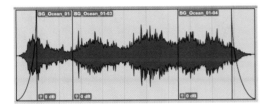

Figure 1.14a
Clip prior to consolidation

Figure 1.14b
Same clip after consolidation

To use the Consolidate command:

1. Select the clip or clips to be consolidated. Be sure to include any fades or crossfades.

2. Select EDIT > CONSOLIDATE or press OPTION+SHIFT+3 (Mac) or ALT+SHIFT+3 (Windows).

Processing Game Audio

When sound designers are building game assets, two techniques come into play: the layering of raw sound elements to create a more complex sound effect, and the application of signal processing to some or all of the layers. In Pro Tools, the layering process is accomplished using additional tracks as well as standard editing and automation techniques like those mentioned in the previous section. The second technique, applying signal processing, is accomplished using plug-ins.

Two types of plug-ins are used in the sound design process: file-based plug-ins and real-time plug-ins. In Pro Tools, these two plug-in types are called AudioSuite and TDM/RTAS respectively.

AudioSuite

AudioSuite plug-ins are used for file based signal processing (see Figure 1.15). While AudioSuite plug-ins can be previewed in real time, the process must be applied to the clip to achieve the desired result. When you apply an AudioSuite process, you can choose to create a new whole file clip or to modify the original whole file clip. Creating a new clip is almost always the best choice.

Figure 1.15
AudioSuite plug-in

Most Pro Tools plug-ins have both real-time and AudioSuite versions. This gives the sound designer a choice either to run the plug-in in real time or to apply the plug-in process to the file. However, certain processes in Pro Tools can only be applied using AudioSuite, such as Gain, Normalize, Reverse, and more.

As you work through this book, you will use the following AudioSuite settings (unless otherwise noted):

- **File Mode:** Create individual files

- **Selection Reference:** Playlist

- **Use In Playlist:** Enabled

- **Process Mode:** Clip by clip

In the Avid Learning Series For more information on file-based plug-ins, see "AudioSuite Overview" in the Pro Tools 110 book.

TDM/RTAS

TDM (Time Division Multiplexing) and RTAS (Real Time AudioSuite) plug-ins are used for real-time signal processing (see Figure 1.16). These plug-ins can be inserted into audio tracks, aux inputs, instrument tracks, and master faders in Pro Tools.

Figure 1.16
SansAmp PSA-1, an example of an RTAS plug-in

TDM and RTAS plug-ins offer similar functionality. However, their computations are powered from two different sources: TDM plug-ins rely upon the processing power of Pro Tools HD hardware, whereas RTAS plug-ins are powered by the host computer.

The primary benefit of real-time plug-ins is that parameter changes are instantly audible on the track. In addition, up to ten plug-ins can run in series on each track in Pro Tools. The sound designer can modify the plug-in settings as necessary during the design process without rendering the results to a new clip. An additional benefit of this real-time processing is that almost all parameters can be automated using Pro Tools automation.

In the Avid Learning Series   For more information on real-time plug-ins, see "Real Time Plug Ins" in the Pro Tools 101 book.

Mastering Sounds

The term mastering has several meanings in the audio industry. In music, mastering engineers apply the finishing touches to a song or collection of songs. In post production, mastering engineers create film soundtrack "printmasters" in a variety of stereo and surround formats. Game audio mastering usually refers to the final tweaking of frequency and amplitude before a sound is implemented in the game. A typical mastering signal path may be composed of a variety of plug-ins including Multi Band Compression, Limiting, EQ, and many more.

Ultra-Maximizer

Game audio mastering almost always manipulates both the average and peak amplitude of the output signal. This is generally accomplished using a plug-in called an ultra-maximizer (see Figures 1.17-1.19). An ultra-maximizer offers peak limiting and sound maximizing in a single plug-in. Most ultra-maximizers have a look-ahead buffer that allows them to anticipate peaks in program material. This zero attack time results in much more predictable performance than a traditional limiter plug-in. Furthermore, the ultra-maximizer offers a ceiling control that can push limits extremely close to 0dBFS without fear of clipping.

Note: dBFS stands for decibels relative to full scale, and is always presented as a negative number. Full scale is the maximum amplitude digital audio can reach without clipping, so audio at –6dBFS is 6dB below that value. For more information on how decibels are measured, see Chapter 1 of the Pro Tools 101 book.

Figure 1.17
A clip before using an ultra-maximizer

Figure 1.18
The same clip after using an ultra-maximizer

Figure 1.19
AudioSuite and RTAS versions of Maxim, an ultra-maximizer included with Pro Tools

Dither

When the session bit depth is 24 bit and the destination file bit depth is 16 bit or 8 bit, dither must be used. Dither is a complex process that adds noise to the signal to minimize the low level quantization errors that occur with bit depth reduction. The result is a destination file that actually preserves some of the additional dynamic range that the higher bit depth can represent. Two dither plug-ins are included with Pro Tools: Dither and POWr Dither (see Figure 1.20). POWr Dither uses an advanced dither algorithm and should always be used over standard Dither. All dither plug-ins should be inserted as the last insert on the Master Fader.

Figure 1.20
Dither (left) and POWr Dither (right) RTAS plug-ins

In the Avid Learning Series   For more information on dither, see "Adding Dither to the Master Fader" in the Pro Tools 110 book.

Exporting Game Audio

Although Pro Tools offers a variety of methods for exporting files, three are used predominantly in game audio:

- Bounce to Disk
- Bounce to Tracks
- Export Clips as Files

Bounce to Disk

Bounce to Disk (see Figure 1.21) records the output of a selected bus or output path to hard disk in real time. This real-time recording capability is both a strength and a weakness. Real-time recording is advantageous because it can combine an entire session's worth of tracks and plug-ins in a single pass. The disadvantage comes when you need to export many small clips, because the process must be repeated for each clip.

Figure 1.21
Bounce to Disk

Bounce to Tracks

The Bounce to Tracks technique is similar to Bounce to Disk in that a selected bus is recorded in real time. The difference with Bounce to Tracks is that multiple buses can be recorded to multiple audio tracks simultaneously (see Figure 1.22). In addition, because the resulting bounced clips are still in the session, additional editing and processing can be applied. Typically, the Export Clips as Files command is used to export the clips that result from using Bounce to Tracks.

Note: Bounce To Tracks is a recording technique, and not actually a specific Pro Tools command like Bounce To Disk or Export Clips as Files.

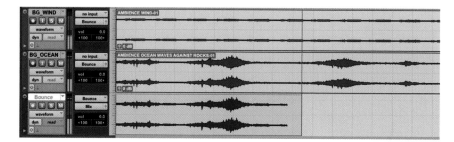

Figure 1.22
The top two tracks are being bounced to the bottom track using the Bounce to Tracks technique

Export Clips as Files

The Export Clips as Files command (see Figure 1.23) provides a faster than real time process which simply copies the contents of all selected clips to new files on disk. This is the only way to export a "batch" of clips from Pro Tools with a single command. Because the clips are copied directly to new files, no automation or real-time processing is applied. Therefore, it's best to use AudioSuite plug-ins, Bounce to Tracks, or the Consolidate command to prepare clips before using Export Clips as Files.

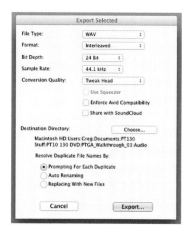

Figure 1.23
The Export Selected dialog box

Implementing Game Audio

Once your clips have been exported from Pro Tools, they are ready to be implemented in the game. For your purposes here, this will be accomplished through Unity 3.4.

The Unity 3.4 Interface

The Unity interface (see Figure 1.24) can seem a bit overwhelming at first glance. Fortunately, you'll be using only a small part of the Unity feature set to implement your game audio.

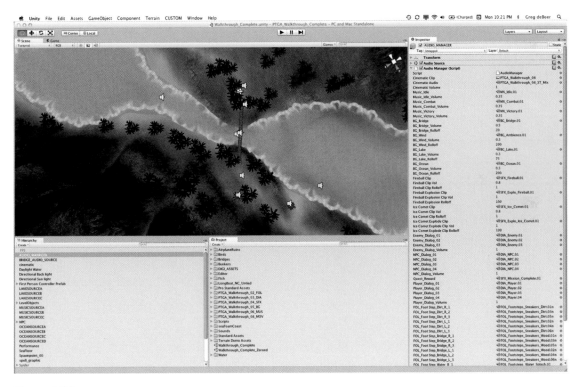

Figure 1.24
Default Unity 3.4 window layout

Caution: You should never move project assets around using the system OS since this will break any metadata associated with the asset. Always use the Project view to organize your assets.

Unity Terminology

You should start by looking at some important Unity terminology:

- **Project file**—A Project file is a complete game. It includes all of the game's scenes, programming code, art, and audio assets.

- **Scene file**—A Scene file is a game "level." Most projects will include many scenes.

- **Project view**—Every Unity project contains an Assets folder; the contents of this folder are presented in the Project view (see Figure 1.25). This is where you view all of the assets that are included in the game. Assets include scenes, scripts, models, textures, audio files, and more. If you right-click on any asset in the Project view, you can choose Reveal in Finder (Mac) or Reveal in Explorer (Windows) to actually see the asset in your file system.

  To add assets to your project, you can drag any file from your OS into the Project view, or use Assets > Import New Asset. The asset can then be implemented in the game. For more information about working with assets, see Importing Audio into Unity in the "Implementing Game Audio" section of this lesson.

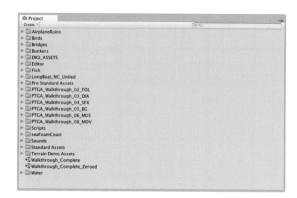

Figure 1.25
Unity 3.4 Project view

- **Scene**—Scenes are also stored in the Project view. Scenes are essentially individual levels of the game. For example, there is usually a Scene entitled "Level 1" that represents the default Scene in a Project. In your Projects, the default scenes are "Walkthrough_01" and "Exercise_01." To save the current Scene including all of your adjustments to game audio assignments and settings, use Command+S (Mac) or Ctrl+S (Windows).

- **Hierarchy view**—The Hierarchy view contains every GameObject in the current scene (see Figure 1.26). Some of these are custom objects, such as the AUDIO_MANAGER that you will be using to adjust game audio assignments and settings. As objects are added to and removed from a scene, they will appear and disappear from the Hierarchy view as well.

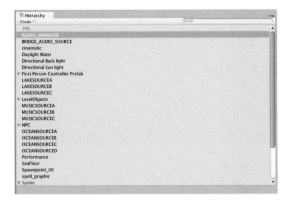

Figure 1.26
Unity 3.4 Hierarchy view

■ **Inspector view**—Games in Unity are made up of multiple GameObjects that include models, scripts, sounds, or other elements. The Inspector view displays detailed information about your currently selected GameObject, including all attached components and their properties (see Figure 1.27). Here, you modify the functionality of GameObjects in your scene.

Figure 1.27
Unity 3.4 Inspector view

Over the course of this book, you will be working with a single GameObject in the Inspector view: AUDIO_MANAGER. This GameObject has been created to simplify audio implementation. It includes assignment, volume, and attenuation controls for every audio asset in the game levels.

Any property that is displayed in the Inspector can be directly modified. You can use the Inspector to change variables at runtime to experiment and find the best settings for your game.

- **Game view**—The Game view is rendered from a "camera" in your game (see Figure 1.28). It is representative of your final, published game. This is the window where the game is displayed when you enter Play mode.

Figure 1.28
Unity 3.4 Game view

- **Play Mode buttons**—Use the Play Mode buttons in the Toolbar (see Figure 1.29) to control the Editor Play mode and to see (and hear) how your published game will play. While in Play mode, any changes you make are temporary and will be reset when you exit Play mode. The Editor UI will darken to remind you of this.

You can also enter and exit Play mode by pressing Command+P (Mac) or Ctrl+P (Windows).

To pause the action, press the Pause button or press Command+Shift+P (Mac) or Ctrl+Shift+P (Windows).

Figure 1.29
Play Mode buttons

■ **Game view control bar**—The first drop-down menu on the Game view control bar is the Aspect drop-down menu (see Figure 1.30). Here, you can force the aspect ratio of the Game view window to different values. This can be used to test how your game will look on monitors with different aspect ratios.

Figure 1.30
Aspect drop-down menu in the Game view control bar

Further to the right is the Maximize on Play toggle (see Figure 1.31). While enabled, the Game view will maximize itself to 100% of your Editor window for a nice full screen preview when you enter Play mode.

Figure 1.31
Additional controls in the Game view control bar

■ **Stats button**—This shows the Rendering Statistics window that is useful for viewing system performance (see Figure 1.32).

Figure 1.32
Game view with the Rendering Statistics window displayed in the upper-right

■ **Scene view**—The Scene view is like an interactive sandbox for the game designer. Scene view is used to select and position environments, the player, the camera, enemies, and all other GameObjects (see Figure 1.33). You won't be working with the Scene view in this book.

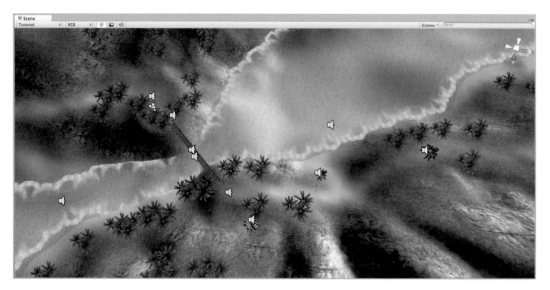

Figure 1.33
Unity 3.4 Scene view

Unity Design Considerations

Unity includes several features in its audio toolset that are important to keep in mind.

Using Positional Audio

Positional audio is audio that has its panning and attenuation properties controlled by Unity. With positional audio, the Unity audio engine simulates the location and distance of sounds by adjusting pan and volume automatically. Dialogue and sound effects are generally enabled for positional audio.

When an audio clip is not enabled for positional audio, it does not have panning or attenuation in the Unity audio engine and, therefore, is always played at the original volume and pan values determined by the asset file. Music and cinematic clips are generally *not* enabled for positional audio.

Tip: Positional audio is also referred to as *3D sound* in Unity.

Audio Source Volume

In Unity, "volume" is defined as how loud a sound is when played at a virtual distance of 1 meter from the player. The valid range is 0.0 (silent) to 1.0 (full scale).

Audio Source Rolloff Factor

In Unity, the "rolloff factor" (also known as the "falloff factor") is defined as how quickly a sound fades as the player travels away from the audio source. In Unity 3.0 and later, the rolloff value is entered in feet. The entered value represents the maximum distance at which a sound source will be audible.

Importing Audio into Unity

To import a folder of audio assets:

1. Open the desired project in Unity.

2. Locate the folder containing clips exported from Pro Tools.

3. Drag and drop the folder into the Project view in Unity. Unity will import the entire folder and copy its contents to the Assets folder for the project.

Or

1. Open the desired project in Unity.

2. Select **ASSETS > IMPORT NEW ASSET** or right-click in the Project view and select **IMPORT NEW ASSET** (see Figure 1.34).

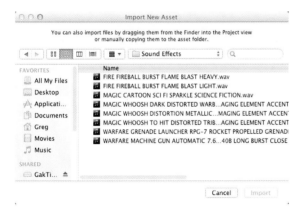

Figure 1.34
Import New Asset dialog box

3. Navigate to the folder containing clips exported from Pro Tools. Select the asset you want to import and click the Import button. Unity will import the individual asset and copy it to the Assets folder for the project.

Assigning Audio Assets to Triggers

Normally, audio assets are assigned directly to individual GameObjects in Unity. For this book, a single GameObject called AUDIO_MANAGER (see Figure 1.35) has been built for you, which places all of the assignment, level, rolloff, and other controls in one place.

To access the settings of the AUDIO_MANAGER GameObject:

1. Double-click the scene in the Project view. The Hierarchy view will change to show all of the GameObjects associated with the scene.

2. Click the AUDIO_MANAGER GameObject in the Hierarchy view. The Inspector view will change to show the AUDIO_MANAGER parameters.

To assign an asset to an audio source in AUDIO_MANAGER:

1. Locate the audio source you want to assign.

Figure 1.35
An audio source and its associated parameters in the AUDIO_MANAGER

2. Click the circle to the right of the currently assigned asset. The Select AudioClip dialog box will open and display the audio assets that have been imported into the project (see Figure 1.36).

Figure 1.36
The Unity 3.4 Select AudioClip dialog box showing available audio assets

3. Select the asset that you want to assign to the audio source.

Tip: In Unity 3.0 or later, you can search through the imported assets by typing a text string into the search field at the top of the Select AudioClip dialog box.

To modify the volume of the audio source:

1. Locate the audio source you want to modify.

2. Type a new value into the Volume field. Although Unity will let you enter any value, the valid range is 0-1, with 1 representing the full volume of the audio file.

To modify the distance rolloff of the audio source:

1. Locate the audio source you want to modify.

2. Type a new value into the Rolloff (or Falloff) field. In Unity 3.0 and later, this value is entered in feet. The entered value represents the maximum distance at which a sound source will be audible.

Walkthrough: Reviewing a Finished Game

In this walkthrough you will learn how to identify the different types of audio used in a game. Before you get started with the first training lesson, take a look at the finished Unity Walkthrough game project that you will be creating during this book. You can find it on the DVD, in the Completed Projects folder (see PTGA Files > Completed Projects > PTGA_Completed_Unity > PTGA_Walkthroughs_ Complete > Assets > PTGA_Walkthroughs_Complete.unity).

Some things to notice in the finished game projects:

■ **Dialogue**—Spoken dialogue to create context and also to enhance gameplay.

■ **Foley**—Foley sounds for footsteps on different materials as well as weapon handling.

■ **Sound effects**—High-impact sounds for the weapons and explosions.

■ **Backgrounds**—Ambient sounds that reinforce the game location.

■ **Music**—Music cues that change to follow the action.

■ **Cinematics**—Video sections, such as the intro cinematic, that establish the game world in just a few seconds.

Summary

In this lesson you were introduced to the game audio workflow. You learned about:

- The critical hardware and software components that are necessary for sound design and implementation.

- Techniques for acquiring sound elements through recording or libraries.

- Pro Tools features for editing, processing, mastering, and exporting game audio assets.

- Audio implementation in Unity with a tour of a finished game level.

Review/Discussion Questions

1. How does field recording differ from traditional studio recording? (See "Acquiring Sound" on page 5.)

2. Which Pro Tools edit tool can function as the Trimmer, Selector, and Grabber tools? (See "Editing Game Audio" on page 8.)

3. What type of Pro Tools plug-in performs file-based processing? (See "Processing Game Audio" on page 13.)

4. When converting audio from a higher bit depth to a lower bit depth, what process should be applied? (See "Mastering Sounds" on page 15.)

5. Which Pro Tools export technique is faster than real time? (See "Exporting Game Audio" on page 17.)

6. In Unity 3.0 and later, the distance rolloff is entered in feet. What does this number represent? (See "Implementing Game Audio" on page 19.)

Working with Dialogue

In this lesson, you'll look at techniques for recording, editing, and processing dialogue.

Media Used: Pro Tools Session: PTGA_Walkthrough_02
Unity Project: PTGA_Walkthroughs

Duration: 90 Minutes

GOALS

- Understand the types of game dialogue
- Record dialogue
- Edit dialogue
- Process dialogue
- Export dialogue
- Implement dialogue

Understanding Game Dialogue

Not all games have or need dialogue. When it's present though, how dialogue is implemented can be critical to a game. Poorly written or poorly recorded dialogue can ruin an otherwise well-crafted game. On the other hand, when dialogue is implemented well, it can draw the players into the virtual world and create a more compelling gaming experience.

Understanding the Types of Game Dialogue

In game audio, the term "dialogue" refers to any audio that is created using voice actors or "voice talent." This might include any of the following:

- **Narration**—Generically referred to as "voiceover." Narration is often used at the beginning or end of game levels to transition to another level. The narrator does not usually appear onscreen.

- **Gameplay Dialogue**—Dialogue that takes place while the player is actually "playing" the game level. This dialogue can be further broken down into two categories:
  - **Dialogue**—Lines of scripted dialogue that are spoken by the player or another character that appears onscreen.
  - **Efforts**—Additional dialogue that is triggered when the player jumps, throws, and so on.

- **Cinematic Dialogue**—Dialogue that takes place during pre-rendered movies. (See Lesson 8 of this book for more about cinematics.)

- **Group Dialogue**—Group dialogue is often referred to as "walla" for the sound that a crowd of people makes when speaking all at once. Group dialogue may have parts where the dialogue is intelligible, but the goal is usually to have no intelligible dialogue so that the audio can be repurposed when localized into other languages.

- **Localized Dialogue**—Most of the previous elements (except group dialogue) are replaced with foreign language dialogue when a game is released in other countries. A common European baseline is to record in French, Italian, German, and Spanish (collectively known by the acronym FIGS), but some larger games can be localized to more than 20 languages across the globe!

Creating Scripts

Most large budget games have a dedicated writer who writes and maintains the script. Don't be surprised if the script is constantly evolving before, during, and after the dialogue-recording process! There are two basic script types in the game dialogue world: the spreadsheet-style script, and the movie-style script. The two types of scripts are not necessarily exclusive—many larger projects will keep their script in a database and export both spreadsheet and movie style scripts, depending on who the script is for.

At a minimum, a script will contain three critical pieces of information for each line:

- **Character**—The name of the character in the game.

- **Filename**—The name of the final edited and mastered audio file that will be implemented in the game.

- **Dialogue**—The line (or lines) of dialogue that the voice actor will perform.

Often additional information is included, such as scene numbering or additional notes, depending on the nature of the script.

Spreadsheet-Style Script

Typically, producers and editors prefer the spreadsheet-style script. They are often interested in viewing the script data in multiple ways. For example an editor would likely want to sort the script by character, so that it's easy to see and edit all of a character's lines at once, whereas a producer may want to see how many lines there are in any given scene. Considering many games have 10,000 lines of dialogue or more, the flexible sorting of a spreadsheet can be invaluable. Let's take a look at a spreadsheet-style script, shown in the following table.

Line #	Scene	Character	Filename	Dialogue	Notes
01	01a	NPC	DIA_NPC_01	Hello. My name is Amanda. Can you help me? There are three spiders on the other side of the bridge and they are blocking my way home.	Offer Quest
02	01a	Player	DIA_Player_01	OK. I think I can help you with that.	Accept Quest
03	01a	Player	DIA_Player_02	That's one down.	First Kill
04	01a	Player	DIA_Player_03	That's two down. One more to go.	Second Kill
05	01a	Player	DIA_Player_04	That's the last one. Now I just need to get back to Amanda.	Third Kill
06	01a	NPC	DIA_NPC_02	Hey! You're not finished yet.	Quest Incomplete
07	01a	NPC	DIA_NPC_03	Thanks for helping me. Now I can go home.	Quest Complete

Line #	Scene	Character	Filename	Dialogue	Notes
08	01a	NPC	DIA_NPC_04	Thanks again for helping me!	Quest Complete. Player Returns
09	01a	Enemy	DIA_Enemy_01	(Small Scream)	Small Damage
10	01a	Enemy	DIA_Enemy_02	(Large Scream)	Large Damage
11	01a	Enemy	DIA_Enemy_03	(Death Scream)	Death
12	01a	Player	DIA_Player_05	Incendia!	Cast Fireball Spell
13	01a	Player	DIA_Player_06	Glacies!	Cast Ice Comet Spell
14	02a	Player	DIA_Player_07	I'd been lost for three days when I spotted an island in the distance...	Cinematic Voiceover

Note: In game terminology, an NPC is a *non-player character*. This refers to any character in the game who is not the one controlled by the person playing the game.

Movie-Style Script

Actors and VO directors tend to prefer the movie-style script, as they typically aren't closely involved with the development of the game, and are coming to the table knowing very little about the story. The movie-style script does a better job of explaining the setting and context, and is much easier to read on the page. In addition, the actor can see the lines spoken by other characters that come before and after the current line, which can help tremendously with performance. However, if you can only have the script in a single format (which will be the case for most independent games) the spreadsheet-style script is a better choice due to its flexibility. Let's take a look at a movie-style script:

Scene 1A (OVER GAMEPLAY)

EXT. ISLAND SAVANNAH

Player is approaching the NPC. He doesn't know what to expect.

(DIA_NPC_01)

Amanda

Hello. My name is Amanda. Can you help me? There are three spiders on the other side of the bridge and they are blocking my way home.

(DIA_Player_01)

Player

OK. I think I can help you with that.

If player returns before completing the mission:

(DIA_NPC_02)

Amanda

Hey! You're not finished yet!

If player returns after completing the mission:

(DIA_NPC_03)

Amanda

Thanks for helping me. Now I can go home.

If player returns again after completing the mission:

(DIA_NPC_04)

Amanda

Thanks again for helping me!

Scene 1B (OVER GAMEPLAY)

EXT. ISLAND SAVANNAH

After player kills first spider:

(DIA_Player_02)

Player

That's one down!

After player kills second spider:

(DIA _Player_03)

Continues...

Player

That's two down. Just one more to go!

After player kills third spider:

(DIA _Player_04)

Player

That's the last one. Now I just need to get back to Amanda.

As player shoots enemy:

(DIA _Enemy_01)

Enemy

(Small Damage Sound)

(DIA _Enemy_02)

Enemy

(Large Damage Sound)

Enemy death:

(DIA _Enemy_03)

Enemy

(Dying sound)

Player spell casting sounds:

(DIA_Player_05)

Player

Incendia! (Cast Fireball spell.)

(DIA_Player_06)

Player

Glacies! (Cast Ice Comet spell.)

Player cinematic narration:

(DIA_Player_07)

Player

I'd been lost for three days when I spotted an island in the distance...

Recording Dialogue

Now that you've got a script, it's time to talk about the actual dialogue-recording process. Game dialogue is typically recorded in a studio environment, although sometimes dialogue recording takes place at a remote location such as a motion capture stage. Voice actors are usually recorded alone, but may be recorded as an ensemble when schedules permit. For the sake of simplicity, this lesson will focus on recording each voice actor independently in a controlled studio environment.

Dialogue-Recording Concepts

A typical game dialogue-recording session usually progresses through all of a particular voice actor's script lines. The actor will read a line from the script, rehearse it a few times (if time permits), and then attempt to record the line. At this point, the producer or director will decide to either try another take or move on to the next line. In some cases, the actor will read lines for multiple characters in the same game, modifying their voice quality or accent to achieve a different sound.

Although the process of recording game dialogue requires a systematic approach, obtaining the ideal performance can be elusive. For this reason, the voice talent is usually given direction by a dialogue producer or, when budget permits, a voiceover director. The goal is usually to record each line several different ways (called "reads" in the industry) so that the dialogue producer has as many options as possible to add variety to the game.

Although some producers prefer to stop a record pass to offer direction, it is beneficial to keep recording until the desired performance for a line is achieved. The latter method allows for the recording of direction to the Slate track for later reference.

Recording Slate

At the beginning of a record pass, it is often desirable to record the recording engineer or the dialogue producer speaking the line number or filename to be recorded. This is generally referred to as "slate," which takes its name from the slate that is used in film production to mark the beginning of each take. In the studio, "slate" is really just a fancy term for recording the talkback mic from the console or control surface onto a track in Pro Tools.

Note: All Avid control surfaces (except Command|8 and Euphonix Artist Series) have a dedicated audio output for talkback.

In addition, talkback between the dialogue producer and the voice talent can be recorded using the same signal path. This can be quite helpful if the Pro Tools session is then handed off to a dialogue editor. The editor can use the Slate track to determine which take or combination of takes the producer liked best.

Timeline Insertion/Play Start Marker Follows Playback

It's a good idea to enable the Timeline Insertion/Play Start Marker Follows Playback preference when recording. You can do this from the Preferences dialog box, from the Edit window toolbar, or from the keyboard (with Commands Keyboard Focus (A-Z) enabled) by pressing the N key.

Creating a Cue Mix

If you have a Pro Tools configuration with a minimum of four audio outputs, you can create a discrete headphone mix for the voice actor. This is called a "cue" mix. The cue mix is created by assigning prefader Sends to all of the relevant tracks in Pro Tools. These can be referred to as "cue sends." The Send levels and Send mutes on these cue sends are then used to balance the individual tracks to create a pleasing mix for the voice actor.

This discrete cue mix offers several advantages:

- The cue mix levels are independent from the main mix.

- The cue mix mutes do not impact the main mix (and vice versa).

Walkthrough: Recording Dialogue

In this walkthrough, you will learn how to record dialogue for the game.

Save a Copy of the Session

To prepare the session:

1. Open the PTGA_Walkthrough_02.ptt session file, which is found on the DVD included with this book.

2. Keep the default session parameters.

3. Click **OK**.

4. Save a copy of the session with your initials added to the filename.

Set Up the Session

To create the cue sends:

1. Create a Send on the DIA_New track and assign it to the Cue output (see Figure 2.1).

Figure 2.1
A Send assigned to the cue output.

2. Set the Send to prefader status (see Figure 2.2)

Figure 2.2
The Send set to prefader status

3. Repeat Steps 1-2 for the Slate track.

Shortcut: You can also Option+click (on the Mac) or Alt+click (on Windows) on the first Cue Send, and then drag it to a Send on the Slate track to make a copy.

Record Dialogue

To slate the filename and record some dialogue:

1. Record-enable the **DIA_NEW** and **SLATE** tracks.

Caution: You'll probably want to mute the Slate track so that you won't hear it in the control room (and to avoid feedback).

2. Check to be sure that signal is coming from the mics. Also, make sure that the control room and Cue output levels are appropriate.

3. Enable **TIMELINE INSERTION/PLAY START MARKER FOLLOWS PLAYBACK** by clicking the button or pressing the **N ALPHANUMERIC KEY** with Commands Keyboard Focus (A-Z) enabled.

4. Press **RECORD** and then **PLAY** in the Transport window or on the Edit window toolbar to begin recording.

5. Slate the first line by stating the filename into the talkback microphone.

6. Have the voice actor perform the first line of the script found on page 33.

7. Provide performance feedback using the talkback microphone.

8. Keep the record pass going and record as many additional takes as necessary.

9. When you are satisfied with the recorded line, press **STOP**.

10. Repeat Steps 4-9 for each additional line and character in the script.

11. Record-disable the **DIA_NEW** and **SLATE** tracks.

Editing Dialogue

Now that you've recorded some dialogue, it's time to look at some dialogue-editing techniques. Right now, you've got a bunch of long, whole file clips composed of many takes of the same line of dialogue. Your next task is to select the best takes and create separate clips for each line. This section offers an overview of some of the techniques used to complete this task.

Capturing Clips

In Pro Tools, there are several ways to edit a whole file clip into one or more smaller clips: Trim, Separate, and Capture. In this section, you'll look at the most commonly used technique for dialogue editing, which is Capture. You can access Capture by choosing Clip > Capture or by pressing Command+R (Mac) or Ctrl+R (Windows).

Why Use Capture?

The reason capture is used for dialogue editing rather than using Edit > Trim Clip > To Selection is because you may need to grab a bunch of subset clips out of one whole file clip (see Figure 2.4a). Trim will remove the rest of the whole file clip from the playlist and leave only the selected portion (see Figure 2.4b). Capture simply moves a copy of the captured selection to the Clip List without removing any of the whole file clips from the playlist (see Figure 2.4d). In addition, Capture automatically brings up the Name dialog box (see Figure 2.3), which allows immediate renaming of the new clip, which is essential for organizing dialogue clips.

Figure 2.3
Name dialog box

Edit > Separate Clip > At Selection has some good features: It doesn't trim away the rest of the whole file clip, and it can bring up the Name dialog box based on the Auto Name Separate Clips preference. However, the reason Capture is used rather than Separate is because the Separate command creates a lot of extraneous clips. Each time the Separate command is used, a new clip is created for the selection, but as many as two additional clips are also created (see Figure 2.4c). This is because the clips bordering the selection are also modified by the Separate command. Needless to say, this can create some serious clutter in the Clip List when you're editing hundreds of lines!

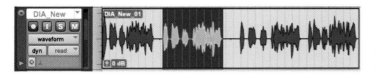

Figure 2.4a
Selection before editing

Figure 2.4b
Selection after Trim command

Figure 2.4c
Selection after Separate command

Figure 2.4d
Selection after Capture command (note that the original clip has not been modified)

Timeline Drop Order

There is one important but little known setting that is hidden in the Pro Tools Clip List menu: Timeline Drop Order (see Figure 2.5). This setting determines whether multiple clips dragged from the Clip List are distributed horizontally on a single track or vertically across multiple tracks.

Figure 2.5
Timeline Drop Order

Timeline Drop Order has the following options:

- **Top to Bottom**—When enabled, this option distributes dropped clips vertically across multiple destination tracks.

- **Left to Right**—When enabled, this option distributes dropped clips horizontally on a single destination track.

When working with dialogue, it's best to set this option to Left to Right. (When you want to apply compression, or any other sort of processing to the file, it's easier to have all of the dialogue on the same track.)

Walkthrough: Editing Dialogue

In this walkthrough, you will learn how to apply the most relevant techniques for editing dialogue.

To select the best takes from the recorded dialogue:

1. Enable the **Slip Edit** mode.

2. Enable the Smart Tool.

3. Set the TIMELINE DROP ORDER to Left to Right.

4. If you're working from the included dialogue clips, drag them all onto the DIA_NEW track. This will speed up the auditioning process.

5. On the DIA_NEW track, locate the whole file clip that includes the takes of the first line from the "Spreadsheet-Style Script" on page 31.

6. Listen to the takes. Once you find the best take, select the take using the Smart Tool as the Selector tool. Be sure to leave some extra room at the start and end of the selection. You'll clean it up in the next section.

7. Select CLIP > CAPTURE or press COMMAND+R (Mac) or CTRL+R (Windows) to create a clip for the selection.

8. The Create Clip dialog box will appear. Name the clip using the filename that is specified in the script, but add "edit" as a suffix to show that it is an unmastered clip. For example, **DIA_NPC_01_edit**.

Note: **You should see the clip appear in the Clip List.**

9. Repeat Steps 4-7 for each additional line in the script.

10. When you're finished, delete all of the whole file clips from the DIA_NEW track. Don't worry, you'll still be able to access them from the Clip List.

Once the best takes are selected, you can edit them more precisely:

1. Select SETUP > PREFERENCES and click the Editing tab. Set the Zoom Toggle settings to the following:

   - **Horizontal Zoom:** Selection
   - **Track Height:** Jumbo
   - **Track View:** Waveform/notes

2. Drag the NPC subset clips you created from the Clip List to the DIA_NPC track.

3. Use the Smart Tool as the Grabber tool to select the first clip.

4. Enable ZOOM TOGGLE by clicking the ZOOM TOGGLE button or by pressing the E KEY on the keyboard with Commands Keyboard Focus (A-Z) enabled (see Figure 2.6). The clip will zoom to fill the screen.

Figure 2.6
Toolbar with the Smart Tool selected and Zoom toggle enabled

5. Using the Smart Tool as the Trimmer tool, trim the start and end of the clip to leave a very small amount of room (a few milliseconds) on either side of the recorded dialogue.

6. Use the Smart Tool to create a small fade in and fade out in the clip.

7. Disable ZOOM TOGGLE to zoom back out.

8. Repeat Steps 2-7 for the remaining lines of dialogue. Be sure to put each line of dialogue on the appropriate track:

   - **NPC:** DIA_NPC (already completed)
   - **Player:** DIA_Player
   - **Enemy:** DIA_Enemy

9. Save the session.

Processing Dialogue

Game dialogue is almost always processed in some way before implementation in the game. This can range from a basic process to make a line sound less like it was recorded in a studio, to the more extreme processes necessary to make a line sound like it was recorded through a radio or telephone.

Making the dialogue sound less like studio dialogue is often called "worldizing." The goal here is to enhance the dialogue clarity, while making it sound like it was recorded in the virtual indoor or outdoor space represented in the game. Generally, the majority of dialogue is processed in this way. Plug-ins used for worldizing often include Compression, EQ, De-Essing, and Reverb.

The process of making dialogue sound like it's being transmitted though a radio or telephone is called a "futz." Nobody knows the origination of the term, but it is used universally in the game and film business. For example, a phone process is simply called a "phone futz" and a radio process a "radio futz." Plug-ins used for futzing often include Compression, EQ, De-Essing, Reverb, Delay, Guitar Amp Simulators, and many more.

The most extreme processing is generally reserved for lines that need a complete character "makeover." Typical applications include robot voices, alien voices, and any other voice whereby clever voice manipulation is desired. Plug-ins used for dialogue sound design include Reverse, Pitch Shift, Time Shift, Modulation Effects, Harmonic Effects, and just about everything else.

Using a Compressor

Compression is one of the most commonly used processes in audio. Compression reduces the dynamic range of signals that exceed a chosen threshold. Compression can help control average volume levels for dialogue and, therefore, increase intelligibility. The Dynamics III Compressor/Limiter plug-in (see Figure 2.7) is included with every copy of Pro Tools.

Figure 2.7
Dynamics III Compressor/Limiter plug-in

The standard compressor controls are as follows:

- **Threshold**—Sets the level that the signal must exceed to trigger compression.

- **Attack**—Sets how quickly the compressor responds to the "front" of an audio signal once it crosses the selected threshold.

- **Release**—Sets the amount of time that it takes for the compressor's gain to return to its original level after the input signal drops below the selected threshold.

- **Ratio**—Sets the compression ratio, or the amount of compression applied as the input signal exceeds the threshold. For example, a 2:1 compression ratio means that a 2dB increase of level above the threshold produces a 1dB increase in output.

- **Gain**—Adds gain to the signal after it has been compressed (sometimes called "makeup gain").

- **Knee**—Sets the rate at which the compressor reaches full compression once the threshold has been exceeded.

Using a De-Esser

De-essers are an essential tool for creating game dialogue. A de-esser is essentially a compressor that only targets a specific frequency. The goal is to find the frequency where "s" sounds occur. Dialogue has a tendency to have exaggerated "s" sounds (known as "sibilants") when exported to an audio file with a reduced bit depth. Careful de-essing can successfully combat this problem. A de-esser should be inserted after a compressor in Pro Tools. The Dynamics III De-Esser plug-in (see Figure 2.8) is included with every copy of Pro Tools.

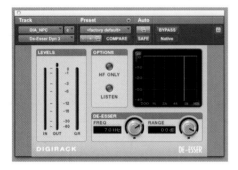

Figure 2.8
Dynamics III De-Esser plug-in

The standard de-esser controls are as follows:

- **Threshold**—Sets the level above which compression starts.

- **Frequency**—Sets the frequency band in which the de-esser operates.

- **Listen**—Lets you monitor the sibilant peaks.

- **HF Only**—When enabled, gain reduction is applied only to the frequency set by the Frequency control. When disabled, gain reduction is applied to the whole signal.

Walkthrough: Processing Dialogue

In this walkthrough, you will learn how to process the clips you have edited and renamed. A compressor has already been inserted on the first insert of each or the dialogue tracks. The compressor will help to control the dynamic range of the recorded dialogue. Now you're going to add plug-ins to create a unique "futz" for each character.

To process the NPC dialogue with pitch shift and reverb:

1. Solo the **DIA_NPC** track.

2. Select the first clip on the **DIA_NPC** track.

3. Open the AudioSuite Pitch Shift plug-in.

4. Set the Coarse setting to +4.00.

5. Press the PREVIEW button to audition the pitch change.

6. Set the AudioSuite File setting to Create Continuous File.

7. Once you're happy with the results, press the PROCESS button to apply the effect.

8. Repeat Steps 2-7 for the remaining clips on the DIA_NPC track, processing them one at a time.

9. Close the Pitch Shift plug-in and switch to the Mix window.

10. Insert an RTAS Air Reverb plug-in on the last insert of the DIA_NPC track.

11. Select the 01 Basic Small preset.

12. Select all of the clips on the track.

13. Press PLAY to hear the clips played through the plug-in.

14. Adjust the plug-in parameters as follows:

    - **Reverb Time:** 0.3

15. Experiment with the settings or try a different preset if desired.

16. Disable SOLO on the DIA_NPC track.

To process the player dialogue with reverb:

1. Solo the DIA_PLAYER track.

2. Insert an Air Reverb plug-in on the last insert of the DIA_PLAYER track.

3. Select the 01 Basic Small preset.

4. Select all of the clips on the track.

5. Press PLAY to hear the clips played through the plug-in.

6. Adjust the plug-in parameters as follows:

    - Reverb Time: 0.3

7. Experiment with the settings or try a different preset if desired.

8. Disable SOLO on the DIA_PLAYER track.

To process the enemy dialogue with a frequency shifter:

1. Solo the DIA_ENEMY track.

2. Insert an Air Frequency Shifter plug-in on the last insert of the DIA_ENEMY track.

3. Select the 02 Infinite Downward Spiral preset.

4. Select all of the clips on the track.

5. Press **PLAY** to hear the clips played through the plug-in.

6. Adjust the plug-in parameters as follows:

    - **Frequency:** 30.0Hz
    - **Mix:** 100%

7. Experiment with the settings or try a different preset if desired.

8. Disable **SOLO** on the **DIA_ENEMY** track.

Mastering Dialogue

Now that you've configured the processing for your dialogue, it's time to maximize levels before exporting.

TDM/RTAS Maxim

As discussed in Lesson 1, "Understanding the Game Audio Workflow," an ultra-maximizer is the ultimate tool for averaging dynamic range. You're going to use the Avid Maxim plug-in, which is included free with every Pro Tools system.

Figure 2.9
Maxim RTAS plug-in

The interface elements in Maxim are as follows:

- **Input Level Meter**—Displays the amplitude of input signals prior to limiting.

- **Histogram**—Displays the distribution of waveform peaks in the audio signal.

- **Threshold Slider**—Sets the threshold level for limiting. Signals that exceed this level will be limited.

- **Output Meter**—Displays the amplitude of the output signal.

- **Ceiling Slider**—Determines the maximum output level.

- **Attenuation Meter**—Displays the amount of gain reduction being applied.

- **Release Slider**—Sets how long it takes for Maxim to ease off of its attenuation after the input signal drops below the threshold level.

- **Mix Slider**—Sets the ratio of dry signal to limited signal. (Normally set to 100% wet.)

- **Link Button**—Links the threshold and ceiling controls.

- **Dither Section**—Applies dither and noise shaping if desired.

Walkthrough: Mastering Dialogue

In this walkthrough you will learn how to maximize the levels before exporting.

To add an ultra-maximizer to the Mastering track:

1. Insert a Maxim plug-in on the first insert of the MASTERING track.

2. Select the Mixing Limiter preset.

3. Solo the DIA_NPC track.

4. Enable the SLIP EDIT mode.

5. Using the Smart Tool as the Grabber tool, select the first clip on the DIA_NPC track.

6. Enable Loop Play by selecting OPTIONS > LOOP PLAYBACK.

7. Press PLAY to hear the clip played through Maxim.

8. Set the Ceiling to 0.1 dB.

9. Experiment with the Threshold setting to get a consistently loud signal.

Walkthrough: Exporting Dialogue

Now that you've mastered the dialogue, you should be ready to bounce and export your clips. As mentioned in Lesson 1, Bounce to Tracks is one of several techniques for exporting audio. Because Bounce to Tracks does not actually export the bounced clips, you'll also use Export Selected as Files once the bounce is completed.

In this walkthrough, you will learn how to use the Bounce to Tracks technique to create processed and mastered clips.

To Bounce to Tracks:

1. Set the Mastering track output to the Bounce bus.

2. Record-enable the **BOUNCE** track.

3. Solo the **DIA_NPC** track.

4. Switch to the Edit window and enable the **SLIP EDIT** mode.

5. Using the Smart Tool as the Grabber tool, select the first clip on the **DIA_NPC** track.

6. Press **RECORD** then **PLAY** in the Transport window or on the Edit window toolbar to begin recording.

7. Listen to be sure that all of the plug-ins are set correctly. If the signal is being compressed too much, increase the Threshold setting in Maxim. If the signal is too quiet, decrease the Threshold setting in Maxim.

8. Repeat Steps 6 and 7 for the remaining clips on the track.

9. Rename the resulting clips to match the filenames from the script.

10. Repeat the Bounce to Tracks process for each track of dialogue. Remember to adjust the Maxim settings for each track to make sure the levels are optimized.

    Because you've already bounced the dialogue to whole file clips, you can use Export Clips as Files for a faster than real-time export.

Note: Export Clips as Files automatically applies dither (without noise shaping) when exporting from 24-bit to 16-bit.

To export the clips:

1. Select all of the final bounced clips in the Clip List.

2. Select **EXPORT CLIPS AS FILES** from the Clip List pop-up menu, or press **COMMAND+SHIFT+K** (Mac) or **CTRL+SHIFT+K** (Windows). The Export Selected dialog box will appear.

3. Set the export settings as follows:

   - **File Type:** WAV
   - **Format:** (Multiple) Mono
   - **Bit Depth:** 16-bit
   - **Sample Rate:** 48kHz

4. Create a folder named **PTGA_Walkthrough_02_DIA** to store the Walkthrough 2 clips.

5. Click **EXPORT**.

Walkthrough: Implementing Dialogue

Now that you've exported your clips from Pro Tools, you're ready to implement them in Unity. In this walkthrough, you will learn how to implement dialogue.

To prepare the Unity project:

1. Open the **PTGA_WALKTHROUGH** Unity project.

2. Select the **WALKTHROUGH_01** scene in the Project window.

3. Duplicate the scene by choosing **EDIT > DUPLICATE** or pressing **COMMAND+D** (Mac) or **CTRL+D** (Windows).

4. Rename the scene **Walkthrough_02** and add your initials to the name of the duplicated level.

5. Double-click the duplicated level to make it active.

To import the audio clips:

1. Navigate to the folder where you bounced your dialogue clips.

2. Drag the folder onto the Unity Project window. The folder and all of its contents will automatically be imported into the project.

To assign the clips in the Inspector:

1. Click the **AUDIO_MANAGER** item in the Hierarchy window.

2. Assign the sounds to specific triggers in the Inspector window as follows:

- **NPC_Dialog_01:** DIA_NPC_01
- **NPC_Dialog_02:** DIA_NPC_02
- **NPC_Dialog_03:** DIA_NPC_03
- **NPC_Dialog_04:** DIA_NPC_04
- **Player_Dialog_01:** DIA_Player_01
- **Player_Dialog_02:** DIA_Player_02
- **Player_Dialog_03:** DIA_Player_03
- **Player_Dialog_04:** DIA_Player_04
- **Enemy_Dialog_01:** DIA_Enemy_01
- **Enemy_Dialog_02:** DIA_Enemy_02
- **Enemy_Dialog_03:** DIA_Enemy_03

Note: The player lines DIA_Player_05 and DIA_Player_06, will be used in Lesson 4, "Working with Sound Effects." The last player line, DIA_Player_07, will be used in Lesson 8, "Working with Cinematics."

Testing the dialogue:

1. Select **EDIT > PLAY** or press **COMMAND+P** (Mac) or **CTRL+P** (Windows) to launch the game.

2. Play through the level as described in Lesson 1, and listen to all of your dialogue files.

3. If anything doesn't sound right, go back and make changes.

4. Press **COMMAND+P** (Mac) or **CTRL+P** (Windows) to exit the game.

Summary

In this lesson, you learned how to work with dialogue. You should now be able to:

■ Understand dialogue terminology and different script types.

■ Use Pro Tools features for recording, editing, mastering, and exporting dialogue.

■ Use plug-ins that are useful for dialogue processing.

■ Implement dialogue in Unity.

Review/Discussion Questions

1. Which script type is best for games with a large number of dialogue lines? (See "Understanding Game Dialogue" on page 30.)

2. Why is it useful to record a Slate track when recording dialogue? (See "Recording Dialogue" on page 35.)

3. What are the advantages of using Capture rather than Trim or Separate to edit dialogue? (See "Editing Dialogue" on page 38.)

4. What are the two options for Timeline Drop Order in Pro Tools? (See "Editing Dialogue" on page 38.)

5. What are some examples of typical dialogue futz processes? (See "Processing Dialogue" on page 42.)

Adding Dialogue to the Game

In this exercise, you will learn how to use dialogue to move the story along by creating and implementing several lines of spoken conversation. For this section of the exercise, you will create a new session from a template file and record lines of dialogue for each character in the first scene of the game, following the provided script (see page 60 of this module). If you do not wish to record the dialogue, you can use the existing clips in the session's Clip List.

Media Used:
Pro Tools: PTGA_Exercise_02.ptt
Unity: PTGA_Exercises

Duration:
60 Minutes

Preparing the Pro Tools Session

Before beginning the recording process, you'll need to prepare the session:

1. Open the PTGA_Exercise_02.ptt session file. A New Session dialog box will open.

2. Keep the default session parameters.

3. Click **OK**.

4. Save a copy of the session with your initials added to the filename.

Recording Dialogue (Optional)

To record the dialogue lines for each character, follow these steps:

1. Record-enable the **DIA_NEW** track.

2. Connect a microphone and verify that signal is coming from the mic.

3. Press **RECORD** then **PLAY** in the Transport window or on the Edit Window toolbar.

4. Perform the first line of the exercise script on page 60.

5. Keep the record pass going and record some additional takes if necessary.

6. When you are satisfied with the recorded content, press **STOP**.

7. Repeat Steps 1-6 for each additional line and character in the script.

8. Disable recording the **DIA_NEW** track.

Using Existing Dialogue (Alternate Option)

To place the dialogue lines for each character onto the track, follow these steps:

1. Click the **CLIP LIST** pop-up menu.

2. At the bottom of the menu, select **TIMELINE DROP ORDER > LEFT TO RIGHT**.

3. Select all the clips in the Clip List.

4. Drag the clips to the start of the **DIA_NEW** track.

Creating Clips

To select the best takes from the recorded dialogue, follow these steps:

1. Enable the **SLIP EDIT** mode.

2. Enable the Smart Tool.

3. On the **DIA_NEW** track, locate the whole file clip that includes the takes of the first line from the exercise script.

4. Listen to the takes. Once you find the best take, select the take using the Smart Tool as the Selector tool. Be sure to leave some extra room at the start and end of the selection. You'll clean it up in the next section.

5. Select **CLIP > CAPTURE** or press **COMMAND+R** (Mac) or **CTRL+R** (Windows) to create a clip for the selection.

6. The Create Clip dialog box will appear. Name the clip using the filename that is specified in the script, but add "edit" as a suffix to show that it is an unmastered clip. For example, **DIA_HQ_01_edit**.

Note: **You should see the clip appear in the Clip List.**

7. Repeat Steps 4-7 for each additional line in the script.

8. When you're finished, delete all of the whole file clips from the **DIA_NEW** track. Don't worry, you'll still be able to access them from the Clip List.

Once the best takes are selected, you can edit them more precisely by following these steps:

1. Select **SETUP > PREFERENCES** and click on the Editing tab. Set the Zoom toggle settings to the following:

   - **Horizontal Zoom:** Selection
   - **Track Height:** Jumbo
   - **Track View:** Waveform/notes

2. Set the Timeline Drop Order to Left to Right.

3. Drag the HQ clips from the Clip List to the **DIA_HQ** track.

4. Use the Smart Tool as the Grabber tool to select the first clip.

5. Enable Zoom toggle by clicking the **ZOOM TOGGLE** button or by pressing the **E KEY** on the keyboard with Commands Keyboard Focus (A-Z) enabled. The clip will zoom to fill the screen.

6. Using the Smart Tool as the Trimmer tool, trim the start and end of the clip to leave a very small amount of room (a few milliseconds) on either side of the recorded dialogue.

7. Use the Smart Tool to create a small fade-in and fade-out in the clip.

8. Disable **ZOOM TOGGLE** to zoom back out.

9. Repeat Steps 3-8 for the remaining lines of dialogue. Be sure to put each line of dialogue on the appropriate track:

   - **HQ**: DIA_HQ (already completed)
   - **Player**: DIA_Player
   - **Enemy**: DIA_Enemy
   - **Turret**: DIA_Turret
   - **Security**: DIA_Security

10. Save the session.

Processing Dialogue

Now that you've edited your clips, it's time to make them sound like real-world dialogue. A compressor, EQ, and de-esser have already been inserted on the first three inserts of each of the dialogue tracks to get you started. The compressor will help to control the dynamic range of the recorded dialogue. The EQ will reduce some of the "studio" quality of the dialogue. The de-esser will reduce sibilants that can be problematic when reducing bit depth.

In the following steps, you will add additional plug-ins to create a unique "futz" for each character.

To process the HQ dialogue using a radio futz, follow these steps:

1. Insert an Eleven Free RTAS plug-in on the last insert of the **DIA_HQ** track.

2. Select the CRUNCH > BLUESY BREAKUP preset.

3. Select the clip on the **DIA_HQ** track.

4. Solo the **DIA_HQ** track.

5. Press PLAY to hear the clip played through Eleven Free.

6. Adjust the plug-in parameters as follows:

   - **Gain:** 2
   - **Bass:** 0
   - **Treble:** 10

7. Experiment with the settings or try a different preset if desired.

8. Unsolo the **DIA_HQ** track.

To process the player dialogue with a reverb:

1. Insert an Air Reverb RTAS plug-in on the last insert of the **DIA_PLAYER** track.

2. Select the 01 Basic Small preset.

3. Select all of the clips on the **DIA_PLAYER** track.

4. Solo the **DIA_PLAYER** track.

5. Press **PLAY** to hear the clips played through the AIR Reverb.

6. Adjust the plug-in parameters as follows:

   - **Reverb Time:** 0.3

7. Experiment with the settings or try a different preset if desired.

8. Unsolo the **DIA_PLAYER** track.

To process the enemy dialogue with a frequency shifter, follow these steps:

1. Insert an Air Frequency Shifter RTAS plug-in on the last insert of the **DIA_ENEMY** track.

2. Select the 02 Infinite Downward Spiral preset.

3. Select all of the clips on the **DIA_ENEMY** track.

4. Solo the **DIA_ENEMY** track.

5. Press **PLAY** to hear the clips played through the plug-in.

6. Adjust the plug-in parameters as follows:

   - **Frequency:** 30Hz
   - **Mix:** 15

7. Experiment with the settings or try a different preset, if desired.

8. Unsolo the **DIA_ENEMY** track.

To process the turret dialogue with Pitch Shift and Delay, follow these steps:

1. Solo the **DIA_TURRET** track.

2. Select the clip on the track.

3. Open the AudioSuite Pitch Shift plug-in.

4. Set the Coarse setting to –4.00.

5. Set the File setting to Create Continuous File.

6. Press the **PREVIEW** button to audition the pitch change.

7. Once you're happy with the results, press the **PROCESS** button to apply the effect.

8. Close the Pitch Shift plug-in.

9. Insert an Air Multi-Delay RTAS plug-in on the last insert of the **DIA_TURRET** track.

10. Select the 12 Afterburner preset.

11. Press **PLAY** to hear the clip played through the plug-in.

12. Experiment with the settings or try a different preset, if desired.

13. Unsolo the **DIA_TURRET** track.

To process the security dialogue with a Modulator and Reverse Reverb effect, follow these steps:

1. Insert an Air Non-Linear Reverb RTAS plug-in on the fourth insert of the **DIA_SECURITY** track.

2. Select the 06 Reversed preset.

3. Select all the clips on the **DIA_SECURITY** track.

4. Solo the **DIA_SECURITY** track.

5. Press **PLAY** to hear the clip played through the plug-in.

6. Experiment with the settings or try a different preset, if desired.

7. Insert an Air Fuzz Wah RTAS plug-in on the last insert of the **DIA_SECURITY** track.

8. Select the 01 Slow Wah preset.

9. Adjust the plug-in parameters as follows:

   - **Mix:** 20%

10. Press **PLAY** to hear the processed clip played through the plug-in.

11. Experiment with the settings or try a different preset, if desired.

12. Unsolo the **DIA_SECURITY** track.

Mastering Dialogue

Now that you've edited and processed your dialogue, it's time to maximize the levels before exporting.

To add an ultra-maximizer to the Mastering tracks, follow these steps:

1. Insert a Maxim RTAS plug-in on the first insert of the Mastering track.

2. Select the Mixing Limiter preset.

3. Set the ceiling to –0.1 dB.

4. Solo the **DIA_HQ** track.

5. Enable the **SLIP EDIT MODE**.

6. Enable Loop Playback by selecting **OPTIONS > LOOP PLAYBACK**.

7. Using the Smart Tool as the Grabber tool, select the clip on the **DIA_HQ** track.

8. Press **PLAY** to hear the clip played through Maxim.

9. Experiment with the Threshold setting to get a consistently loud signal.

Note: You'll repeat Steps 7-9 to adjust the Maxim settings for each of the other tracks in the next section, after you've exported the files from the DIA_HQ track.

Exporting Dialogue

Your dialogue clips are now ready to be exported. Because you are running real-time plug-ins on the tracks, you'll need to use Bounce to Tracks to export the files.

To use Bounce to Tracks to create processed and mastered clips, follow these steps:

1. Enable the **SLIP EDIT** mode.

2. Set the Mastering track output to the Bounce bus.

3. Record-enable the Bounce track.

4. Solo the **DIA_HQ** track.

5. Using the Smart Tool as the Grabber tool, select the clip on the **DIA_HQ** track.

6. Press **RECORD** then **PLAY** in the Transport window or on the Edit Window toolbar to begin recording.

7. Listen to be sure that all of the plug-ins are set correctly. If needed, stop the record pass, make adjustments as noted here, and repeat the record pass.

   ● If the signal is being compressed too much, increase the Threshold setting in Maxim.

   ● If the signal is too quiet, decrease the Threshold setting in Maxim.

8. Rename the resulting clip to match the filename from the script.

9. Unsolo the **DIA_HQ** track.

10. Repeat Steps 4-9 to bounce each dialogue clip on each of the tracks. Remember to adjust the Maxim settings for each clip and track to make sure the levels are optimized. Because you've already bounced your dialogue to whole file clips, you can use Export Clips as Files for a faster than real-time export.

Tip: The Export Clips as Files command automatically applies dither (without noise shaping) when exporting from 24-bit to 16-bit.

Export the Clips

To export your final clips, follow these steps:

1. Select all of the final bounced clips in the Clip List.

2. Select **EXPORT CLIPS AS FILES** from the Clip List pop-up menu, or press **COMMAND+SHIFT+K** (Mac) or **CTRL+SHIFT+K** (Windows). The Export Selected dialog box will appear.

3. Set the export settings as follows:

   - **File Type:** WAV
   - **Format:** (Multiple) Mono
   - **Bit Depth:** 16-Bit
   - **Sample Rate:** 48 kHz

4. Create a folder named **PTGA_Exercise_02_DIA** to store all of the Exercise 2 clips.

5. Click **EXPORT**. All of the selected clips will be converted and saved in the folder you created.

Implementing Dialogue

Now that you've exported your clips from Pro Tools, you're ready to implement them in Unity.

To prepare the Unity project, follow these steps:

1. Launch the Unity application and choose **FILE > OPEN PROJECT** to open the PTGA_Exercises Unity project.

2. Select the Exercise_01 scene in the Project window.

3. Duplicate the scene by choosing **EDIT > DUPLICATE** or pressing **COMMAND+D** (Mac) or **CTRL+D** (Windows). A new scene named Exercise_01 will appear in the Project window.

4. Rename the scene **Exercise_02** and add your initials to the name of the duplicated level by clicking on the Exercise_01 file to rename it. Press Return to apply the new name.

5. Double-click the duplicated level to make it active.

To import the audio files, follow these steps:

1. Navigate to the folder where you exported your dialogue clips.

2. Drag the folder to the top of the Unity Project window. The folder and all of its contents will automatically be imported into the project.

To assign the clips in the Inspector, follow these steps:

1. Click the **AUDIO_MANAGER** item in the Hierarchy window.

2. Assign the sounds to specific triggers in the Inspector window by clicking on the small black circle to the right of a trigger item. Triggers with no assigned sounds read None (Audio Clip). Sounds should be assigned as follows:

   - **Intro_Dialog:** DIA_HQ_01
   - **Intro_Hero_Dialog:** DIA_Player_01
   - **Player_Pain_Small:** DIA_Player_02
   - **Player_Pain_Big:** DIA_Player_03
   - **Player_Death:** DIA_Player_04
   - **Enemy_Hit_01:** DIA_Enemy_02
   - **Enemy_Hit_02:** DIA_Enemy_03
   - **Enemy_Die:** DIA_Enemy_04
   - **Enemy_Turret_Dialog:** DIA_Turret_01
   - **Alarm_Loop:** DIA_Security_01

Note: The last player line, DIA_Player_05, will be used in Lesson 8, "Working with Cinematics."

To test the dialogue, follow these steps:

1. Select **EDIT > PLAY** or press **COMMAND+P** (Mac) or **CTRL+P** (Windows) to launch the game.

2. Using the **A**, **S**, **D**, and **W** keys (or arrow keys) and the mouse, navigate your character through the level, and listen for your dialogue cues.

3. Press **COMMAND+P** (Mac) or **CTRL+P** (Windows) to exit the game.

Exercise Script

Use the following script for this exercise:

Line Number	Character	Filename	Dialogue	Notes
1	HQ	DIA_HQ_01	Bravo, you've got a tango inside the building, and two more in the loading yard out back. Sensors are detecting several gun emplacements as well. Your mission is to eliminate all hostiles. You are weapons free.	Mission briefing
2	Player	DIA_Player_01	Got it. Thanks HQ. Let's get some bad guys.	Accept mission
3	Player	DIA_Player_02	(Wounded sound)	Player small damage
4	Player	DIA_Player_03	That's going to leave a bruise.	Player large damage
5	Player	DIA_Player_04	(Dying sound)	Player dies
6	Player	DIA_Player_05	HQ, this is Bravo. I've tracked the enemy ship to New Europa. I'm going in.	Cinematic Intro
7	Enemy	DIA_Enemy_01	Stop! You've entered a secure area!	Spots player
8	Enemy	DIA_Enemy_02	(Wounded sound)	Small damage
9	Enemy	DIA_Enemy_03	(Small scream)	Large damage
10	Enemy	DIA_Enemy_04	(Large scream)	Enemy dies
11	Security	DIA_Security_01	Intruder alert!	Intruder alarm goes off
12	Turret	DIA_Turret_01	Target acquired.	Turret senses player

Working with Foley

Foley is a design technique in which you create a sense of realism by emphasizing the small details. In this lesson, you'll look at techniques for recording and editing footsteps.

Media Used: Pro Tools Session: PTGA_Walkthrough_03
Unity Project: PTGA_Walkthroughs

Duration: 90 Minutes

GOALS

- Understand Foley
- Record Foley
- Edit Foley
- Master Foley
- Export Foley
- Implement Foley

Understanding Foley

Foley sounds are essential to creating realism in a game. *Foley* takes its name from Jack Foley, an employee at Universal Pictures, who invented the technique. In film, Foley sounds are created by a Foley artist (or "Foley walker") who actually recreates the sounds of a scene while watching it on a television or projection screen. Most film Foley is recorded in a dedicated studio (or "Foley stage," as shown in Figure 3.1) where a large assortment of props and surfaces are available. In addition, a Foley stage often has a collection of basins (or "pits") that are filled with a variety of substances including hardwood, marble, gravel, and sand. These pits are then used for footsteps and other Foley elements.

Figure 3.1
Foley Stage at Post Creations *Photo by Kyle Billingsley and Nick Neutra*

In game audio, the term "Foley" is used to describe any sounds that convey the movement of characters. Game Foley is typically not recreated while watching pre-rendered gameplay (although it can be helpful). Although not technically Foley in the strictest sense of the term, these sounds achieve a similar result when properly implemented.

There is one major difference between film Foley and game Foley: film Foley requires an action to be performed once and matched precisely to actions onscreen, whereas game Foley requires a collection of sounds that can be triggered based on gameplay. For example, imagine a film scene showing a female character walking across a marble floor. For this scene, the film Foley artist must recreate ten steps with high-heeled shoes on marble and match the precise timing of the scene. In a game, the same character and floor may exist, but we have no way of knowing how many steps the character will take on that particular floor. They might walk around in that virtual room for hours! Therefore, the game Foley must include a collection of sounds of high-heeled shoes on marble, which can be randomly triggered by the game audio engine and matched precisely to actions onscreen.

Categories of Foley Sounds

There are several categories of Foley sounds. The terminology for these categories is borrowed directly from film Foley. The three main types include the following:

- **Movement**—The sound of clothing or equipment moving and rustling as the character moves around in the game. An individual movement record take is sometimes called a "cloth pass" or "clothing pass."

- **Footsteps**—The sound of footsteps with appropriate shoes on each of the surfaces present in the game.

- **Specifics**—Any other sound that is necessary to reinforce character movements. Generally, specifics are focused on items that are handled by a game character.

The following table shows some common Foley effects and the props used to make them:

Effect	Prop
Gun handling	Handling wrenches
Kissing	Kissing hand
Horses galloping	"Galloping" coconuts by hand
Bones breaking	Breaking celery stalks
Punch to the body	Punching phone book
Bird wings flapping	Flapping a pair of gloves
Fire	Crunching cellophane
Body falling	Dropping a melon

Assessing Foley Requirements

The three main types of Foley sounds (movement, footsteps, and specifics) are present in most games, and the majority of Foley needs for a particular game level can be easily classified into one of these types.

For movement, observe the clothing that is being worn by the game characters. Is it cloth? Is it leather? Are they carrying any equipment that might make noise as the character moves?

For footsteps, check out the footwear of each of the characters. Are they wearing boots? High heels? Sneakers? Take note of all of the surfaces where the character might step. Typical surfaces include concrete, grass, metal, and sand. The game may even include some special surfaces, like creaky rope bridges or puddles of water.

For specifics, look for anything that is handled by the characters. Do they handle a gun, type at a computer, write with a pencil or pen, or drink from a glass or bottle? All of these sounds are easily created with Foley techniques.

Recording Foley

A typical film Foley recording process progresses through each of the Foley categories in a linear fashion: The movement tracks are recorded first, then the footsteps, and then specifics. For practical reasons, this lesson focuses on recording footsteps.

Because you're not working with picture, you'll simply work your way through the list of sound elements that you need for the game level. Remember, for the purpose of game Foley, you need both quality and variety.

Some Foley teams prefer to stop a record pass to discuss the performance. While this is a perfectly acceptable way of working, it can also be beneficial to keep the record pass rolling so that the slate and listen mics are recorded.

Listen Mics

Foley is often recorded with shotgun mics that have a hyper-cardioid polar pattern. This means that the mic will do a great job of recording Foley elements, but won't necessarily allow the Foley artist to communicate with the recording engineer. Placing one or two mics around the recording space can assist this communication.

Pro Tools Settings

Pro Tools provides several Preference settings that can assist in Foley recording.

Mute Record-Armed Tracks While Stopped (Pro Tools HD Only)

The Mute Record-Armed Tracks While Stopped preference (Preferences > Operation Tab) is particularly useful for Foley recording (see Figure 3.2). In a typical Foley recording scenario, the Foley artist frequently moves and adjusts the microphone. Microphone preamplifier gain can be set extremely high in Foley recording situations, so even small movements of the mic or mic stand can create loud transients that can damage speakers. When Mute Record-Armed Tracks While Stopped is enabled, the record-armed tracks are automatically muted whenever the transport is stopped.

One issue comes into play when enabling this preference, however. Because the mic that is being used for Foley recording is muted between record passes, a listen mic *must* be used for communication between the Foley artist and the recording engineer.

Figure 3.2
Mute Record-Armed Tracks While Stopped
(Pro Tools HD Only)

Note: Mute Record-Armed Tracks While Stopped is also referred to as Foley record mute.

Timeline Insertion/Play Start Marker Follows Playback

Whenever Foley is being recorded, it's a good idea to enable the Timeline Insertion/Play Start Marker Follows Playback preference in Pro Tools. When enabled, Timeline Insertion (see Figure 3.3) and the Play Start Marker both move to the point in the Timeline where playback stopped. This puts the Transport in the correct position to immediately begin the next record take.

Figure 3.3
Timeline Insertion point during a record pass

Figure 3.4 displays the Timeline Insertion point after the record pass. In this example, the Timeline Insertion/Play Start Marker Follows Playback is disabled.

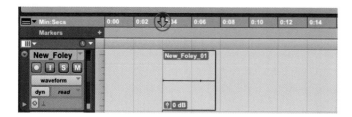

Figure 3.4
Timeline Insertion/Play Start Marker
Follows Playback is disabled

Note: The Timeline Insertion point stays at the previous location.

If the Timeline Insertion/Play Start Marker Follows Playback is enabled, you'll see what's shown in Figure 3.5.

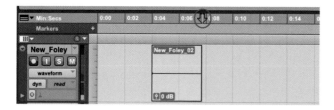

Figure 3.5
Timeline Insertion/Play Start Marker
Follows Playback is enabled

Note: The Timeline Insertion point moves to the point where recording was
stopped.

To toggle Timeline Insertion/Play Start Marker Follows playback, you need to either click the Insertion Follows Playback button in the toolbar, as shown in Figure 3.6, or use the following steps.

Figure 3.6
Timeline Insertion/Play Start Marker
Follows Playback button in the toolbar

To toggle Timeline Insertion/Play Start Marker Follows Playback:

1. Enable Commands Keyboard Focus by clicking the **COMMANDS KEYBOARD FOCUS (A-Z)** button in the Edit window (see Figure 3.7) or pressing **OPTION+COMMAND+1** (Mac) or **CTRL+ALT+1** (Windows).

2. Press the **N KEY** on the computer keyboard.

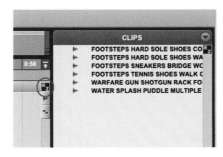

Figure 3.7
Commands Keyboard Focus (A-Z)
button in the Edit window

Tip: It's not a good idea to enable Timeline Insertion/Play Start Marker Follows Playback when Loop Recording. This is because the original selection will be lost after the first loop record pass is stopped.

Creating a Cue Mix

If you have a Pro Tools configuration with a minimum of four audio outputs, you can create a discrete headphone mix for the Foley artist. This is called a "cue" mix. The cue mix is created by assigning prefader Sends to all of the relevant tracks in Pro Tools. The Send levels and Send mutes are then used to balance the individual tracks to create a pleasing mix for the Foley talent.

This discrete cue mix offers several advantages:

■ The cue mix levels are independent from the main mix.

■ The cue mix mutes do not impact the main mix (and vice versa).

Walkthrough: Recording Foley

In this walkthrough, you learn how to record some simple Foley footsteps.

In this case, you need three kinds of footsteps:

■ Dirt

■ Water

■ Wooden bridge

To prepare the working area:

1. Set up three areas or pits that have the surfaces you need. For this example, fill a large shallow pan or bucket with dirt or gravel, a second pan with water, and gather some loose 2x4s or other boards.

2. Set up a microphone pointing at one of these Foley pits. When you finish your first pass, you will move the microphone to the next pit.

3. Set up listen mics, if you are using them.

To prepare the Pro Tools session:

1. Open the PTGA_Walkthrough_03.ptt session file.

2. Keep the default session parameters.

3. Click **OK**.

4. Save a copy of the session with your initials added to the filename.

To create the Cue Sends:

1. Create a Send on the **NEW_FOLEY** track and assign it to the Cue output (see Figure 3.8).

Figure 3.8
Creating a Send

2. Set the Send to prefader status by clicking on the Pre button in the Send window (see Figure 3.9).

Figure 3.9
Send set to prefader status

To record Foley:

1. Record-enable the **NEW_FOLEY** track.

2. Check to be sure that signal is coming from the mic.

3. Press **RECORD** then **PLAY** in the Transport window or on the Edit window toolbar.

4. Perform the actions required to create the Foley sounds. For example, you can either actually walk in the pits or put various types of shoes on your hands and simulate walking.

5. Keep the record pass going and record some additional takes, if necessary.

6. When you are satisfied with the recorded content, press **STOP**.

7. Name the recorded clip so that you'll remember what it contains. For example, **FOL_Footsteps_Boots_Dirt**.

8. Repeat Steps 3-7 for each additional Foley sound.

9. Disable recording on the **NEW_FOLEY** track.

Editing Foley

Now that you've finished recording Foley, it's time to look at some Foley editing techniques. At this point, you have a series of long, whole file clips composed of multiple Foley elements. Your next task is to select the best takes and create a variety of clips for each movement. This section offers an overview of some of the techniques used to complete this task.

Tab To Transients

For Foley editing, the Tab To Transients function is a tremendous time-saver. See Lesson 1, "Understanding the Game Audio Workflow" for a complete overview. The Tab To Transients function can be enabled from the Edit window toolbar or from the keyboard using Option+Command+Tab (Mac) or Ctrl+Alt+Tab (Windows).

Nudging

Many novice Pro Tools editors struggle to move the cursor or selected clips with precision. This is usually due to an over-reliance on the mouse. Using the mouse to move the cursor in precise intervals is difficult and time consuming. It can require a complex series of steps, such as changing the Edit mode, changing the grid value, and zooming. You then need to reverse all of those steps to get back to where you started!

Nudge uses key commands to move the cursor forward or backward by the value specified in the Nudge Value menu. If you watch Pro Tools experts edit (or mix), you'll see them use Nudge constantly. Nudging is the easiest way to move the cursor (or a selection) in precise intervals. In fact, Nudge is probably the most used command in Pro Tools.

To use Nudge, do one of the following:

- Press the + and – keys on the numeric keypad.
- With Commands Keyboard Focus (A-Z) enabled, press the , or . alphanumeric keys.

To nudge by the next largest Nudge value:

- With Commands Keyboard Focus (A-Z) enabled, press the M or / alphanumeric keys.

To modify the Nudge value, do one of the following:

- Click on the Nudge Value pop-up selector in the Edit window toolbar and choose a new time scale and/or Nudge value (see Figure 3.10).

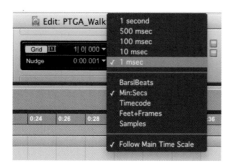

Figure 3.10
Nudge Value pop-up menu

To step through the default Nudge values, do the following:

- Hold Command+Option (Mac) or Ctrl+Alt (Windows) and press the + and – keys on the numeric keypad or alphanumeric keys.

Separate Clips

In Pro Tools, there are several ways to edit a whole file clip into one or more smaller clips: Trim, Separate, and Capture. This section focuses on the most commonly used technique for editing Foley: Separate.

The Edit > Separate Clip > At Selection command is particularly well suited for Foley editing. When editing for variety, you want to find multiple usable instances of a sound in each whole file clip. In cases like footsteps, you may even use a series of Foley elements in the exact sequence in which they were recorded. This gives an automatic balance of left foot and right footsteps, which is important for randomization. In this case, you can use Tab To Transients to quickly position the cursor at the attack of each footstep. Then Nudge allows you to back up a small distance to preserve the attack. Finally, the Separate command is used to create a new edit at the precise location. The process is repeated for each subsequent footstep. See Figures 3.11-3.13.

It is certainly possible to use Clip > Capture to edit Foley. In fact, when dealing with a small number of Foley elements, Capture could be the better choice. However, when creating a large number of clips, it is usually faster to use Tab, Nudge, and Separate.

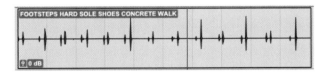

Figure 3.11
Unedited clip with the cursor positioned arbitrarily

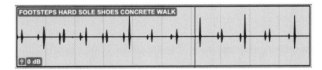

Figure 3.12
Cursor position after pressing the Tab key with Tab To Transients enabled

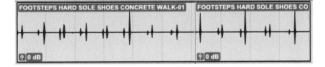

Figure 3.13
Newly created clips after the Separate command has been applied

Key Shortcuts

There are many important single key commands in Pro Tools. Fortunately, you can increase your Foley editing efficiency with just a few.

- **A**   Trim Clip Start To Insertion
- **S**   Trim Clip End To Insertion
- **B**   Separate Clip at Selection
- **,**   Nudge Backward by Nudge Value
- **.**   Nudge Forward by Nudge Value

Tip: You must have Commands Keyboard Focus (A-Z) enabled for all of these commands to function. See Lesson 1 for more information.

Batch Fades

Creating fades is an important part of any audio workflow. By now, you're probably familiar with the standard methods for creating fades in Pro Tools. Let's take a look at a method for quickly creating fades across multiple clips: batch fades.

There is no specific command for "batch fades" in Pro Tools. Selecting multiple clips and using the standard fade commands is all it takes.

To create batch fades:

1. Select multiple clips in Pro Tools.

2. Do one of the following:

   - Select **EDIT > FADES > CREATE**
   - Press **COMMAND+F** (Mac) or **CTRL+F** (Windows)

The Batch Fades dialog box will appear (see Figure 3.14).

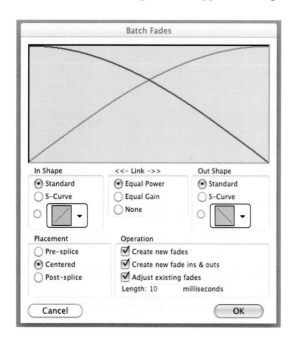

Figure 3.14
Batch Fades dialog box

3. Adjust the settings for Shape, Link, Placement, and Operation. Pay particular attention to the Length setting under Operation, as this determines the duration for each of the fades to be created.

4. Click the **OK** button to create the fades.

Walkthrough: Editing Foley

In this walkthrough, you will learn how to select and edit the best Foley elements. If you were not able to record your own Foley elements, import the following Foley elements to the Clip List from the BlastwaveFX folder:

- Footsteps Sneakers Bridge Wood Suspended

- Footsteps Tennis Shoes Walk On Earth Mix

- Water Splash Puddle Multiple Small

To edit the Foley elements:

1. Set the Nudge value to one millisecond.

2. Drag the first footsteps clip from the Clip List to the **NEW_FOLEY** track.

3. With the Smart Tool as Selector tool, place the cursor near the beginning of the first clip.

4. Verify that **TAB TO TRANSIENTS** is enabled.

5. Zoom in slightly (if necessary), so that you can see the individual footstep transients.

6. Press the **TAB KEY** to move the cursor to the initial transient of the first footstep.

7. Nudge back by five milliseconds using the comma (,) alphanumeric key or the minus – key on the numeric keypad.

8. Press the **A KEY** or choose **EDIT > TRIM CLIP > START TO INSERTION** to eliminate the extra material at the beginning of the clip.

9. Press the **TAB KEY** to move the cursor to the initial transient of the second footstep.

10. Nudge back by five milliseconds using the comma (,) alphanumeric key or the minus – key on the numeric keypad.

11. Press the **B KEY** or select **EDIT > SEPARATE CLIP > AT SELECTION** to add an edit at the current cursor position. Do not add fades for now; you'll learn about them in the next section.

12. Use **TAB**, **NUDGE**, and **SEPARATE** to add edits for each of the remaining footsteps.

13. When you've separated six footsteps, Tab to the initial transient of the seventh footstep, Nudge back by two milliseconds, and press the **S KEY** or choose **TRIM CLIP > END TO INSERTION** to trim the extra material from the end of the clip.

14. If time allows, repeat all of the previous steps to edit your remaining foot-steps.

To use batch fades to quickly add fades to a bunch of clips:

1. Select all of the Foley clips.

2. Press **COMMAND+F** (Mac) or **CTRL+F** (Windows) or choose **EDIT > FADES > CREATE**. The Batch Fades dialog box will appear.

3. Deselect **CREATE NEW FADES**. This will disable crossfades and only create new fade ins and fade outs.

4. Set the Length to five milliseconds.

Note: The fade shape doesn't make much difference with such a short fade duration.

5. Click **OK** to create the fades.

To consolidate the edited and faded clips:

1. Select the clip to be consolidated. Be sure that the selection includes the fade in and fade out.

2. Select **EDIT > CONSOLIDATE** or press **OPTION+SHIFT+3** (Mac) or **ALT+SHIFT+3** (Windows).

3. Repeat Steps 1 and 2 for the remaining clips.

Mastering Foley

Before exporting the Foley clips, you need to take a moment to maximize all of the levels. You could use a simple Normalize process to make sure all of the files peak near full scale. But Normalize won't bring out any of the quieter details in the recordings. So you'll turn again to an ultra maximizer to maximize levels and increase the overall volume. The exaggerated, hyper-real result is exactly what you're looking for to bring the small Foley details to life.

AudioSuite Maxim

In this section, you'll take a look at the AudioSuite version of Maxim (see Figure 3.15).

There are fewer interface elements in the AudioSuite version than in the TDM/RTAS version (as you'll see later in this book). That's because some of the functionality (like dither) wouldn't make sense in an AudioSuite processor.

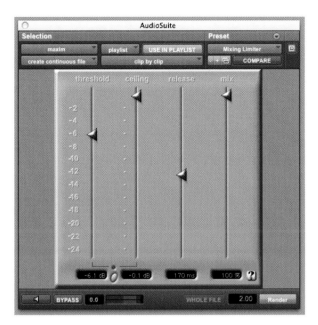

Figure 3.15
AudioSuite Maxim plug-in

Other interface items, like the output meters, have been replaced by the default AudioSuite output meters at the bottom of the interface. Let's take a look at the remaining controls:

- **Threshold slider**—Sets the threshold level for limiting. Signals that exceed this level will be limited.

- **Ceiling slider**—Determines the maximum output level.

- **Release slider**—Sets how long it takes for Maxim to ease off of its attenuation after the input signal drops below the threshold level.

- **Mix slider**—Sets the ratio of dry signal to limited signal. (Normally set to 100% wet.)

- **Link button**—Links the threshold and ceiling controls.

- **Output meter**—Displays the amplitude of the output signal. In addition, you have all of the standard AudioSuite controls.

Note: For more information about AudioSuite, refer to Lesson 1.

Walkthrough: Mastering Foley

In this walkthrough you will learn how to maximize the levels before exporting. Because you're not running any real-time plug-ins, you can use an AudioSuite Limiter to maximize the levels quickly.

To run an AudioSuite Limiter on the clips:

1. Select the first group of footsteps (footsteps on dirt) on the NEW_FOLEY track.

2. Select AUDIOSUITE > DYNAMICS > MAXIM.

3. Select the Mixing Limiter preset.

4. Press PREVIEW to hear the clips played through Maxim.

5. Adjust the plug-in parameters as follows:

   - **File Mode:** Create Individual Files
   - **Selection Reference:** Playlist
   - **Use In Playlist:** Enabled
   - **Playlist Mode:** Clip by Clip

6. Further adjust the Threshold setting to get a consistently loud signal.

7. Click the PROCESS button to apply the effect to all of the selected clips.

8. Repeat the previous steps for the remaining groups of footsteps.

Exporting Foley

You've mastered your clips, but you still need to rename them in a logical fashion. Fortunately, you can batch rename them in Pro Tools. Then you'll be ready to export. Because you've been working with file-based processing exclusively in this lesson, you don't need to perform either of the real-time exporting techniques: Bounce To Disk and Bounce To Tracks. You can use the Export Clips as Files function instead.

Batch Renaming

Pro Tools includes a little known feature that can be used to "batch rename" a group of clips. This function is actually built into the Clip List menu.

To batch rename:

1. Select the clips to be renamed.

2. Open the Clip List pop-up menu and select Auto Rename. The Rename Selected Clips dialog box will appear, as shown in Figure 3.16.

Figure 3.16
Rename Selected Clips dialog box

3. Enter a name to use as the base for the renamed clips.

4. Enter the desired starting number for the renamed clips. (You will generally start at 1.)

5. Enter the desired number of places. ("1" will create single digit numbers [1, 2, 3...]; "2" will create double digit numbers [01, 02, 03...]; "3" will create three digit numbers [001, 002, 003...]; and so on.)

6. Click **OK**. Pro Tools will automatically name and number each of your clips.

Tip: You can also add a suffix to the end of the new clip names if you desire.

Export Clips as Files

You will use the Export Clips as Files function to export the mastered and renamed clips. You're able to use this export technique because you've already completed all of your processing.

Note: For more information about Export Clips as Files, see Lesson 1.

Walkthrough: Exporting Foley

In this walkthrough you will learn how to export Foley. Because you are not running plug-ins on the tracks, you can use Export Clips as Files for a faster than real-time export.

To automatically rename all of the footstep clips:

1. Select all of the clips of a particular type (dirt, wood, or water) on the NEW_FOLEY track.

2. Click the Clip List pop-up menu and select AUTO RENAME. The Rename Selected Clips dialog box will appear.

3. Enter the appropriate name for the footstep clips: **FOL_Footsteps_Sneakers_Dirt_**, **FOL_Footsteps_Sneakers_Wood_**, or **FOL_Footsteps_Water_**.

4. Be sure to put an underscore _ at the end of the name.

5. Enter a starting number of 1.

6. Enter a value for Number of Places of 2.

7. Click **OK**. Pro Tools will automatically name and number each of your footstep clips.

8. Repeat the steps for the other groups of footsteps.

To export the footstep clips:

1. Select all of the clips on the New_Foley track.

2. Select **EXPORT CLIPS AS FILES** from the Clip List pop-up menu, or press **COMMAND+SHIFT+K** (Mac) or **CTRL+SHIFT+K** (Windows). The Export Selected dialog box will appear.

3. Set the export settings as follows:
   - **File Type:** WAV
   - **Format:** (Multiple) Mono
   - **Bit Depth:** 16-bit
   - **Sample Rate:** 48kHz

4. Click **CHOOSE**.

5. Create a folder named **PTGA_Walkthrough_03_FOL** to store all of the clips for this walkthrough. Click **CHOOSE**.

6. Click **EXPORT**.

Implementing Foley

You implement Foley slightly differently than other sound effects. This is because you've created a group of sounds that the game engine will randomize. Fortunately, the game engine does all of the heavy lifting. All you need to do is correctly assign the Foley sounds.

Walkthrough: Implementing Foley

In this walkthrough, you will learn how to implement your exported clips in Unity.

To prepare the Unity project:

1. Open the PTGA_Walkthrough project.

2. Select the Walkthrough_02 scene.

3. Duplicate the scene by choosing EDIT > DUPLICATE or pressing COMMAND+D (Mac) or CTRL+D (Windows).

4. Name the duplicated scene **Walkthrough_03** and add your initials.

5. Double-click the duplicated scene to make it active.

To import the audio files:

1. Navigate to the folder where you exported your Foley clips.

2. Drag the folder onto the Unity Project window. The folder and all of its contents will automatically be imported into the project.

To assign the assets in the Inspector:

1. Click the **AUDIO_MANAGER** object in the Hierarchy window.

2. In the Inspector window, assign the Foley sounds to specific triggers by clicking on the small black circle to the right of each trigger. Sounds should be assigned as follows:

    ● **Dirt footsteps:** FOL_Footsteps_Sneakers_Dirt
    ● **Bridge footsteps:** FOL_Footsteps_Sneakers_Wood
    ● **Water footsteps:** FOL_Footsteps_Water

To test the Foley:

1. Select EDIT > PLAY or press COMMAND+P (Mac) or CTRL+P (Windows) to launch the game.

2. Using the **A**, **S**, **D**, and **W** KEYS (or arrow keys) and the mouse, test the footsteps by walking on the three different surfaces—Dirt, Water, and Wooden Bridge.

3. Press COMMAND+P (Mac) or CTRL+P (Windows) to exit the game.

Summary

This lesson included an overview on how to work with Foley. You should now be able to:

- Work with different types of Foley and commonly used props.
- Use Pro Tools features for recording, editing, mastering, and exporting Foley sounds.
- Implement Foley in Unity.

Review/Discussion Questions

1. What are the three main types of Foley? How are they different? (See "Understanding Foley" on page 62.)

2. Why are listen mics helpful when recording Foley? (See "Recording Foley" on page 64.)

3. What are the key commands for nudging? (See "Editing Foley" on page 69.)

4. Which edit command allows you to quickly divide a clip into smaller clips? (See "Editing Foley" on page 69.)

5. In Pro Tools, which window can be used for batch renaming? (See "Exporting Foley" on page 76.)

Adding/Editing Foley Elements

In this exercise you learn how to emphasize the small details to create a sense of realism. In this exercise you create footsteps and other Foley sounds.

Media Used:
Pro Tools: PTGA_Exercise_03
Unity: PTGA_Exercises

Duration:
60 Minutes

Assessing Foley Requirements

The Foley sounds needed for this exercise include the following.

Footsteps:

- Boots on Concrete—Walk
- Boots on Metal—Walk

Specifics:

- Gun Handling—Switching Weapons, short duration (250 to 750 ms)

Prop Suggestions

Gun handling:

- Wrenches (especially sliding and locking types) make a great substitute for weapons Foley.

Preparing the Pro Tools Session

Before beginning the recording process, you need to prepare the session:

1. Open the PTGA_Exercise_03.ptt session template file. A New Session dialog box will open.

2. Keep the default session parameters.

3. Click **OK**.

4. Save a copy of the session with your initials added to the filename.

5. Prepare the session with the following settings:
   - **Nudge Value:** One Millisecond
   - **Keyboard Focus:** Commands Keyboard Focus (A-Z)
   - **Timeline Drop Order:** Left to Right
   - **Tab To Transients:** Enabled

Recording Foley (Optional)

If you have the ability to record Foley, go ahead and record your own unique elements. Otherwise, the Foley elements in the Clip List can be used.

To record Foley:

1. Record-enable the NEW_FOLEY track.

2. Check to be sure that signal is coming from the mic.

3. Press RECORD then PLAY in the Transport window or on the Edit Window toolbar.

4. Perform the actions required (footsteps and wrench handling) to create the desired Foley sound. For the gun-handling Foley, simulate the sound of switching weapons. (In the game, this will occur when switching between the machine gun and the grenade launcher.)

5. Keep the record pass going and record some additional takes, if necessary. If you're recording the footsteps, try to get a dozen good steps (you will be using the best six of these).

6. When you are satisfied with the recorded content, press STOP.

7. Name the recorded clip so that you'll remember what it contains. For example, **FOL_Boots_Concrete** or **FOL_Gun_Handling**.

8. Repeat Steps 3-7 for each additional Foley sound, as needed.

9. Disable recording on the NEW_FOLEY track.

Using Existing Foley (Alternate Option)

If you are not able to record your own Foley elements, import the following Foley elements to the Clip List from the BlastwaveFX folder:

- ■ Footsteps Hard Sole Shoes Concrete Walk

- ■ Footsteps Hard Sole Shoes Walk On Metal Surface

- ■ Warfare Gun Shotgun Rack Foley Movement

Editing Foley

Once you have all of the Foley elements, it's time to create clips from the best takes. Because some Foley sounds (like footsteps) are repeated many times in the game, it is necessary to create a variety of similar steps that can be randomized by the game engine.

Select and edit the best Foley elements:

1. Drag the first footsteps clip from the Clip List to the NEW_FOLEY track.

2. With the Smart Tool as Selector tool, place the cursor near the beginning of the first clip.

3. Verify that **TAB TO TRANSIENTS** is enabled.

4. Press the **TAB KEY** as needed to move the cursor to the peak transient of the first footstep.

5. Nudge back by two milliseconds using the comma (,) alphanumeric key or the minus – key on the numeric keypad.

6. Press the **A KEY** or chose **EDIT > TRIM CLIP > START TO INSERTION** to eliminate the extra material at the beginning of the clip.

7. Press the **TAB KEY** to move the cursor to the peak transient of the second footstep.

8. Nudge back by two milliseconds using the comma (,) alphanumeric key or the minus – key on the numeric keypad.

9. Press the **B KEY** or select **EDIT > SEPARATE CLIP > AT SELECTION** to add an edit at the current cursor position. Do not add fades at this point; you'll learn about them in the next section.

10. Use **TAB**, **NUDGE**, and **SEPARATE** to add edits for the remaining footsteps.

11. When you've separated six footsteps, tab to the initial transient of the seventh footstep, nudge back by two milliseconds, and press the **S KEY** or choose **TRIM CLIP > END TO INSERTION** to trim the extra material from the end of the clip.

12. Repeat all of these steps to edit the other types of footsteps.

Note: You will need only one edited clip for the gun-handling Foley. Trim the start and end of this clip to isolate the desired take.

Using Batch Fades

To use batch fades to quickly add fades to a selection of clips, follow these steps:

1. Select all of the edited Foley clips on the **NEW_FOLEY** track.

2. Press **COMMAND+F** (Mac) or **CTRL+F** (Windows) or choose **EDIT > FADES > CREATE**. The Batch Fades dialog box will appear.

3. Deselect **CREATE NEW FADES**. This will disable crossfades and only create new fade-ins and fade-outs.

4. Set the Length to two milliseconds.

5. Click **OK** to create the fades.

Consolidating Edited and Faded Clips

1. Select the first clip to be consolidated on the NEW_FOLEY track. Be sure that the selection includes the fade-in and fade-out.

2. Select EDIT > CONSOLIDATE or press OPTION+SHIFT+3 (Mac) or ALT+SHIFT+3 (Windows).

3. Repeat Steps 1 and 2 for the remaining clips on the track.

Mastering Foley

Now that you've edited your Foley, it's time to maximize the levels before exporting. Because you're not running any real-time plug-ins, you can use an AudioSuite ultra-maximizer to maximize the levels.

To run an AudioSuite limiter on the clips, follow these steps:

1. Select the first set of footstep clips on the NEW_FOLEY track.

2. Select AUDIOSUITE > DYNAMICS > MAXIM.

3. Select the Mixing Limiter preset.

4. Press PREVIEW to hear the clips played through Maxim.

5. Adjust the plug-in parameters as follows:

    - **File Mode:** Create Individual Files
    - **Selection Reference:** Playlist
    - **Use In Playlist:** Enabled
    - **Playlist Mode:** Clip by Clip

6. Further adjust the Threshold setting to get consistently loud signal.

7. Click the PROCESS button to apply the effect to all of the selected clips.

8. Repeat these steps for the second set of footsteps and the gun-handling.

Exporting Foley

Your clips are now ready to be renamed and exported. You will use the Auto Rename function to quickly rename the files. Afterward, because you are not running plug-ins on the tracks, you can use Export Selected as Files for a faster than real-time export.

To automatically rename all of the clips:

1. Select all of the clips of a footstep group (concrete or metal) on the NEW_FOLEY track.

2. Open the Clip List pop-up menu and select AUTO RENAME. The Rename Selected Clips dialog box will appear.

3. Enter the appropriate name for the clips: **FOL_Footsteps_Boots_Concrete_**, **FOL_Footsteps_Boots_Metal_**, or **FOL_Gun_Handling_**.

4. Be sure to put an underscore (_) at the end of the name.

5. Enter a starting number of 1.

6. Enter 2 in the Number of Places option.

7. Click **OK**. Pro Tools will automatically name and number each of your footstep clips.

8. Repeat all of these steps for the other Foley clips.

Tip: If you prefer, you can manually rename the gun-handling clip, as you will have only one.

To export Foley:

1. Select all of your finished Foley clips in the Clip List.

2. Select EXPORT CLIPS AS FILES from the Clip List pop-up menu, or press COMMAND+SHIFT+K (Mac) or CTRL+SHIFT+K (Windows). The Export Selected dialog box will appear.

3. Set the export settings as follows:
   - **File Type:** WAV
   - **Format:** (Multiple) Mono
   - **Bit Depth:** 16
   - **Sample Rate:** 48kHz

4. Click the CHOOSE button and create a folder to store all of the Exercise 03 clips. Name the folder **PTGA_Exercise_03_FOL** and click Choose.

5. Click EXPORT.

Implementing Foley

Now that you've exported your Clips from Pro Tools, you're ready to implement them in Unity.

To prepare the Unity project, follow these steps:

1. Launch Unity and open the PTGA_Exercises Unity project.

2. Select the Exercise_02 scene.

3. Duplicate the scene by choosing **EDIT > DUPLICATE** or pressing **COMMAND+D** (Mac) or **CTRL+D** (Windows).

4. Name the duplicated scene **Exercise_03** and add your initials.

5. Double-click the duplicated scene to make it active.

To import the audio files, follow these steps:

1. From a Finder or Explorer window, navigate to the folder where you exported your Foley sounds.

2. Drag the folder to the top of the Unity Project window. The folder and all of its contents will automatically be imported into the project.

To assign the Foley sounds in the inspector, follow these steps:

1. Click the **AUDIO_MANAGER** item in the Hierarchy window.

2. Assign the sounds to specific triggers in the Inspector window as follows:

   - **Footstep_Right01_Cement:** FOL_Footsteps_Boots_Concrete_01
   - **Footstep_Left01_ Cement:** FOL_Footsteps_Boots_Concrete_02
   - **Footstep_Right02_ Cement:** FOL_Footsteps_Boots_Concrete_03
   - **Footstep_Left02_ Cement:** FOL_Footsteps_Boots_Concrete_04
   - **Footstep_Right03_ Cement:** FOL_Footsteps_Boots_Concrete_05
   - **Footstep_Left03_ Cement:** FOL_Footsteps_Boots_Concrete_06
   - **Footstep_Right01_Metal:** FOL_Footsteps_Boots_Metal_01
   - **Footstep_Left01_Metal:** FOL_Footsteps_Boots_Metal_02
   - **Footstep_Right02_Metal:** FOL_Footsteps_Boots_Metal_03
   - **Footstep_Left02_Metal:** FOL_Footsteps_Boots_Metal_04
   - **Footstep_Right03_Metal:** FOL_Boots_Metal_05
   - **Footstep_Left03_Metal:** FOL_Boots_Metal_06
   - **Switch Weapon Clip:** FOL_Gun_Handling_01

To test the Foley, follow these steps:

1. Select **EDIT > PLAY** or press **COMMAND+P** (Mac) or **CTRL+P** (Windows) to launch the game.

2. Using the **A**, **S**, **D**, and **W** KEYS (or arrow keys) and the mouse, navigate your character into the building and up the stairs. You should hear the footsteps on concrete on the concrete surfaces, and the footsteps on metal on the metal stairs and walkway.

3. Press the **2 ALPHANUMERIC KEY** to switch weapons to the grenade launcher; press the 1 key to switch back to the machine gun. You will hear your gun-handling sound with each weapon change.

4. Press **COMMAND+P** (Mac) or **CTRL+P** (Windows) to exit the game.

Working with Sound Effects

Great sound effects are one of the key elements that can create excitement in a game. In this lesson, you'll look at techniques for creating weapon and pick-up sounds.

Media Used: Pro Tools Session: PTGA_Walkthrough_04.ptt
PTGA_Walkthroughs

Duration: 90 Minutes

GOALS

- Understand sound effects
- Acquire sound effects
- Process sound effects
- Master sound effects
- Export sound effects
- Implement sound effects

Understanding Sound Effects

In game audio, sound effects are king. Compelling dialogue may help to move the story forward, and great music may help to illicit a certain emotion from a player, but sound effects bring a whole world to life. Great sound design keeps a player coming back for more!

Most of the concepts and techniques for sound design come from the film world. Film sound designers have been pushing the limits of sound for quite some time. They've used ingenious recording techniques, unusual props, and cutting edge technology to manipulate sound in unimaginable ways. In the process, the great film sound designers have paved the way for a new generation of game sound designers. And best of all, the technology available today is much faster and easier to use than tools from just a few years ago. Pro Tools is at the forefront of this revolution. The ease with which sounds can be edited and processed is incredible.

Weapons, magic spells, explosions, and power ups are just a few of the typical sound effects in games (see Figure 4.1). These sounds provide the primary opportunity for sound designers to make their mark on a title.

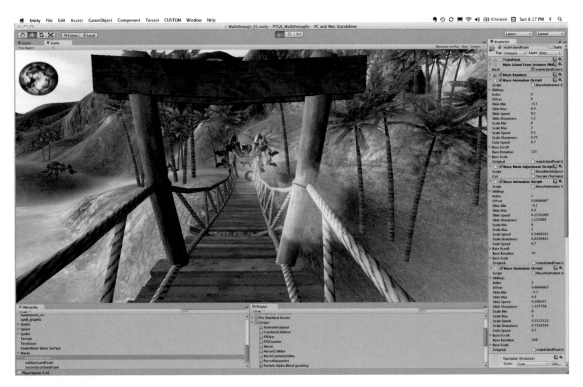

Figure 4.1
An opportunity for great sound design

Assessing Sound Effects Requirements

Unlike dialogue or music, it is often up to the sound designer to determine how sound effects are implemented in the game. While dialogue and music needs can be fairly obvious, a game will have numerous graphical elements that could have a sound effect component. The sound designer shapes the overall sound of the game by deciding which sound elements will be featured, which will be subtle, and which will be silent. This may be accomplished by simply adjusting the volume of various elements, or it may be done through more sophisticated techniques like using EQ.

In addition, it is useful to create a common nomenclature for sound design approach or style. While there are numerous of ways to describe a sound design style, certain terms are commonly used in film, game audio, and related industries.

- **Real**—This style is often described as TV news style, documentary film style, or independent film style. Sounds are generally represented in a low fidelity manner, and are not accentuated with extensive EQ.

- **Hyper-real**—This style can be described as action movie style. (Although, even a Hollywood romantic comedy can sometimes incorporate a hyper-real approach to sound design.) Sounds are generally over the top with extreme detail and extensive EQ.

- **Surreal**—This style can be described as fantasy or science fiction style. Surreal sound design goes beyond simple EQ manipulation, often exploring time-based effects (reverb and delay) and modulation effects (flange, pitch shifting, and more).

Acquiring Sound Effects

As mentioned previously, source sounds are gathered in two primary ways to create finished elements for a game: recording sounds and working with sound libraries. However, sound effects design often incorporates a third technique: synthesis.

Methods for acquiring sound elements:

- **Recording sounds:** Studio and field recording.

- **Browsing sound libraries:** Proprietary and commercial sound libraries.

- **Using synthesis:** Using real or virtual instruments to create sounds. For this lesson, you'll use sound libraries and synthesis to build sounds for your game level.

Note: For more information on studio and field recording, see Lesson 3, "Working with Foley" and Lesson 5, "Working with Backgrounds."

Browsing Sound Libraries

As mentioned in Lesson 1, "Understanding the Game Audio Workflow," most sound elements in a game are designed by combining elements that are transferred (or "pulled") from sound libraries. Just a few years ago, this required the sound designer to look through the library manufacturer's spreadsheet to find a potential sound, locate the appropriate audio CD where the sound was stored, and record the sound effect from a CD player into Pro Tools.

Fortunately, almost all sound effects libraries are now copied to hard disks. But, this still leaves the problem of efficiently browsing the available sound effects to find the handful of sounds that are needed for a particular task. Two primary options are available for browsing and searching sound effects libraries: DigiBase and third-party applications.

DigiBase

Pro Tools has a built-in set of browsers, collectively known as DigiBase, that can be used for locating, auditioning, and importing sound effects. Audio files can be imported directly into Pro Tools by simply dragging and dropping from a DigiBase browser window into the Edit window. Files imported in this manner are automatically converted to the session's bit depth, sample rate, and file format.

To search for sound effects using DigiBase:

1. Choose **WINDOWS > WORKSPACE** or press **OPTION+;** (Mac) or **ALT+;** (Windows). The Workspace browser will open (see Figure 4.2).

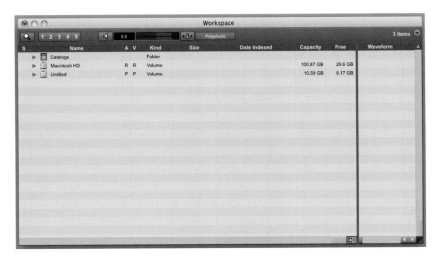

Figure 4.2
Workspace browser

2. In the Workspace browser, click the **Find** button, which looks like a magnifying glass (see Figure 4.3).

The Find button ———

Figure 4.3
Workspace browser Find button

3. Select the volumes you want to search by clicking the checkboxes (see Figure 4.4).

Figure 4.4
Workspace browser with only one volume selected

Tip: Limiting the volumes (drives) that are included in your search can speed up the process dramatically. You can also expand a volume's contents by clicking the triangle next to it and further limit your search to specific directories (folders) within the volume.

4. Click the **drop-down** button in the **Kind** column (see Figure 4.5) and choose **Audio File** (see Figure 4.6).

Figure 4.5
Kind column set to Audio File

Figure 4.6
Options available in the Kind pop-up menu

5. Enter a search term in the **Name** field, and click the **Search** button. The search results will appear in the bottom half of the Workspace browser (see Figure 4.7).

Figure 4.7
Results of a
Workspace search

To audition sound effects using DigiBase:

1. Select an audio file in the DigiBase browser.

2. Do one of the following:

   ● Click the **WAVEFORM PREVIEW** button (the speaker icon) (see Figure 4.8).

Figure 4.8
Auditioning from the start of a file in DigiBase

   ● Press the **SPACEBAR**. (Requires the option for Spacebar Toggles File Preview to be enabled in the Browser menu.)

   ● Press **COMMAND+P** (Mac) or **CTRL+P** (Windows).

Note: If the Auto Preview option is enabled in the Browser menu, previewing starts as soon as a file is selected.

To audition from a specific location in the audio file:

   ■ Click the Waveform Display at the desired location. The audio will play starting at that point in the file (see Figure 4.9).

Figure 4.9
Auditioning from a specific location in a file by clicking the waveform

To import an audio file to the Clip List:

■ Drag the audio file from the Workspace browser onto the Clip List.

To import an audio file onto an existing audio track:

■ Drag the audio file from the Workspace browser onto the track in the Pro Tools Edit window.

To import an audio file onto a new track, do one of the following:

■ Drag the audio file from the Workspace browser onto the Tracks list. A new track will be created, and the file will be placed at the session start.

■ Drag the audio file from the Workspace browser onto the empty space at the bottom of the Edit window. A new track will be created and the file will be placed at the location where it was dropped (see Figure 4.10).

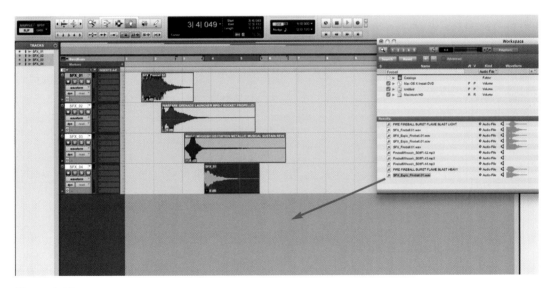

Figure 4.10
Dragging and dropping a file onto the empty space in the Edit window

Using Synthesis to Create Sound Effects

Many sound designers make use of synthesizers to generate new sound effects or to complement existing sound effects. Synthesizers have a lot of great uses for game sound design: game menu elements, low frequency "sweeteners" for impacts and explosions, quick "stingers" for in game pick ups, and much more.

A synthesizer can be an actual musical instrument that exists in the real world, or it can be a virtual synth in the form of a Pro Tools plug-in. In Pro Tools, you're fortunate to have access to a huge variety of quality virtual instruments and synthesizers. Take a closer look at a free synth that is included with every version of Pro Tools: Xpand!2.

Xpand!2

Xpand!2 (see Figure 4.11) is a virtual workstation plug-in. The Xpand!2 engine consists of a sample playback, FM, wavetable, and virtual analogue synth architecture, capable of creating complex sounds very efficiently, allowing for multiple simultaneous patches with integrated effects on any Pro Tools system.

Figure 4.11
Xpand!2 plug-in interface

Some Xpand!2 features include the following:

- More than 1,000 factory patches and 500 combinable part presets
- Multi-synthesis engine
- Four layerable parts for millions of combinations
- 64-note polyphony
- Quick and easy sound tweaking
- Sample playback and virtual tonewheels
- Two built-in effect sections and four arpeggiators/phrase generators

- Highly efficient on system resources
- RTAS format

How Is a Synthesizer Different from a Sampler?

With modern electronic instruments, there is very little difference between a synthesizer and a sampler. Both synths and samplers can offer envelopes, filters, effects processors, arpeggiators, and other sound manipulation tools. The only absolute difference is that a synthesizer uses an oscillator as its fundamental sound source, whereas a sampler uses a sampled waveform instead. Therefore, a synth is great for creating elements that sound "electronic," but not so good at creating elements that sound "acoustic." On the other hand, a sampler can play a "snapshot" of any type of waveform, and so is quite capable of imitating a synthesizer while also being able to reproduce natural acoustic sounds. Many modern electronic instruments, including Xpand!2, incorporate both technologies.

Using the Pencil Tool

The Pencil tool (see Figure 4.12) is particularly important when working with MIDI data. In fact, the Pencil is essentially a Smart Tool for working with MIDI.

Figure 4.12
Pencil tool selected in the toolbar

To use the Pencil tool to create a MIDI note:

1. Click and hold the **PENCIL TOOL** icon in the toolbar.

2. Select the **FREEHAND** shape (see Figure 4.13).

Figure 4.13
Pencil tool pop-up menu

3. Click a MIDI or Instrument Track while in Notes view. A MIDI note will be created at the click location (see Figure 4.14). Clicking and dragging will create a note the length of the drag.

Figure 4.14
Using the Pencil tool to draw a MIDI note

Tip: If the track is in a view other than Notes (the default view of clips), clicking on the track with the Pencil tool will automatically change the view to Notes. You will then need to click a second time to create a midi note.

4. To use the Pencil tool to modify a MIDI note, do one of the following:

- **Transpose**—To transpose a MIDI note, select the middle portion of the note with the Pencil tool and drag up or down. The Pencil tool will switch to the Grabber tool (see Figure 4.15).

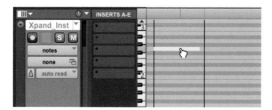

Figure 4.15
Using the Pencil tool to transpose a MIDI note

- **Trim**—To trim the start or end time of a MIDI note, select near the start or end of the note with the Pencil tool and drag left or right. The Pencil tool will switch to the Trimmer tool (see Figure 4.16).

Figure 4.16
Using the Pencil tool to trim a MIDI note

In the Avid Learning Series For more information about the Pencil tool, see "Edit Tool Functions" in the "Pro Tools 101: An Introduction to Pro Tools 10" book by Avid.

Recording Virtual Instruments

In Pro Tools, the output from a virtual instrument cannot be recorded onto the track where the virtual instrument is inserted. Instead, the output of the virtual instrument's track must be routed to an audio track using a bus.

First in bulleted list 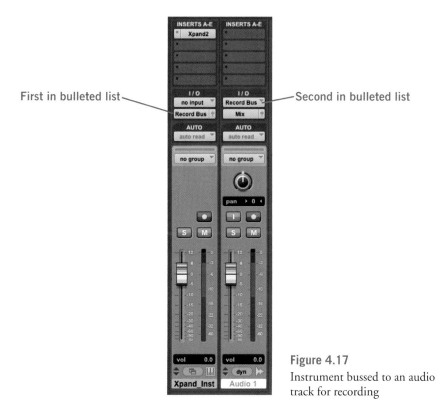 Second in bulleted list

Figure 4.17
Instrument bussed to an audio
track for recording

To record the output of a virtual instrument:

1. Set the AUDIO OUTPUT PATH selector of the virtual instrument track to an available bus (see Figure 4.17).

2. Set the AUDIO INPUT PATH selector of the audio track you want to use for recording to the same bus (see Figure 4.17).

3. Click on the RECORD ENABLE button for the audio track. The button will begin to flash.

4. Position the PLAYBACK cursor in the desired location.

5. Press RECORD then PLAY in the Transport window or on the Edit window toolbar.

6. When the desired output has been recorded, press STOP. Don't forget to name the newly recorded clip.

**In the Avid
Learning Series**   For more information, see "Recording Audio" in the Pro Tools 101 book.

Walkthrough: Acquiring Sound Effects

In this walkthrough you will learn how to browse and search for sound effects to be used in a game. You can find any files you need on the DVD.

Sound design elements needed:

- Fireball Spell
- Ice Comet Spell
- Mission Complete

Suggested sound design search terms:

- Spells—Fireball, whooshes, magic spell
- Mission Complete—Synth patches from Hits, Percussion, or FX

To prepare the session:

1. Open the PTGA_Walkthrough_04.ptt session template file.

2. Keep the default session parameters.

3. Click **OK.**

4. Save a copy of the session with your initials added to the filename.

5. Prepare the session with the following settings:

   - **Nudge Value:** One Millisecond
   - **Keyboard Focus:** Commands Keyboard Focus (A-Z)
   - **Timeline Drop Order:** Left to Right
   - **Tab To Transients:** Enabled

Typically, the sound design process begins by browsing or searching existing SFX libraries. Let's look at how to use DigiBase to browse and search for useful elements.

To use DigiBase to browse sound effects elements (Option 1):

1. Press **OPTION+;** (Mac) or **ALT+;** (Windows) or select **WINDOW > WORKSPACE** to open the Workspace browser.

2. Navigate to the location of the BlastwaveFX folder on your system (included on the DVD).

3. Browse through the assets in the folder.

4. Click the **SPEAKER** icon or the **WAVEFORM** to audition the files.

To use DigiBase to search for sound effects elements (Option 2):

1. Press **OPTION+;** (Mac) or **ALT+;** (Windows) or select **WINDOW > WORKSPACE** to open the Workspace browser (if it's not already open).

2. Click the **FIND** button (magnifying glass) in the Workspace, or press **COMMAND+F** (Mac) or **CTRL+F** (Windows) to initiate a search.

3. Select the volumes you want to search by clicking the checkboxes. Be sure you have selected the volume that contains the BlastwaveFX folder.

4. Type a search term like "fireball" into the search field. Press **RETURN** or **ENTER** or click the **SEARCH** button to execute the search. After a few moments, the assets that match "fireball" will appear.

5. Browse through the found assets.

6. Click on the **SPEAKER** icon or the **WAVEFORM** to audition the files.

7. Repeat Steps 1-6 for the other sound design elements.

Importing Sound Effects into Pro Tools

Once you've found a variety of elements for the magic spells, import them into the session.

To import the sound elements to the Clip List:

1. Select the desired element(s) in the Workspace browser.

2. Drag and drop the elements into the Clip List.

Note: You'll also want to import the DIA_Player_05 and DIA_Player_06 dialogue lines that you recorded in Lesson 2.

Using Synthesis to Create Sound Elements

In this section, you'll use a virtual instrument to create the Mission Complete sound effect.

To create an instrument track and an audio track:

1. Select **TRACK > NEW TRACK** or press **COMMAND+SHIFT+N** (Mac) or **CTRL+SHIFT+N** (Windows). The New Tracks dialog box will open.

2. Configure a new Mono Instrument track and a new Mono Audio track. (Remember to use the Add Row **+** button to create tracks with different track formats.)

3. Click **CREATE** to add the tracks to Pro Tools.

4. Name the new tracks **Xpand_Inst** and **Xpand_Rec**.

To insert Xpand!2 on the instrument track and audition patches:

1. Insert an instance of Xpand!2 on the Xpand_Inst track. The track's MIDI output will be automatically assigned to the Xpand!2 plug-in (see Figure 4.18).

Figure 4.18
Instrument track with Xpand!2 inserted

2. Return to the **EDIT** window, and zoom in so that single bars are visible.

3. Use the **PENCIL** tool (or a MIDI keyboard) to create a single MIDI note with approximately a one bar duration on the track (see Figure 4.19).

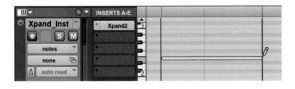

Figure 4.19
Using the Pencil tool to create a MIDI note

4. Select the bar that contains the MIDI note with the Smart Tool as the Selector tool.

5. Enable loop playback by pressing **COMMAND+SHIFT+L** (Mac) or **CTRL+SHIFT+L** (Windows).

6. Press **PLAY** to begin playback.

7. Use the **PLUG-IN LIBRARIAN** menu (see Figure 4.20 A) or the **PREVIOUS SETTING** and **NEXT SETTING** buttons (see Figure 4.20 B) to audition different patches. (The Hits folder is a good place to start.)

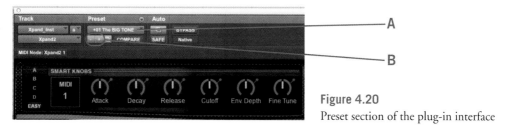

Figure 4.20
Preset section of the plug-in interface

To record the output of Xpand!2:

1. Switch to the **MIX** window and route the output of the Xpand_Inst track to a bus (see Figure 4.21 A).

2. Route the same bus to the input of the Xpand_Rec track (see Figure 4.21 B).

3. Record-enable the Xpand_Rec track (see Figure 4.21 C).

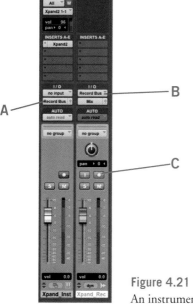

Figure 4.21
An instrument track routed to an audio track for recording

4. Position the playback cursor in the desired location and begin recording.

5. When the desired output has been recorded, press **STOP** and name the new clip.

6. Right-click the Xpand_Inst track and choose **HIDE AND MAKE INACTIVE** from the pop-up menu.

Editing Sound Effects

Sound effects editing makes use of many of the techniques discussed previously, like Tab To Transients. However, editing for sound design also presents some opportunities to use additional techniques to layer and arrange sound elements.

Layering Sound Elements

One of the fundamental sound design techniques for building complex sound effects is to layer multiple sound elements. Some typical functions for layering sound elements include adding tracks, trimming clips, and creating fades.

Adding Tracks

Layering multiple, separate sound elements requires multiple tracks in Pro Tools. Often, sound designers will create a new Pro Tools session for each required sound effect (or group of sound effects) in a game. This guarantees that all of the resources (tracks and plug-ins) of the Pro Tools system will be available during the sound design process.

Don't hesitate to create plenty of additional tracks in Pro Tools when designing a sound effect. Experimentation with various sound elements (and plug-ins— discussed later in this lesson) is the key to creating unique sound effects.

Note: For more information about adding tracks to a session, see "Creating New Tracks" in Lesson 1, "Understanding the Game Audio Workflow."

Trimming Clips

Creatively trimming clips is an important component of making multiple sound elements work together. Even when you're working with the Smart Tool, you still have access to all of the Trimmer Tool modes (see Figure 4.22). Let's take a quick look at all of them in the next sections.

Figure 4.22
Trimmer tool pop-up menu

Standard Trim

You're probably already familiar with the Standard mode for the Trimmer tool (see Figure 4.23). In this mode, you can quickly shorten or lengthen a clip, trimming off unwanted audio or revealing previously trimmed audio (up to the full length of the whole file clip).

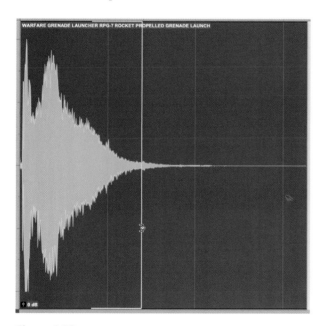

Figure 4.23
Before and after using the standard Trimmer tool

TCE Trim

The TCE mode for the Trimmer tool (see Figure 4.24) appears to function like Standard mode. But, it's actually invoking your preferred Time Compression/Expansion plug-in and using that algorithm to process the selected clip, shrinking or stretching the audio to match the new length.

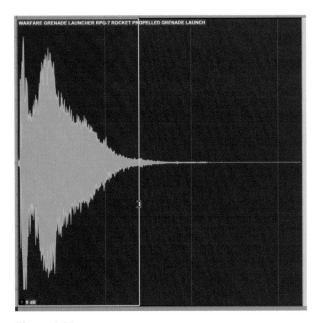 

Figure 4.24
Before and after using the TCE Trimmer tool

To set the AudioSuite plug-in that is used by the TCE Trimmer tool:

1. Choose **SETUP > PREFERENCES**.

2. Select the **PROCESSING** tab (see Figure 4.25).

3. From the TC/E plug-in pop-up menu, select the desired **AUDIOSUITE** plug-in (see Figure 4.26).

Figure 4.25
TC/E preferences

Figure 4.26
TC/E plug-in pop-up menu

4. From the **DEFAULT SETTINGS** pop-up menu, select the plug-in setting best suited to the material you work with most. (The **< FACTORY DEFAULT >** setting is fine for most material; see Figure 4.27.)

5. Click **OK**.

Figure 4.27
TC/E Default Settings pop-up menu

Scrub Trim

Scrub Trim requires Pro Tools HD or Pro Tools software with Complete Production Toolkit 2. The Scrub mode for the Trimmer tool allows you to scrub audio while adjusting the length of the clip. This allows you to use your ears to find the perfect clip length. When you release the mouse, the clip will be trimmed to the Scrub Trim location (see Figure 4.28).

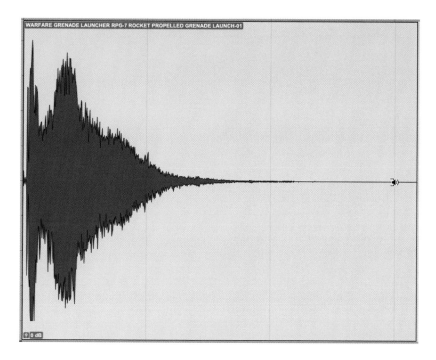

Figure 4.28
Scrub Trimmer in action

Loop Trim

The Loop mode for the Trimmer tool automatically creates a clip loop when the clip is trimmed beyond its current length. When you release the mouse, loop iterations are generated as needed to fill the trim length (see Figure 4.29).

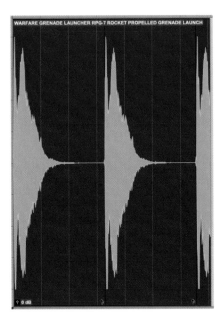

Figure 4.29
Before and after using the Loop Trimmer tool

> **Note:** The Loop Trim mode is discussed in detail in Lesson 8, "Working with Cinematics."

Creating Fades

Used in conjunction with trimming, adding fades is a critical technique for blending sound elements into a cohesive sound effect. You've looked at basic fades and batch fades in previous lessons. When using the Smart Tool (or single key commands) to create fades, the fade shape is determined by the Pro Tools preferences. Let's look at these fade preferences in a little more detail.

To change the default fade shape:

1. Choose **SETUP > PREFERENCES**.

2. Select the **EDITING** tab (see Figure 4.30).

3. In the Fades section, click one of the following buttons:

- Fade In
- Fade Out
- Crossfade

The relevant Fades dialog box will appear.

Figure 4.30
Fades preferences

Fade Shapes

While many fade shapes are available in each Fades dialog box, they are built from three basic types: Standard, S Curve, and Preset Curves. Of the available Preset Curve options, the middle three are probably used the most.

Shortcut: All of these fade shapes can be modified by clicking and dragging with the mouse.

- **Preset Shape 3** (see Figure 4.31)—Keeps the volume relatively high during the duration of the fade.

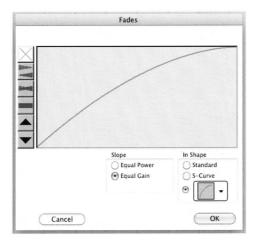

Figure 4.31
Preset shape 3

■ **Preset Shape 4** (see Figure 4.32)—Modifies volume in a linear fashion.

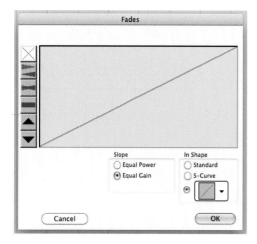

Figure 4.32
Preset shape 4

■ **Preset Shape 5** (see Figure 4.33)—Keeps the volume relatively low during the duration of the fade.

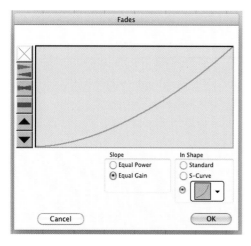

Figure 4.33
Preset shape 5

Arranging Sound Elements

Another important sound design technique involves adjusting the timing of the different layers of a sound effect. Pro Tools provides several particularly useful features for changing clip timing, including nudging, using sync points, and using clip align modifiers.

Nudging

The importance of *nudging* in Pro Tools cannot be overstated. As mentioned previously, nudging is the easiest way to move the cursor or a selection in precise intervals.

To nudge something, do one of the following:

■ Press the **+** and **–** keys on the numeric keypad.

■ With Commands Keyboard Focus enabled, press the **,** or **.** alphanumeric keys.

Note: For more about nudging, see Lesson 3, "Working with Foley."

Sync Points

Sync points provide a powerful feature for marking and aligning locations within a clip. As discussed previously, using the Tab key in Pro Tools will move the cursor through clip boundaries. However, if you want to Tab to a location inside the clip, you've got two options: Enable Tab To Transients or use a sync point. If you enable Tab to Transients and then press Tab repeatedly you'll eventually arrive at the desired location in the clip (assuming the location corresponds to a transient). However, a sync point placed at the desired location creates a Tab destination that avoids the hassle and limitations of using Tab To Transients. Standard Tab key functionality will stop on the sync point in addition to clip boundaries. Furthermore, sync points are invaluable for aligning clips (as discussed in the "Aligning Clips" section, next).

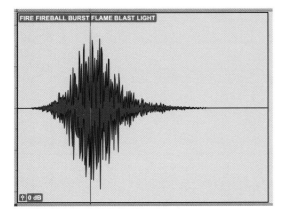

Figure 4.34
Cursor positioned prior to adding the sync point

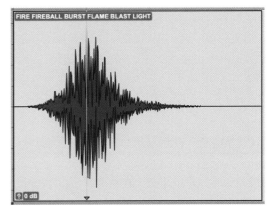

Figure 4.35
Clip after the sync point has been added

To identify a sync point in a clip:

1. Using the Smart Tool as the Selector tool, place the cursor at the desired location inside the clip. (It can be helpful to use Tab To Transients to quickly find the correct location; see Figure 4.34.)

2. Choose **CLIP > IDENTIFY SYNC POINT**, or press **COMMAND+,** (Mac) or **CTRL+,** (Windows) (see Figure 4.35).

To move an existing sync point, do one of the following:

- Use the Smart Tool as the Grabber tool and drag the **SYNC POINT** to a new location.

- Hold **CONTROL** (Mac) or **START** (Windows) while using the Smart Tool as the Grabber tool to drag the sync point while scrubbing.

To delete a sync point from a clip, do one of the following:

- Using the Smart Tool as the Grabber tool, Option-click on an existing sync point.

- Select the clip containing the sync point and choose **CLIP > REMOVE SYNC POINT**, or press **COMMAND+,** (Mac) or **CTRL+,** (Windows).

Aligning Clips

When working with multiple sound elements, it is often necessary to align the clips using the clip start, clip end, or sync point. Fortunately, aligning clips can be accomplished quickly with key modifiers in Pro Tools.

To align the clip start:

1. Using the Smart Tool as the Grabber tool, select the clip that you want to align *to* (typically on another track); see Figure 4.36.

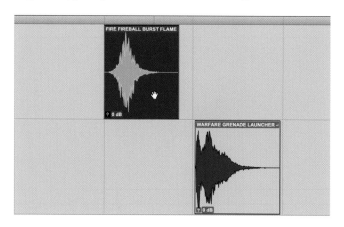

Figure 4.36

Selecting the clip you want to align to

2. Control-click (Mac) or Start-click (Windows) the clip that you want to have aligned (see Figure 4.37). The clicked clip will instantly move to align its start with the previously selected clip (see Figure 4.38).

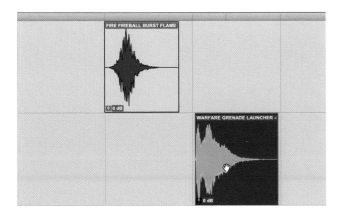

Figure 4.37
When the clip to be aligned is clicked, a highlight will appear to show the clip destination

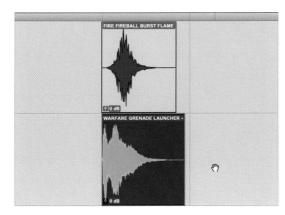

Figure 4.38
After the mouse is released, the clip is aligned

To align the clip end:

1. Using the Smart Tool as the Grabber tool, select the clip that you want to align to (see Figure 4.36).

2. Control+Command-click (Mac) or Ctrl+Start-click (Windows) on the clip that you want to have aligned (see Figure 4.39). The clicked clip will instantly move to align its end with the start of the previously selected clip (see Figure 4.40).

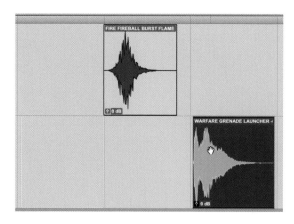

Figure 4.39
Notice that the tail of the highlight is aligned to the head of the guide clip

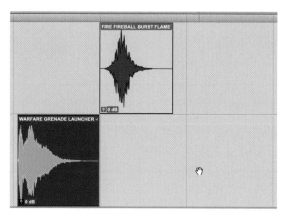

Figure 4.40
After the mouse is released, the clip is aligned

To align the clip sync point:

1. Using the Smart Tool as the Grabber tool, select the clip that you want to align to (refer back to Figure 4.36).

2. Find the clip you want to have aligned, make sure it has a sync point marked, and press Control+Shift-click (Mac) or Start+Shift-click (Windows) (see Figure 4.41). The clicked clip will instantly move to align its sync point with the start of the previously selected clip (see Figure 4.42).

Tip: All of these alignment functions can also be performed with the cursor location rather than with a selection.

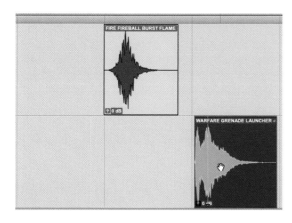

Figure 4.41
Notice that the sync point is being used to align the highlight to the guide clip

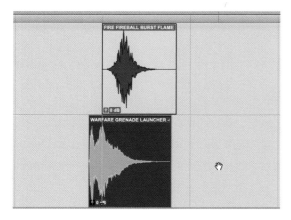

Figure 4.42
After the mouse is released, the clip is aligned

Walkthrough: Editing Sound Effects

In this walkthrough, you will learn how to edit the sound effects you have imported for the game.

Now that you've imported your sound elements, you can choose to use them in their original form or combine them with other elements. Let's start with the fireball. For the purposes of this walkthrough, you will build this sound from three parts—a burning element for the fireball, a more magical sound to support the idea that a spell is being cast, and a vocalized incantation.

To edit the fireball element:

1. Enable the SLIP EDIT mode.

2. Create three new Mono Audio tracks and name the tracks **Fireball_01**, **Fireball_02**, and **Fireball_03**.

3. Drag a **FIREBALL** clip from the Clip List onto the Fireball_01 track. Leave a few seconds of space between the clip and the session start.

4. Enable **ZOOM TOGGLE** to get a better look at the clip.

5. Using the Smart Tool as the Trimmer tool, trim the start and end of the clip to eliminate the silent portions.

6. Using the Smart Tool, create a small fade (around 50 milliseconds) at the beginning and end of the clip.

7. Disable **ZOOM TOGGLE**.

To edit the magic element and add a sync point:

1. Drag a **MAGIC** clip from the Clip List to the Fireball_02 track.

2. Enable **ZOOM TOGGLE** to get a better look at the clip.

3. Using the Smart Tool as the Trimmer tool, trim the start and end of the clip to eliminate the silent portions.

4. Using the Smart Tool, create a very small fade (around 50 milliseconds) at the beginning and end of the clip.

5. Using the Smart Tool as the Selector tool, place the cursor at the peak of the waveform.

6. Add a sync point by choosing **CLIP > IDENTIFY SYNC POINT** or by pressing **COMMAND+,** (Mac) or **CTRL+,** (Windows).

7. Disable **ZOOM TOGGLE**.

To position the magic element relative to the fireball element:

1. Using the Smart Tool as the Grabber tool, select the **FIREBALL** clip.

2. Control+Shift-click (Mac) or Start+Shift-click (Windows) on the **MAGIC** clip.

3. Audition the results and use the **NUDGE** tool to adjust the timing as needed.

To position the dialogue element relative to the fireball element:

1. Drag the DIA_Player.05 clip from the Clip List to the Fireball_03 track.

2. Disable **TAB TO TRANSIENTS**.

3. Use the **TAB KEY** to position the cursor at the sync point of the **MAGIC** clip on the Fireball_02 track.

4. Using the Smart Tool as the Grabber tool, Control+Command-click (Mac) or Ctrl+Start-click (Windows) on the dialogue clip to align the end of the clip with the sync point.

5. Audition the results and use NUDGE to adjust the timing as needed.

6. Once you're happy with the Fireball, repeat all of these steps for the Ice Comet using another FIREBALL clip and MAGIC clip and the DIA_Player.06 clip. Don't worry about making the sound shorter. You'll deal with that in the "Processing Sound Effects" section that follows.

7. Name the tracks and place the clips as follows:

   - **Ice_Comet_01:** Fireball clip
   - **Ice_Comet_02**: Magic clip
   - **Ice_Comet_03**: Dia_Player_06 clip

Processing Sound Effects

Perhaps the most creative aspect of designing sound effects is the use of signal processing. In Pro Tools, signal processing is accomplished using AudioSuite and TDM/RTAS plug-ins. In previous lessons, you've already looked at the basics of inserting plug-ins and adjusting plug-in parameters. Now you'll dig deeper to look at some specific plug-ins and how they can be used for sound design.

AudioSuite

As you may recall, AudioSuite plug-ins are non-real-time. Some powerful sound design processes can only be applied in this manner.

Time Shift

The Time Shift plug-in (see Figure 4.43) provides high-quality time compression and expansion (TCE) algorithms and formant correct pitch shifting. It uses an algorithm that is superior to the standard Time Compression/Expansion or Pitch Shift plug-ins.

Time Shift controls include the following:

- **Audio**—Use these controls to select the time compression and expansion algorithm (mode), and to attenuate the gain of the processed audio to avoid clipping.

- **Time**—Use these controls to specify the amount of time compression or expansion you want to apply.

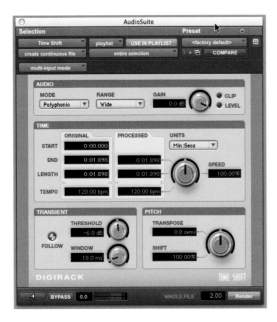

Figure 4.43
AudioSuite Time Shift plug-in interface

- **Formant or Transient**—Use these controls to adjust either the amount of formant shift or the transient detection parameters, depending on the mode selected in the Audio section.

- **Pitch**—Use these controls to apply pitch shifting.

TDM/RTAS

TDM/RTAS plug-ins are real-time processors that are inserted on a track. In Pro Tools, TDM/RTAS parameter changes are instantly audible on the track.

Air Flanger

The Air Flanger plug-in (see Figure 4.44) applies a short modulation delay to an audio signal.

Air Flanger controls include the following:

- **Sync**—When enabled, the Flanger Rate control synchronizes to the Pro Tools session tempo.

- **Rate**—When Sync is enabled, lets you select a rhythmic subdivision of the beat for the Flanger Modulation Rate.

- **Depth**—Lets you adjust the amount of modulation applied to the delay time.

- **Pre Delay**—Controls the minimum delay time in milliseconds.

Figure 4.44
RTAS AIR Flanger plug-in interface

- **LFO Section**—Provides controls for the Low Frequency Oscillator (LFO) used to modulate the delay time.

- **EQ Section**—Provides controls for cutting lows from the Flanger signal and inverting phase.

- **Feedback**—Lets you adjust the amount of delay feedback for the Flanger. At +/− 100%, the Flanger feeds back on itself.

- **Mix**—Lets you balance the amount of dry signal with the amount of wet (flanged) signal.

Air Dynamic Delay

The Air Dynamic Delay (see Figure 4.45) plug-in is a delay line that can synchronize to Pro Tools session tempo and be modulated by an envelope follower.

Figure 4.45
RTAS AIR Dynamic Delay plug-in interface

Air Dynamic Delay controls include the following:

- **Sync**—When enabled, the Delay control synchronizes to the Pro Tools session tempo.

- **Delay**—When Sync is enabled, lets you select a rhythmic subdivision of the beat for the Delay time.

- **Feedback**—Lets you adjust the amount of delay feedback. At 0%, the delayed signal repeats only once. As you increase the feedback, the number of repetitions increases.

- **Delay Section**—Lets you adjust the Left/Right Ratio and the Stereo Width of the delay effect.

- **EQ Section**—Lets you adjust Low Cut and High Cut filters.

- **Envelope Modulation Section**—Lets you control the parameters of the envelope follower.

- **Feedback Mode**—Controls how the input signal is processed and fed to the outputs.

- **Mix**—Lets you adjust the balance of the dry signal against the wet (delayed) signal.

Basic Plug-In Automation

Plug-in automation is a large topic in its own right. Fortunately, only a basic understanding of automation is necessary to begin using plug-ins for sound design. Let's take a look at some fundamental information you'll need to perform simple automation.

Enabling Plug-In Parameters for Automation

Before a plug-in parameter can be automated, it must be automation enabled. You can enable plug-in parameters for automation from a couple of different locations: the Plug-In Automation dialog box and the plug-in window itself.

To enable a parameter for automation using the Plug-In Automation dialog box:

1. Open the plug-in window for the plug-in you want to automate (see Figure 4.46).

Figure 4.46
Plug-In Automation Enable button

2. In the Plug-In Automation dialog box, choose the controls to automate and click **ADD** (see Figure 4.47).

Figure 4.47
Plug-In Automation dialog box

3. Click **OK** to close the dialog box.

To enable a parameter for automation directly in the plug-in window:

1. Open the plug-in window for the plug-in you want to automate.

2. Control+Option+Command-click (Mac) or Ctrl+Start+Alt-click (Windows) on the parameter that you want to automate (see Figure 4.48). Select the **ENABLE AUTOMATION FOR** option from the pop-up menu.

Figure 4.48
Enable Automation
For pop-up menu

Automating Plug-In Parameters in the Track View

Once a plug-in parameter has been enabled for automation, an automation playlist for the parameter is automatically created. This automation playlist can be accessed from the Track View selector on the track where the plug-in is inserted.

To display an automation playlist in the Track view:

1. Locate the track where the plug-in is inserted in the Edit window.

2. Click the **TRACK VIEW** selector and select the automation type corresponding to the automation enabled plug-in parameter (see Figure 4.49).

Figure 4.49
Track View selector and pop-up menu

Shortcut: **You can also press Control+Command (Mac) or Ctrl+Start (Windows) and click on the control in the plug-in window to automatically display the automation playlist for the selected parameter.**

To create automation on the automation playlist, do either of the following:

■ Use the Pencil tool to draw automation directly on the automation playlist. You can also use any of the Pencil tool shapes (see Figure 4.50).

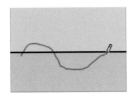

Figure 4.50
Using the Pencil tool to draw automation

■ Click with the Grabber tool to add individual automation breakpoints to the automation playlist (see Figure 4.51).

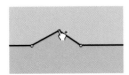

Figure 4.51
Using the Grabber tool to add automation breakpoints

To edit automation on the automation playlist, do either of the following:

■ Click and drag with the Grabber tool to reposition an individual automation breakpoint.

■ Option-click (Mac) or Alt-click (Windows) with the Grabber tool to delete an individual breakpoint.

In the Avid Learning Series   For more information about automation, see "Basic Automation" in the Pro Tools 101 book.

Walkthrough: Processing Sound Effects

In this walkthrough you will learn how to make some final adjustments and add some signal processing.

The Ice Comet effect is sounding pretty good, but it's too long for your purposes. Let's assign a high-quality plug-in to the TCE Trimmer and shorten the Ice Comet elements.

To set the TCE Trimmer plug-in:

1. Choose SETUP > PREFERENCES.

2. Select the PROCESSING tab.

3. From the TC/E plug-in pop-up menu, select TIME SHIFT.

4. From the Default Settings pop-up menu, select < FACTORY DEFAULT >.

5. Click OK.

To use the TCE Trimmer to shorten an element:

1. Locate the Ice_Comet_01 track.

2. Consolidate the clip on the track.

3. Using the Smart Tool as the TCE Trimmer tool, click near the end of the Fireball element and shorten it by about 50%.

4. Audition the shortened element. If it's too short or too long, undo the TCE Trim and try again.

Caution: Whenever you need to re-process a sound with Time Compression/ Expansion, always undo the previous process. This is because each application of a TCE algorithm degrades the sound quality of the source sound.

5. If needed, use **Nudge** to adjust the clip placement on the Ice_Comet_01 track.

6. Repeat Steps 3-4 for the Ice Comet's magic element as well.

Now that the Ice Comet has the correct duration, let's apply some processing to the Fireball and Mission Complete sounds.

To put a flanger on the Fireball_01 track:

1. Insert the **Air Flanger** on the last insert of the Fireball_01 track.

2. Select the 05 Soft Flanger preset.

3. Enable automation for the **Mix** parameter by holding **Control+Option+ Command** (Mac) or **Ctrl+Start+Alt** (Windows) and clicking on the control in the plug-in window.

4. Return to the Fireball_01 track in the Edit window and change the Track View to see the **Air Flanger > Mix** parameter.

Shortcut: Pressing Control+Command (Mac) or Ctrl+Start (Windows) and clicking on the control in the plug-in window will automatically change the Track View to the selected parameter.

5. Use the **Pencil** tool to draw some automation for the **Mix** parameter. Try increasing the **Mix** percentage from 0% up to 50% as the sound trails off.

Finally, you'll accentuate the synthesized Mission Complete sound by adding some delay.

To put a delay on the Mission Complete hit:

1. Insert the **Air Dynamic Delay** on the last insert of the Xpand_Rec track.

2. Select the 10 Spin Delay preset.

3. Reduce the **Feedback** parameter to around 33%.

Mastering Sound Effects

Now that you've configured the processing for the sound effects, it's time to maximize levels before exporting.

Walkthrough: Mastering Sound Effects

In this walkthrough, you learn how to master the sound effects for the game.

To modify the I/O setup:

1. Select SETUP > I/O. The I/O Setup window will open.

2. Create two new mono busses and name them **Master** and **Bounce**.

3. Close the I/O Setup window.

To add an ultra-maximizer to the mastering track:

1. Show the I/O view in the Edit window.

2. Set the outputs of all the audio tracks to the Master bus.

Shortcut: **Holding the Option modifier (Mac) or Alt modifier (Windows) while changing the output on one track will change the output on all tracks simultaneously.**

3. Create a new mono Auxiliary Input track and name it **Mastering**.

4. Set the Mastering track to Solo Safe.

5. Set the input of the Mastering track to the Master bus.

6. Insert a Maxim plug-in on the first insert of the Mastering track.

7. Select the MIXING LIMITER preset.

8. Solo the Fireball_01, Fireball_02, and Fireball_03 tracks.

9. Enable the SLIP EDIT mode.

10. Using the Smart Tool as the Grabber tool, select the clip on the Fireball_01 track, and then Shift-click to select the clips on the Fireball_02 and Fireball_03 tracks.

11. Enable Loop Play by selecting OPTIONS > LOOP PLAYBACK.

12. Press PLAY to hear the clip played through Maxim.

13. Set the Ceiling to 0.1 dB.

14. Experiment with the Threshold setting to get a consistently loud signal.

Exporting Sound Effects

Now that you've mastered your sound effects you're ready to bounce and export your clips. As mentioned in Lesson 1, "Understanding the Game Audio Workflow,"

Bounce To Tracks is one of several techniques that can be used to prepare for exporting audio. Because Bounce To Tracks does not actually export the bounced clips, you'll also use the Export Clips As Files function once the bounce is completed.

Walkthrough: Exporting Sound Effects

In this walkthrough you will learn how to export the sound effects for the game.

To use the Bounce To Tracks technique to create processed, mixed, and mastered clips:

1. Create a new Mono Audio track and name it **Bounce**.

2. Set the Bounce track input to the Bounce bus.

3. Set the Mastering track output to the Bounce bus.

4. Record-enable the Bounce track.

5. Solo the Fireball_01, Fireball_02, and Fireball_03 tracks.

6. Enable **SLIP EDIT** mode.

7. Using the Smart Tool as the Grabber tool, select the clip on the Fireball_01 track, and then Shift-click to select the clips on the Fireball_02 and Fireball_03 tracks.

8. Press **RECORD** then **PLAY** in the Transport window or on the Edit window toolbar to begin recording.

9. Listen to be sure that all of the plug-ins are set correctly. When satisfied, rename the recorded clip as **SFX_Fireball_01**.

10. Repeat the **BOUNCE TO TRACKS** process for the Ice Comet and Mission Complete sound effects. Remember to adjust the **MAXIM** settings for each track to make sure the levels are optimized.

11. Rename the resulting clips **SFX_Ice_Comet_01**, and **SFX_Mission_Complete_01**. Because you've already bounced your dialogue to whole file clips, you can use Export Clips As Files for a faster than real-time export.

Note: The Export Clips as Files function automatically applies dither (without noise shaping) when exporting from 24-bit to 16-bit.

12. Don't forget to disarm **RECORD** on the Bounce track.

To export the clips:

1. Select all of the final bounced clips in the Clip List.

2. Select EXPORT CLIPS AS FILES from the Clip List pop-up menu, or press COMMAND+SHIFT+K (Mac) or CTRL+SHIFT+K (Windows). The Export Selected dialog box will appear.

3. Set the export settings as follows:

   - **File Type:** WAV
   - **Format:** (Multiple) Mono
   - **Bit Depth:** 16-bit
   - **Sample Rate:** 48kHz

4. Create a folder named **PTGA_Walkthrough_04_SFX** to store all of the Walkthrough 4 clips.

5. Click EXPORT.

Implementing Sound Effects

Now that you've exported your clips from Pro Tools, you're ready to implement them in Unity.

Walkthrough: Implementing Sound Effects

In this walkthrough, you will learn how to implement the sound effects in Unity. You will be building upon the unity project that you used in Lesson 3.

To prepare the Unity project:

1. Launch Unity and open the PTGA_Modules project.

2. Select the Walkthrough_03 file that you created in Lesson 3.

3. Duplicate the file by choosing EDIT > DUPLICATE or pressing COMMAND+D (Mac) or CTRL+D (Windows).

4. Name the duplicated level **Walkthrough_04** and add your initials.

5. Double-click the duplicated level to make it active.

To import your audio files:

1. Navigate to the folder where you exported your sound effects clips.

2. Drag the folder onto the Unity Project view. The folder and all of its contents will automatically be imported into the project.

To assign the clips in the Inspector:

1. Click the **AUDIO_MANAGER** item in the Hierarchy window.

2. Assign the sounds to specific triggers in the Inspector window as follows:
    *   **Fireball clip:** SFX_Fireball_01
    *   **Ice Comet clip:** SFX_Ice_Comet_01
    *   **Quest Reward:** SFX_Mission_Complete_01

To test your sound effects:

1. Select **EDIT > PLAY** or press **COMMAND+P** (Mac) or **CTRL+P** (Windows) to launch the game.

2. Use the **1 ALPHANUMERIC KEY** to switch between the two spells. Use the mouse button to cast the spells.

3. Press **COMMAND+P** (Mac) or **CTRL+P** (Windows) to exit the game.

Summary

In this lesson, you learned how to work with sound effects. You should now understand how to:

*   Identify different styles of sound design.

*   Use Pro Tools features to record, edit, master, and export sound effects.

*   Use automation plug-ins to process sound effects.

*   Implement sound effects in Unity.

Review/Discussion Questions

1. What are the three styles of sound design?
   (See "Understanding Sound Effects" on page 90.)

2. What are the three methods for acquiring assets for sound design?
   (See "Acquiring Sound Effects" on page 91.)

3. Which tool is like a Smart Tool for editing MIDI?
   (See "Acquiring Sound Effects" on page 91.)

4. What are the four modes of the Trimmer tool?
   (See "Editing Sound Effects" on page 104.)

5. What key command allows you to identify a sync point in a clip?
   (See "Editing Sound Effects" on page 104.)

6. What are the two ways to enable a plug-in parameter for automation?
   (See "Basic Plug-In Automation" on page 120.)

Adding/Editing Sound Effects

In this exercise you learn how to design the blockbuster sound effects that create excitement in the game. For this exercise, you create some weapon sounds.

Media Used:
Pro Tools: PTGA_Exercise_04
Unity: PTGA_Exercises

Duration:
60 Minutes

Acquiring Sound Effects

Sound design elements needed:

■ Machine gun

■ Rocket propelled grenade

Suggested search terms:

■ Machine gun: Warfare, guns

■ Rocket propelled grenade: Warfare, RPG

Preparing the Pro Tools Session

Before beginning the recording process, you'll need to prepare the session:

1. Open the PTGA_Exercise_04.ptt session template file.

2. Keep the default session parameters.

3. Click **OK**.

4. Save a copy of the session with your initials added to the filename.

5. Prepare the session with the following settings:

   ● **Nudge Value:** One Millisecond
   ● **Keyboard Focus:** Commands Keyboard Focus (A-Z)
   ● **Timeline Drop Order:** Left to Right
   ● **Tab To Transients:** Enabled

Browsing Sound Effects

Typically, the sound design process begins by browsing or searching existing SFX libraries. In this section, you use DigiBase to search for useful elements for the machine gun and rocket propelled grenade sound effects.

Use DigiBase to search for sound effects elements:

1. Press **Option+;** (Mac) or **Alt+;** (Windows) or select **Window > Workspace** to open the Workspace browser.

2. Click the **Find** (magnifying glass) button in the Workspace browser, or press **Command+F** (Mac) or **Ctrl+F** (Windows) to initiate a search.

3. Navigate to the BlastwaveFX folder, and click the checkbox next to it to limit the search.

4. Type **gun** into the search field. Press RETURN or ENTER or click the SEARCH button to execute the search. After a few moments, the assets that match your search will appear in the results pane at the bottom.

5. Browse through the results and find the gun elements.

6. Click the SPEAKER icon to audition each file and identify appropriate gun sounds for the game.

Importing Sound Effects into Pro Tools

Once you've found elements for the gun and grenade launcher, import them into the session.

To import the sound elements to the Clip List, follow these steps:

1. Select the desired element(s) in the Workspace browser.

2. Drag and drop the elements into the Clip List.

Editing Sound Effects

Now that you've imported your sound elements, you can edit them to create useable assets. You should start with the gunshots.

To trim the gunshot clip down to one repeatable gunshot, follow these steps:

1. Drag the MACHINE GUN clip from the Clip List to the Gun track.

2. Use TAB TO TRANSIENTS to navigate to the last shot in the clip. Typically, a gunshot needs to be useable both as a one-shot sample and as a repeating "automatic weapon" sample. The last shot in a recording is usually well suited for this purpose.

3. Nudge two milliseconds earlier and press the **A** KEY or select EDIT > TRIM CLIP > START TO INSERTION. The clip will be trimmed down to just the last gunshot.

4. Nudge two milliseconds later and press the **D** KEY or select EDIT > FADES > FADE CLIP START TO SELECTION. A small fade will be added at the beginning of the clip.

5. Place the cursor somewhere after the decay of the gunshot ends and press the **S** KEY or select EDIT > TRIM CLIP > END TO INSERTION. The tail of the clip will be trimmed to the insertion point.

6. Nudge two milliseconds earlier and press the **G KEY** or select **EDIT >
   FADES > FADE CLIP END TO SELECTION**. A small fade will be added at the
   end of the clip.

To clean up the RPG clip, follow these steps:

1. Drag the **RPG** clip from the Clip List to the RPG track.

2. Using the same technique as before, trim the start of the RPG clip so that
   the attack is right at the beginning, with a 2ms buffer.

3. Create a small fade over the first 2ms at the beginning of the clip.

4. Place the cursor somewhere after the tail of the RPG trails off, and trim
   the clip.

5. Create a small fade over the last 2ms at the end of the clip.

Processing Sound Effects

Now it's time to process the RPG clip with a real-time plug-in.

To put a flanger on the RPG track, follow these steps:

1. Insert the **AIR FLANGER** on the last insert of the RPG track.

2. Select the 05 Soft Flanger preset.

3. Enable automation for the **MIX** parameter by holding
   CONTROL+OPTION+COMMAND (Mac) or **CTRL+START+ALT** (Windows)
   while clicking on the control in the plug-in window.

4. Return to the RPG_Trail track in the Edit window and change the Track
   View to see the **AIR FLANGER > MIX** automation graph.

Shortcut: Pressing Control+Command (Mac) or Ctrl+Start (Windows) and clicking
           on the control in the plug-in window will automatically change the
           Track view to the selected parameter's automation graph.

5. Use the **GRABBER** or **PENCIL** tool to draw some automation for the **MIX**
   parameter. Generally, you'll want to increase the **MIX** percentage as the
   sound trails off.

Bouncing the Sound Effects

You will need to bounce and maximize your sound effects to prepare to export
them.

Because you are using a real-time plug-in on one of the tracks, you'll need to bounce the sound to another track inside the session.

To record the processed RPG sound effect to another track in the session, follow these steps:

1. Set the output of the RPG track to the RPG Bounce bus.

2. Using the Smart Tool as the Grabber tool, select the RPG clip.

3. Record-enable the Bounce track.

4. Press RECORD then PLAY to record the processed RPG sound effect.

5. Disarm-record on the Bounce track.

Mastering the Sound Effects

Now that you've bounced your sound effects, it's time to maximize the levels before exporting. Because you've bounced the RPG to a new clip, you can use an AudioSuite ultra-maximizer to maximize the levels.

To run an ultra-maximizer on the clips, follow these steps:

1. Select the GUN clip.

2. Select AUDIOSUITE > DYNAMICS > MAXIM.

3. Select the MIXING LIMITER preset.

4. Press PREVIEW to hear the clip played through Maxim.

5. Adjust the plug-in parameters as follows:

    - **File Mode:** Create Continuous File
    - **Selection Reference:** Playlist
    - **Use In Playlist:** Enabled
    - **Playlist Mode:** Clip by Clip

6. Further adjust the Threshold setting to get consistently loud signal.

7. Press the PROCESS button to apply the effect to the selected clip.

8. Name the mastered clip **SFX_Machine_Gun_01**.

9. Repeat Steps 1-7 for the bounced RPG clip.

10. Name the mastered **RPG** clip **SFX_RPG_01**.

Exporting Sound Effects

With the mastering complete, you're ready to export your sound effects. To do so, follow these steps:

1. Select the final gunshot and RPG clips in the Clip List.

2. Select **EXPORT CLIPS AS FILES** from the Clip List pop-up menu, or press **COMMAND+SHIFT+K** (Mac) or **CTRL+SHIFT+K** (Windows). The Export Selected dialog box will appear.

3. Set the export settings as follows:

   - **File Type:** WAV
   - **Format:** (Multiple) Mono
   - **Bit Depth:** 16-bit
   - **Sample Rate:** 48kHz

4. Create a folder named **PTGA_Exercise_04_SFX** to store all of the Lesson 4 clips.

5. Click **EXPORT**.

Implementing Sound Effects

Now that you've exported your clips from Pro Tools, you're ready to implement them in Unity.

To prepare the Unity project, follow these steps:

1. Launch Unity and open the PTGA_Exercises Unity project.

2. Select the Exercise_03 file that you created in Lesson 3.

3. Duplicate the file by choosing **EDIT > DUPLICATE** or pressing **COMMAND+D** (Mac) or **CTRL+D** (Windows).

4. Name the duplicated level **Exercise_04** and add your initials.

5. Double-click the duplicated level to make it active.

To import the audio files, follow these steps:

1. Navigate to the folder where you exported your sound effects clips.

2. Drag the folder onto the Unity Project view. The folder and all of its contents will automatically be imported into the project.

To assign the audio files in the Inspector, follow these steps:

1. Click the **AUDIO_MANAGER** item in the Hierarchy window.

2. Assign the sounds to specific triggers in the Inspector window as follows:
   - **Machine Gun Clip:** SFX_Machine_Gun_01
   - **Rocket Launcher Clip:** SFX_RPG_01

To test the sound effects, follow these steps:

1. Select EDIT > PLAY or press COMMAND+P (Mac) or CTRL+P (Windows) to launch the game.

2. Use the **1** and **2** ALPHANUMERIC KEYS to switch between weapons. Use the mouse button to fire the weapons.

3. Press COMMAND+P (Mac) or CTRL+P (Windows) to exit the game. You're done!

Working with Backgrounds

In this lesson, you explore techniques for designing ambient sounds to bring the game world to life.

Media Used: Pro Tools session: PTGA_Walkthrough_05
Unity project: PTGA_Walkthroughs

Duration: 90 Minutes

GOALS

- Understand backgrounds
- Acquire backgrounds
- Edit backgrounds
- Export backgrounds
- Implement backgrounds

Understanding Backgrounds

Backgrounds are really just a particular category of sound effects. Backgrounds (also called ambient sounds) are the sounds that reinforce the feeling of being in a particular setting or location. Generally, the virtual environment in which the game exists dictates the backgrounds. For example, an island level like the one you've been working with (see Figure 5.1) typically has ocean waves and birds and wind blowing through tall grass. A warehouse level, on the other hand, might have ventilation sounds and dripping water and the hum of fluorescent lighting.

Figure 5.1
An island level

As you'll see, most of the techniques presented in this lesson have already been covered in the previous lesson. However, some aspects of working with backgrounds are quite different from regular sound effects and, therefore, merit a closer inspection.

Assessing Background Requirements

It's usually pretty easy to determine which backgrounds are needed for a game level. The real creativity comes with deciding how many different layers are required for each element. Too many layers can make for a muddy mess. Not enough and the environment can be less immersive than it should be.

Another consideration when creating backgrounds is the placement and density of sound emitters. Sound emitters are objects placed in the game environment that play sounds when the player is within a certain range. It's essential to know how many different emitters will be used in a game level, and how many of each type will be scattered around the environment. Unless the sound designer is also the person placing the emitters, this will require communication with the game programmer(s).

Notice the placement of the background sound emitters in the level you've been working on, as shown in Figure 5.2.

Figure 5.2
Top-down view of the main game environment

You'll be preparing sounds for these emitters throughout this lesson.

Acquiring Backgrounds

As discussed previously, source sounds can be gathered either by recording sounds or by browsing sound libraries.

- **Recording sounds**—Studio and field recording
- **Browsing sound libraries**—Proprietary and commercial sound libraries

Field Recording

Previous lessons discussed techniques for studio recording of dialogue and Foley sounds. Backgrounds offer a great opportunity to make use of another recording method: field recording.

As mentioned in Lesson 1, field recording refers to the practice of taking portable recorders to a non-studio location to record new sound elements. Backgrounds are a great application for field recorders because they require very little external equipment to record well. (Unlike some other field recording tasks such as recording a tank or a fighter plane!) However, you will need to find an appropriate location to record your backgrounds.

Mono vs. Stereo

Because you'll be assigning sounds to multiple sound emitters, you'll be creating mono backgrounds to enhance directionality and prevent phase problems. Regardless, it's a great idea to field record the backgrounds in stereo. The stereo files will make a great addition to your personal sound effects library, and they might also come in useful for the game cinematics or some other application where stereo is desired.

Field Recording Tips

Here are some basic field recording tips that are important to consider.

Recording Duration

When field recording, unlike studio recording, it's important to get long takes of each environment that you're recording. A one-minute take is the absolute minimum that you should record. Ideally, you should try to get five minutes or more in any location. This extra duration serves two purposes. First, it allows for multiple long backgrounds in the game with minimal looping. Second, it gives you a "buffer" of extra audio for those (inevitable) times when you have to remove unwanted noises, such as a car honk or a plane flying overhead.

Equipment

Many an amateur field recording session has been ruined by wind noise. Even if you're using a relatively inexpensive mic (of which there are many excellent choices), it's a great idea to invest in the best windscreen you can afford. In addition, a good shock mount with a pistol grip will reduce mic handling noise (see Figure 5.3).

Figure 5.3
Windscreen and pistol grip

Slate

As in dialogue recording, it is a very good idea to slate each of your field recorded takes. Simply stating the recording location, mic position, and take number can save a lot of headaches when you start editing the material. This can be accomplished with a minimum of effort by simply speaking into the field recording mic. Just be careful not to deafen yourself when speaking into a high-gain shotgun while wearing headphones!

Walkthrough: Field Recording Session

In this walkthrough you learn how to create a basic field recording. You can find any files you need on the DVD.

To create a basic field recording:

1. Record-arm the recorder.

2. Check the levels to make sure they're loud enough without clipping. Be sure to keep the headphones at a reasonable volume and use the recorder's meters to set the levels!

Note: **If your field recorder has a Confidence Monitor capability, you should
      enable it now.**

3. Begin recording.

4. Slate the recording with the location, mic position, and take. For example, "creek bed—three feet above the water—take two...."

5. Record the longest duration possible. Try to record at least one minute, ideally two or more minutes.

6. Pause the recorder. Most recorders will automatically create a discrete audio file each time you pause.

7. Repeat Steps 2-6 for each additional location and record take.

Tip: Don't forget to name the files with descriptive terms on the recorder (if possible) or after you've copied them to your Pro Tools computer.

Walkthrough: Acquiring Sound Elements

In this walkthrough, you learn how to acquire sound elements for the session.

The backgrounds you need are as follows:

- Ocean waves
- Lake or creek
- General ambience (wind, insects, and so on)
- Creaking bridge

Suggested sound design elements you need are as follows:

- Water—Ocean, lake, or creek elements
- General ambience—Light wind, wind through grass or trees, and insects
- Creaking bridge—Wood creaks, rope stretch

To prepare the session:

1. Open the PTGA_Walkthrough_05.ptt session file.

2. Keep the default session parameters.

3. Click **OK**.

4. Save a copy of the session with your initials added to the filename.

5. Prepare the session with the following settings:
   - **Nudge Value:** One Second
   - **Keyboard Focus:** Commands Keyboard Focus (A-Z)
   - **Edit Mode:** Absolute Grid

- **Grid Value:** One Second
- **Tab To Transients:** Disabled
- **Loop Playback:** Enabled

Browsing Backgrounds

Like sound effects design, the background design process usually begins by browsing or searching existing SFX libraries. Let's look at how to use DigiBase to browse and search for useful elements.

To use DigiBase to browse background elements:

1. Press **OPTION+;** (Mac) or **ALT+;** (Windows) or select **WINDOW > WORKSPACE** to open the Workspace browser.

2. If you've field recorded any elements, navigate to the folder containing them. Otherwise, navigate to the location of the BlastwaveFX folder on your system.

3. Browse through the assets in the folder and find the background elements.

4. Click the **SPEAKER** icon to audition the files.

To use DigiBase to search for background elements:

1. Press **OPTION+;** (Mac) or **ALT+;** (Windows) or select **WINDOW > WORKSPACE** to open the Workspace browser (if it's not already open).

2. Click the **FIND** button (magnifying glass) in the Workspace, or press **COMMAND+F** (Mac) or **CTRL+F** (Windows) to initiate a search.

3. Select the volumes you want to search by clicking the checkboxes.

4. Type a search term like "wind" or "ambience" into the Search field. Press **RETURN** or **ENTER** or click the **SEARCH** button to execute the search. After a few moments, the assets that match your search will appear.

5. Browse through the assets in the folder.

6. Click the **SPEAKER** icon to audition the files.

7. Repeat Steps 1-6 for the other background elements.

Once you've found a variety of elements for the ocean, lake, general ambience, and bridge, you need to import them into the session.

To import the sound elements to the Clip List:

1. Select the desired element(s) in the Workspace browser.

2. Drag and drop the elements onto the Clip List.

Editing Backgrounds

Editing backgrounds is similar to general sound effects editing. In film, where a scene may last for a few minutes, a recorded background may be long enough to play without looping. In game audio, the sound designer won't know how long a player will be playing a given level, so backgrounds must be carefully edited so that they can loop seamlessly.

Using the Edit Selection Indicators

When editing backgrounds, it is often desirable to create selections of a pre-determined length. The Edit Selection indicators in the Edit window (see Figure 5.4) can be used to precisely create and modify selections.

Figure 5.4

Edit Selection indicators in the Edit window toolbar

To create a new selection using the Edit Selection indicators:

1. Click the Start field and enter the desired starting value for the selection. Press **RETURN** or **ENTER** to confirm the entry (see Figure 5.5A).

Figure 5.5

Using the Edit Selection indicators to create a selection

2. To specify the length of the selection, do one of the following:

    ● Click in the End field and enter the desired ending value for the selection. Press **RETURN** or **ENTER** to confirm the entry (see Figure 5.5B).

    ● Click in the Length field and enter the desired length for the selection. Press **RETURN** or **ENTER** to confirm the entry (see Figure 5.5C).

Edit Selection shortcuts:

■ **Up/Down arrows**—Increment or decrement the highlighted number.

■ **Left/Right arrows**—Cycle through the selection fields.

■ **Slash key (/)**—Cycle through the selection indicators.

In the Avid Learning Series   For more information on edit selections, see "Types of Selections" in the "Pro Tools 101: An Introduction to Pro Tools 10" book by Avid.

Trimming a Clip to a Selection

Lesson 2, "Working with Dialogue," describes three ways to edit a whole file clip into a smaller clip: Trim, Separate, and Capture. In this section, you'll take a closer look at the most commonly used technique for editing backgrounds: Trim.

Trim is often the best choice for editing backgrounds because it removes the unselected parts of the whole file clip from the playlist and leaves you with only the selected portion. This will prepare the clip for further editing and looping.

To trim a clip to a selection:

1. Do one of the following:

    ● Using the Smart Tool as the Selector tool, select a portion of the whole file clip (see Figure 5.6).

    ● Create a selection using the Edit Selection indicators.

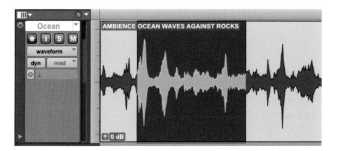

Figure 5.6
Edit selection before using the Trim command

2. Choose **EDIT > TRIM CLIP > TO SELECTION** or press **COMMAND+T** (Mac) or **CTRL+T** (Windows) (see Figure 5.7).

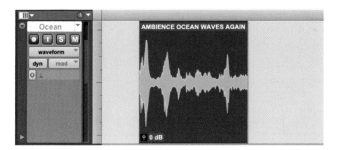

Figure 5.7
After using Trim, only the selection remains

Nudging a Clip's Contents

Sometimes, after a clip has been trimmed to the approximate loop duration, you'll discover that the clip contains some undesirable content. For example, you might have a steady city traffic background with one obnoxious car honk. Or you might have a peaceful rain background with a single thunder crack. Fortunately, you can nudge the contents of the clip to keep the clip start and end points intact while eliminating the undesirable content.

To nudge the contents of a clip without changing the clip start and end points:

1. Use the **NUDGE VALUE POP-UP** selector in the Toolbar to choose the Time Scale and Nudge value (see Figure 5.8).

Figure 5.8
Nudge Value pop-up selector

2. Using the Smart Tool as the Grabber tool, select the clip (see Figure 5.9).

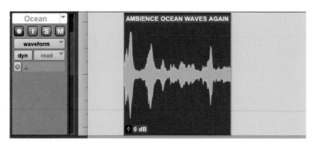

Figure 5.9
The selection as it was trimmed in Figure 5.7

3. While holding **CONTROL** (Mac) or **START** (Windows), press the **+** or **−** KEYS on the numeric keypad. The clip contents will nudge forward or backward by the Nudge value, without affecting the clip location or duration (see Figure 5.10).

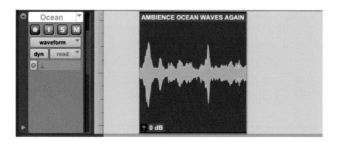

Figure 5.10
After nudging, clip start and end points are maintained while the content is nudged

Backgrounds and Batch Fades

In Lesson 3, "Working with Foley," you looked at how to create batch fades. When you use crossfades to edit backgrounds, you have a couple of additional considerations to address. You'll want to pay particular attention to the Link and Operation settings in the Batch Fades dialog box (see Figure 5.11).

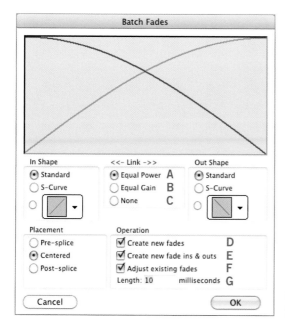

Figure 5.11
Batch Fades dialog box

Link

The Link section of the Batch Fades dialog box provides you with a choice between three options: Equal Power, Equal Gain, and None.

■ **Equal Power (see Figure 5.11A)**—Use this option when crossfading non-phase-coherent material, such as when crossfading between different types of material or non-identical sounds. The fade occurs at –3dB, which allows non-phase-coherent material to crossfade smoothly. This link type is ideal for crossfading backgrounds and will not result in a noticeable drop in volume.

■ **Equal Gain (see Figure 5.11B)** —Use this option when crossfading phase-coherent or nearly phase-coherent material, such as when crossfading between identical clips or instruments (for example, when creating music loops). The fade occurs at –6dB, which prevents phase-coherent material from growing too loud during the fade. This link type may cause a noticeable drop in volume when used on backgrounds, unless the sound source is very steady (for example, an ambient AC hum).

- **None (see Figure 5.11C)**—This option allows the users to create a custom crossfade, which can be useful when crossfading clips with unusual amplitude characteristics.

Operation

The Operation section of the Batch Fades dialog box provides four controls:

- **Create New Fades (see Figure 5.11D)**—This option enables the creation of crossfades. Crossfades are perfect for combining multiple clips into one long background, or for repeating and looping a background.

- **Create New Fade Ins & Outs (Figure 5.11E)**—This option enables the creation of fade ins and fade outs at clip boundaries that aren't crossfaded. You'll want to disable this control when working on background clips, since they will typically be looped. (A possible exception might be backgrounds for a cinematic—see Lesson 8, "Working with Cinematics.")

- **Adjust Existing Fades (Figure 5.11F)**—Use this option to replace existing fades with new fades, based on the current settings for shape, link, duration, and length. Disable this option to keep existing fades while adding fades to clips that do not already have them.

- **Length (see Figure 5.11G)**—Use this field to set the length of crossfades, as well as fade ins and outs. Generally, the more complex the background, the higher this value will need to be. For background editing, 500 milliseconds is a good starting point.

Using Strip Silence Extract

Another common problem when editing backgrounds is a lack of steady content. For example, suppose you need a quiet ocean ambience but find that all you have to work with is big waves breaking on the shore. Fortunately, Pro Tools provides a function that can help to turn that busy clip into a more subtle background: Strip Silence Extract.

In the Strip Silence window, the Extract function is the opposite of the standard Strip function. Instead of removing the quiet portions of clip, it removes the loud portions. The result is a series of clips that, when spliced together, can create a more useful background.

To use Strip Silence Extract:

1. Using the Smart Tool as the Grabber tool, select the **BACKGROUND** clip (see Figure 5.12).

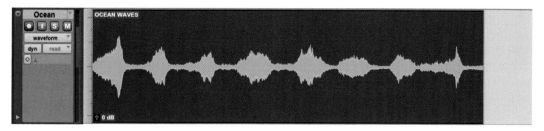

Figure 5.12
Selected clip prior to opening the Strip Silence window

2. Choose **EDIT > STRIP SILENCE** or press **COMMAND+U** (Mac) or **CTRL+U** (Windows) to bring up the Strip Silence window shown in Figure 5.13.

Figure 5.13
Strip Silence window

3. Adjust the settings for the Strip Threshold and the Minimum Strip Duration (see Figure 5.13, A and B). Do this until the Strip Silence rectangles appear in the selection around the areas you want to eliminate.

   As you adjust the settings in the Strip Silence window, the Strip Silence rectangles will appear in the selected clip (see Figure 5.14).

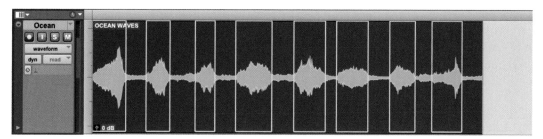

Figure 5.14
Strip Silence rectangles in the selected clip

4. Tune the settings using the Clip Start Pad and Clip End Pad (see Figure 5.13, C and D).

5. Press the **EXTRACT** button (Figure 5.13E). The content inside the rectangles will be deleted, leaving only the content that fell below the Strip Threshold on the track, as shown in Figure 5.15.

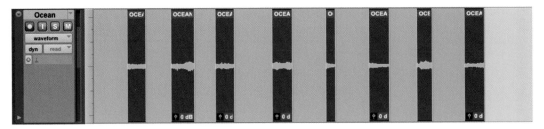

Figure 5.15
Results of the Strip Silence Extract

To combine the extracted clips into one clip:

1. Enable the **SHUFFLE EDIT** mode.

2. Using the Smart Tool as the Grabber tool, move each clip adjacent to the previous clip to form one long continuous string of clips.

3. Enable the **SLIP EDIT** mode. (It's a good idea to exit Shuffle mode as soon as you no longer need it!)

4. Click on the first clip, then Shift-click on the last clip to select them all.

5. Do one of the following to open the Batch Fades dialog box:
   - Select **EDIT > FADES > CREATE**
   - Press **COMMAND+F** (Mac) or **CTRL+F** (Windows)

6. Set the **LINK** setting to Equal Power.

7. Enable **CREATE NEW FADES**.

8. Disable **CREATE NEW FADE INS & OUTS**.

9. Enter a Length of at least 500 milliseconds

10. Click **OK**. The batch fades will be created.

11. Select **EDIT > CONSOLIDATE** or press **OPTION+SHIFT+3** (Mac) or **ALT+SHIFT+3** (Windows) to consolidate the smaller clips into one long clip.

You're now ready to loop the clip.

Dynamic Transport

Dynamic Transport is a powerful tool for auditioning looped clips. It allows you to decouple the playback location from the timeline selection. Translated into plain English, this means that you can preview the loop point of a selected clip without having to listen through the whole clip. This can save a lot of time when you're working with long clips like backgrounds, which typically have a duration of 30 seconds or longer!

You'll use Dynamic Transport as part of a workflow for creating loopable clips, to test the loop point and ensure that it is seamless.

To enable Dynamic Transport:

1. Ensure LINK TIMELINE AND EDIT SELECTION is enabled, as shown in Figure 5.16, and then follow these steps:

Figure 5.16
Link Timeline and Edit Selection enabled

2. Ensure LOOP PLAYBACK is enabled (choose OPTIONS > LOOP PLAYBACK or COMMAND+SHIFT+L (Mac) or CTRL+SHIFT+L (Windows).

3. Select OPTIONS > DYNAMIC TRANSPORT or press CONTROL+COMMAND+P (Mac) or CTRL+START+P (WINDOWS). The Main Timebase ruler will expand to double-height, showing the Play/Start Marker as a blue triangle in the lower half of the ruler, as shown in Figure 5.17.

Figure 5.17
Main Timebase ruler expands to show the Play/Start Marker

To position the Play/Start Marker, do one of the following:

■ Click on the PLAY/START MARKER and drag it to a new position.

■ Click anywhere in the PLAY/START MARKER STRIP in the Main Timebase ruler to move the Play Start Marker to that location.

Workflow for Creating Loopable Clips

To make your background audio usable for a game, you'll need to create a version that loops smoothly and seamlessly. Although this requires a multi-step process, it is easy to do using techniques you've already learned.

The basic steps involved are as follows:

1. Trim the clip to ensure it has room for crossfades.

2. Duplicate or repeat the clip to create three copies end-to-end.

3. Create crossfades on either end of the middle clip.

4. Test the loop point on the middle clip using Dynamic Transport.

5. Consolidate the middle clip to render the crossfades into the audio file.

Before you begin, you need to configure the following Pro Tools settings:

- **Edit Mode:** Absolute Grid
- **Main Time Scale:** Minutes:Seconds
- **Nudge Value:** One Second
- **Grid Value:** One Second
- **Tab To Transients:** Disabled
- **Loop Playback:** Enabled
- **Timeline Insertion/Play Start Marker Follows Playback:** Disabled

Trim the Clip

When you're working with a whole file clip (such as a clip that was previously consolidated), you'll need to trim the clip start and end points to create room in the underlying file for crossfades.

Note: If you're working with a subset clip that was not consolidated, you can skip this step.

To trim the loop slightly to create room for crossfades:

- Using the Smart Tool as the Trimmer tool, TRIM at least ONE SECOND from the beginning and end of the clip.

Repeat the Clip

In order to create a clip that will loop seamlessly, you need to crossfade the clip start and end points together. To do this, you'll need three copies on the playlist, end-to-end.

To repeat the clip:

1. Using the Smart Tool as the Grabber tool, select the clip.

2. Do one of the following:

- Choose **EDIT > REPEAT** or press **OPTION+R** (Mac) or **ALT+R** (Windows). The Repeat dialog box will appear. Enter **2** into the Number Of Repeats field and click **OK**.

- Choose **EDIT > DUPLICATE** twice, or press **COMMAND+D** (Mac) or **CTRL+D** (Windows) twice.

Fade the Clip

Now that you have three copies of the clip on the playlist, you can add crossfades to create a single middle clip that loops smoothly.

To fade the clips:

1. Select all three clips on the track.

2. Press **COMMAND+F** (Mac) or **CTRL+F** (Windows) or select **EDIT > FADES > CREATE CROSSFADE**. The Batch Fades dialog box will appear.

3. Select the **EQUAL POWER** setting, since you are crossfading between two non-phase-coherent clips.

4. In the Operation section of the Batch Fades dialog box, check the **CREATE FADES** box. This will enable the creation of crossfades.

5. Set the Length to 500 milliseconds.

6. Press **OK** to create the crossfades.

Test the Loop

Now that you've added crossfades, you're ready to test the loop point to ensure that the clip loops smoothly.

To use Dynamic Transport to test the loop:

1. Using the Smart Tool as the Grabber tool, select the middle clip. This will create a selection that encompasses the second clip and half of each of the crossfades.

2. Select **OPTIONS > DYNAMIC TRANSPORT** or press **CONTROL+COMMAND+P** (Mac) or **CTRL+START+P** (Windows) to enable Dynamic Transport.

3. Place the **PLAY/START MARKER** a few seconds before the end of the selected clip.

4. Press **PLAY** to audition the loop point. If the loop sounds good, move on to the next section. Otherwise, undo the crossfade, return to the "Fade the Clip" section, and try longer crossfades.

5. Select **OPTIONS > DYNAMIC TRANSPORT** or press **CONTROL+COMMAND+P** (Mac) or **CTRL+START+P** (Windows) a second time to disable Dynamic Transport.

Consolidate the Loop

If the clip is looping smoothly, you need to consolidate it to render the fades and create a single, loopable clip.

To consolidate the loop:

1. Make sure the entire middle clip is still selected.

2. Select **EDIT > CONSOLIDATE** or press **OPTION+SHIFT+3** (Mac) or **ALT+SHIFT+3** (Windows) to consolidate the clip.

3. Press **PLAY** to confirm that the consolidated clip still loops smoothly.

Using Zoom Presets

Zoom presets provide a quick way to zoom to a specific level in Pro Tools. Each of the five Zoom Preset buttons (shown in Figure 5.18) can store a user-defined zoom setting. The factory default settings range from a view that encompasses several minutes (preset one) to a view that encompasses several samples (preset five).

Figure 5.18
Zoom Preset buttons in the Edit window toolbar

To recall a Zoom preset, do one of the following:

- Click on the Zoom Preset button in the Edit window toolbar.

- With Commands Keyboard Focus (A-Z) enabled, press one of the alphanumeric keys, 1-5.

To store a custom zoom setting as a Zoom preset:

1. Set the screen to the desired zoom setting using the Zoomer tool or the Zoom buttons.

2. Hold COMMAND (Mac) or CTRL (Windows) and click on a ZOOM PRESET button.

For more information on Zoom presets, see "Zoom Presets" in the Pro Tools 101 book.

Finding Zero Crossings

Although a well-edited background clip may loop without popping at the loop point, it's generally a good idea to trim the start and end of the clip to zero crossings. A zero crossing is a point where the waveform is at zero amplitude on the vertical axis of the track, shown as the midpoint of the track's amplitude scale.

To trim the start and end of a clip to zero crossings:

1. Enable SLIP EDIT mode.

2. Use the Smart Tool as the Grabber tool to select the clip to be edited.

3. Press the LEFT ARROW KEY to center the beginning of the selected clip.

4. Do one of the following to recall the Zoom preset:

   - Click on the ZOOM PRESET 5 button in the Edit window toolbar.
   - With Commands Keyboard Focus enabled, press the 5 ALPHANUMERIC KEY.

5. Using the Smart Tool as the Trimmer tool, trim the clip start to a zero crossing.

6. Press the RIGHT ARROW KEY to center the end of the selected clip.

7. Using the Smart Tool as the Trimmer tool, trim the clip end to a zero crossing.

8. Press PLAY to verify that the loop point is still clean. If the loop point pops, repeat Steps 3-7 and try different zero crossings.

Walkthrough: Editing Background Elements

In this walkthrough you learn how to trim and loop the background elements you have imported.

The following background elements are used:

- Ocean waves
- Lake or creek
- General ambience (wind, insects, and so on)
- Creaking bridge

To trim each clip to a 10-second section:

1. Drag the first clip to be looped from the Clip List to the Track list. Pro Tools will automatically create a new track and place the clip at the session start.

2. Use the Edit Selection indicators to select a 10-second section of the clip.

3. Press **COMMAND+T** (Mac) or **CTRL+T** (Windows) to trim the clip to the selection.

To nudge the contents of the clip:

If there is an undesirable sound in the clip, nudge the contents of the clip.

1. Make sure the clip is still selected.

2. While holding **CONTROL** (Mac) or **START** (Windows), press the **+** or **−** **KEYS** on the numeric keypad to nudge the contents of the clip earlier or later and find a clean 10-second section.

To repeat the clip to prepare for looping:

1. Make sure the clip is still selected.

2. Press **OPTION+R** (Mac) or **ALT+R** (Windows) to activate the **REPEAT** command and create two more copies of the clip (for a total of three).

To create crossfades to smoothly loop the clip:

1. Select all three clips on the track.

2. Press **COMMAND+F** (Mac) or **CTRL+F** (Windows) or select **EDIT > FADES > CREATE CROSSFADE**. The Batch Fades dialog box will appear.

3. Select the **EQUAL POWER** setting, since you are crossfading between two non-phase-coherent clips.

4. In the Operation section, check the **CREATE FADES** box. This will create crossfades.

5. Set the Length to 500 milliseconds.

6. Press **OK** to create the crossfade.

To use Dynamic Transport to test the loop:

1. Using the Smart Tool as the Grabber tool, select the second (middle) clip.

2. Enable **DYNAMIC TRANSPORT** by pressing **CONTROL+COMMAND+P** (Mac) or **CONTROL+START+P** (Windows).

3. Place the **PLAY/START MARKER** a few seconds before the end of the selected clip.

4. Audition the loop point to verify that it loops smoothly. If not, undo and repeat the crossfades, using different settings.

To consolidate the clip to create a new clip:

1. Make sure the entire second clip is still selected.

2. Consolidate the clip by pressing OPTION+SHIFT+3 (Mac) or ALT+SHIFT+3 (Windows).

3. Press PLAY to confirm that the consolidated clip sounds good. If you're satisfied, delete the unused clips.

To trim the clip start and end points to zero crossings:

1. Enable SLIP EDIT mode.

2. Use the Smart Tool as the Grabber tool to select the clip to be edited.

3. Press the LEFT ARROW KEY to center the beginning of the selected clip.

4. Zoom in as necessary to view the waveform at the sample level.

5. Using the Smart Tool as the Trimmer tool, trim the clip start to a zero crossing.

6. Press the RIGHT ARROW KEY to center the end of the selected clip.

7. Using the Smart Tool as the Trimmer tool, trim the clip end to a zero crossing.

8. Audition the loop. If you're satisfied, disable DYNAMIC TRANSPORT.

Repeat the entire Edit Backgrounds workflow for the remaining backgrounds.

Mastering Backgrounds

Now that you've edited your backgrounds, it's time to maximize the levels before exporting. Because you're not running any real-time plug-ins, you can use AudioSuite Normalize to increase the background's maximum level to full scale. You could use a limiter, but that would reduce the dynamic range of the backgrounds unnecessarily.

Normalizing

Normalize (see Figure 5.19) optimizes the volume level of a selection. Unlike compression and limiting, it preserves dynamics by uniformly increasing or decreasing amplitude. Normalize is perfect for maximizing levels on your background.

Figure 5.19
The Normalize AudioSuite plug-in

This will make your finished backgrounds sound more realistic. Normalize controls include:

- **Max Peak At**—Specifies how close to maximum level (clipping threshold) the peak level is boosted. You can set this value by moving the slider, entering a decibel value, or entering a percentage.

- **RMS/Peak Toggle**—Switches the calibration mode between Peak and RMS modes.

- **Chan/Track Process Mode Selector**—Offers two modes for determining how clips are processed. The first mode, Level On Each Chan/Track, searches for the peak level on a channel-by-channel or track-by-track basis. The second mode, Level On All Chans/Tracks, searches for the peak level of the entire selection.

Walkthrough: Mastering Background Elements

In this walkthrough you learn how to master background elements using Normalize.

To apply AudioSuite Normalize processing to the backgrounds:

1. Select the EDITED BACKGROUND clips.

2. Select AUDIOSUITE > OTHER > NORMALIZE.

3. Adjust the plug-in parameters as follows:
   - **Level:** Create Individual Files
   - **Selection Reference:** Playlist
   - **Use In Playlist:** Enabled
   - **Playlist Mode:** Clip by Clip
   - **Level:** –0.1dBFS

4. Press the PROCESS button to apply the effect to the selected clip.

5. Right-click on each final background clip and select RENAME CLIP.

6. Name the resulting clips **BG_Ocean_01**, **BG_Lake_01**, **BG_Bridge_01**, and **BG_Ambience_01**, as applicable.

Walkthrough: Exporting Backgrounds

Next, you'll need to export your finished backgrounds. Because you're not using real-time plug-ins, you can use the Export Clips as Files command for a faster than real-time export.

In this walkthrough you learn how to export the final backgrounds.

To export the final backgrounds:

1. Select all of your normalized and renamed backgrounds in the Clip List.

2. Select EXPORT CLIPS AS FILES from the Clips List pop-up menu, or press COMMAND+SHIFT+K (Mac) or CTRL+SHIFT+K (Windows). The Export Selected dialog box will appear.

3. Set the export settings as follows:

   • **File Type:** WAV Format: (Multiple)
   • **Mono Bit Depth:** 16-bit
   • **Sample Rate:** 48kHz

4. Click the CHOOSE button and create a folder named **PTGA_Walkthrough_05_BG** to store all of the Walkthrough 5 clips and select it.

5. Back in the Export Selected dialog box, click EXPORT.

Walkthrough: Implementing Backgrounds

Now that you've exported your clips from Pro Tools, you're ready to implement them in Unity. In this walkthrough you learn how to implement the background elements.

To prepare the Unity project:

1. Open the PTGA_Chapters Unity project.

2. Select the Chapter_04 scene that you created in Lesson 4.

3. Duplicate the scene by choosing EDIT > DUPLICATE or pressing COMMAND+D (Mac) or CTRL+D (Windows).

4. Name the duplicated scene **Chapter_05** and add your initials.

5. Double-click the duplicated level to make it active.

To import the audio files:

1. Navigate to the folder where you exported your backgrounds.

2. Drag the folder onto the Unity Project window. The folder and all of its contents will automatically be imported into the project.

To assign the clips in the Inspector:

1. Click the **AUDIO_MANAGER** item in the Hierarchy window.

2. Assign the backgrounds to specific triggers in the Inspector window as follows:

   - **BG_Ocean:** BG_Ocean_01
   - **BG_Lake:** BG_Lake_01
   - **BG_Bridge:** BG_Bridge_01
   - **BG_Wind:** BG_Ambience_01

3. Set the following parameters in the Inspector window:

   - **BG_Ocean_Volume:** 0.5
   - **BG_Ocean_Rolloff:** 200
   - **BG_Lake_Volume:** 0.3
   - **BG_Lake_Rolloff:** 75
   - **BG_Bridge_Volume:** 0.5
   - **BG_Bridge_Rolloff:** 20
   - **BG_Wind_Volume:** 0.3
   - **BG_Wind_Rolloff:** 200

To test the backgrounds:

1. Select **EDIT > PLAY** or press **COMMAND+P** (Mac) or **CTRL+P** (Windows) to launch the game.

2. Use the **A, S, D,** and **W KEYS** (or arrow keys), and the mouse, to navigate through the level. Be sure to listen to the backgrounds for the ocean and lake, the rope bridges, and the general ambience.

3. Press **COMMAND+P** (Mac) or **CTRL+P** (Windows) to exit the game.

Summary

In this lesson you learned how to work with background sound. You should now understand how to:

- Acquire background elements including field recording.
- Use Pro Tools features for editing, mastering, and exporting background sounds.
- Implement background elements in Unity.

Review/Discussion Questions

1. Why is Trim the best command for editing backgrounds?
   (See "Editing Backgrounds" on page 146.)

2. What are the key commands for nudging a clip's contents?
   (See "Nudging a Clip's Contents" on page 147.)

3. Which fade link type is commonly used for crossfading backgrounds?
   Why? (See "Backgrounds and Batch Fades" on page 149.)

4. Which Strip Silence mode will leave the portions of the selection that fall below the threshold value on the track? (See "Using Strip Silence Extract" on page 150.)

5. What is the advantage of using Dynamic Transport to audition background loop points? (See "Dynamic Transport" on page 153.)

Adding/Editing Background Elements

In this exercise you learn how to develop an immersive soundscape. During the exercise, you create background sounds to attach to elements of the game environment.

Media Used:

Pro Tools: PTGA_Exercise_05
Unity: PTGA_Exercises

Duration:

60 Minutes

Assessing Background Requirements

Backgrounds needed:

- Ocean Waves
- Computer Control Room (2)

Suggested search terms:

- Ocean waves: Ocean
- Computer room: Computer, Electronic

Making a Field Recording (Optional)

If you have access to the proper equipment and an appropriate location/environment, you can conduct a basic field recording session to capture some of the necessary backgrounds.

To make a field recording, follow these steps:

1. Record-arm the recorder.

2. Check the levels to make sure they're loud enough without clipping. Be sure to keep the headphones at a reasonable volume and use the recorder's meters to set the levels!

Tip: If your field recorder has a **Confidence Monitor** capability, you should enable it now.

3. Begin recording.

4. Slate the recording with the location, mic position, and take. For example, "computer sounds - six inches from rear of cpu - take three..."

5. Record the longest duration possible. Try to record at least one minute, ideally two or more.

6. Pause the recorder. Most recorders will automatically create a discrete audio file each time you pause.

7. Repeat Steps 2-6 for each additional location and record take.

Tip: Don't forget to name the files with descriptive terms on the recorder (if possible) or after you've copied them to your Pro Tools computer.

Preparing the Pro Tools Session

Before beginning the editing process, you need to prepare the session:

1. Open the PTGA_Exercise_05.ptt session file.

2. Keep the default session parameters.

3. Click **OK**.

4. Save a copy of the session with your initials added to the filename.

5. Prepare the session with the following settings:

    - **Nudge Value:** One Second
    - **Keyboard Focus:** Commands Keyboard Focus (A-Z)
    - **Timeline Drop Order:** Left to Right
    - **Edit Mode:** Absolute Grid
    - **Grid Value:** One Second
    - **Tab To Transients:** Disabled
    - **Loop Playback:** Enabled
    - **Dynamic Transport:** Enabled

Browsing Backgrounds

Typically, the sound design process begins by browsing or searching existing SFX libraries. For this exercise, you use DigiBase to search for appropriate sound elements.

To use DigiBase to search background elements, follow these steps:

1. Press **OPTION+;** (Mac) or **ALT+;** (Windows) or select **WINDOW > WORKSPACE** to open the Workspace browser.

2. Click the **FIND** button (magnifying glass) in the Workspace, or press **COMMAND+F** (Mac) or **CTRL+F** (Windows), to initiate a search.

3. Navigate to the BlastwaveFX folder, and click the checkbox next to it to limit the search.

Note: If you recorded your own backgrounds, you should limit the search to the folder where you copied the recorded elements from the field recorder.

4. Type **ocean** into the **SEARCH** field. Press **RETURN** or **ENTER** or just click the **SEARCH** button to execute the search. After a few moments, the assets that match ocean will appear.

5. Browse through the assets in the folder.

6. Click the SPEAKER icon to audition the files.

7. If you're satisfied with the sound effect, drag and drop it into the Clip List in Pro Tools.

8. Repeat Steps 4-7 for each of the other backgrounds needed (searching for "computer" and "electronic").

Editing Backgrounds

Once you've imported your background elements, you will need to trim and loop them. You'll need to complete all of the following sections for each background, starting with the ocean clip and then repeating the sections and steps for each of the others.

To trim each clip down to a 10-second section, follow these steps:

1. Drag the clip from the Clip List to the Track List. Pro Tools will automatically create a new track and place the clip at the session start.

2. Use the EDIT SELECTION indicators to select a 10-second section of the clip.

3. Press COMMAND+T (Mac) or CTRL+T (Windows) to trim the clip to the selection.

To nudge the contents of the clip (if there is an undesirable fade or sound in the clip), follow these steps:

1. Make sure the clip is still selected.

2. Hold CONTROL (Mac) or START (Window) while pressing the + or – keys on the numeric keypad to nudge the contents of the clip earlier or later. Find a clean 10-second section.

To repeat the clip to prepare for looping, follow these steps:

1. Make sure the clip is still selected.

2. Press OPTION+R (Mac) or ALT+R (Windows) to activate the Repeat command and create two more copies of the clip (for a total of three).

To create crossfades to smoothly loop the clip, follow these steps:

1. Select all three clips on the track.

2. Press COMMAND+F (Mac) or CTRL+F (Windows) or select EDIT > FADES > CREATE CROSSFADE. The Batch Fades dialog box will appear.

3. Select the EQUAL GAIN setting in the Batch Fades dialog box, since you are crossfading between two non-phase-coherent clips.

4. In the Operation section of the Batch Fades dialog box, check the **CREATE FADES** box. This will enable the creation of crossfades.

5. Set the Length to 500 milliseconds.

6. Press **OK** to create the crossfades.

To use Dynamic Transport to test the loops, follow these steps:

1. Using the Smart Tool as the Grabber tool, select the second (middle) clip.

2. Press **CONTROL+COMMAND+P** (Mac) or **CTRL+START+P** (Windows) to enable Dynamic Transport.

3. Place the **PLAY/START MARKER** a few seconds before the end of the middle clip.

4. Press **PLAY** to audition the loop point. If needed, undo the crossfade, make adjustments, and repeat the process.

To consolidate the loop, follow these steps:

1. Make sure the entire second clip is still selected.

2. Press **OPTION+SHIFT+3** (Mac) or **ALT+SHIFT+3** (Windows) to consolidate the clip.

3. Press **PLAY** to confirm that the consolidated clip sounds good.

4. When satisfied with the results, discard the unused clips before and after the consolidated clip.

To trim the clip start and end points to zero crossings, follow these steps:

1. Enable **SLIP EDIT** mode.

2. Use the Smart Tool as the Grabber tool to select the clip to be edited.

3. Press the **LEFT ARROW KEY** to center the beginning of the selected clip.

4. Recall **ZOOM PRESET 5**.

5. Using the Smart Tool as the Trimmer tool, trim the clip start to a zero crossing.

6. Press the **RIGHT ARROW KEY** to center the end of the selected clip.

7. Using the Smart Tool as the Trimmer tool, trim the clip end to a zero crossing.

8. Press **PLAY** to audition the loop. (You may want to mute the other tracks to hear the results.) If needed, repeat the trimming process at different zero crossings to ensure a clean loop.

Repeat the entire workflow for the control room backgrounds. Note that you may be able to skip the trim, repeat, and crossfade steps when looping the control room backgrounds.

As always, use your ears to determine the best approach.

Mastering Backgrounds

Now that you've edited and processed your backgrounds, it's time to maximize the levels before exporting. Because you're not running any real-time plug-ins, you can use AudioSuite Normalize to increase the background's maximum level to full scale.

To run an AudioSuite Normalize on the backgrounds, follow these steps:

1. Select the clips you've prepared for looping.

2. Select AUDIOSUITE > OTHER > NORMALIZE.

3. Adjust the plug-in parameters as follows:
   - **Level:** Create Individual Files
   - **Selection Reference:** Playlist
   - **Use In Playlist:** Enabled
   - **Playlist Mode:** Clip by Clip
   - **Level:** –0.1dBFS

4. Press the PROCESS button to apply the effect to the selected clips.

5. Right-click the final background clips and select RENAME CLIP.

6. Name the clips **BG_Ocean_01**, **BG_Control_Room_01**, and **BG_Control_Room_02**.

Exporting Backgrounds

Next you need to prepare your finished background for export. Since you're not using plug-ins, you can use Export Clips as Files for a faster than real-time export.

To export the backgrounds, follow these steps:

1. Select the final normalized clips for both the ocean and control room backgrounds.

2. Select EXPORT CLIPS AS FILES from the Clip List pop-up menu, or press COMMAND+SHIFT+K (Mac) or CTRL+SHIFT+K (Windows). The Export Selected dialog box will appear.

3. Set the export settings as follows:

- **File Type:** WAV
- **Format:** (Multiple) Mono
- **Bit Depth:** 16-bit
- **Sample Rate:** 48kHz

4. Click the **CHOOSE** button to create a folder named **PTGA_Exercise_05_BG** to store all of the Exercise 5 clips and select the folder.

5. Back in the Export Selected dialog box, click the **EXPORT** button to export the files.

Implementing Backgrounds

Now that you've exported your clips from Pro Tools, you're ready to implement them in Unity.

To prepare the Unity project, follow these steps:

1. Open the PTGA_Exercises Unity project.

2. Select the Exercise_04 scene that you created in Exercise 4.

3. Duplicate the file by choosing **EDIT > DUPLICATE** or by pressing **COMMAND+D** (Mac) or **CTRL+D** (Windows).

4. Name the duplicated scene **Exercise_05** and add your initials.

5. Double-click the duplicated level to make it active.

To import the audio files, follow these steps:

1. Navigate to the folder where you exported your background sounds.

2. Drag the folder onto the Unity Project window. The folder and all of its contents will automatically be imported into the project.

To assign the audio files in the Inspector, follow these steps:

1. Click the **AUDIO_MANAGER** item in the Hierarchy window.

2. Assign the sounds to specific triggers in the Inspector window as follows:

- **Ocean_Loop:** BG_Ocean_01
- **Control Room Clip 1:** BG_Control_Room_01
- **Control Room Clip 2:** BG_Control_Room_02

3. Set the following parameters in the Inspector window:

- **Ocean_Volume:** 0.3
- **Ocean_Falloff:** 50
- **Control_Room_Volume:** 0.8
- **Control_Room_Falloff:** 5

To test the backgrounds, follow these steps:

1. Select EDIT > PLAY or press COMMAND+P (Mac) or CTRL+P (Windows) to launch the game.

2. Use the **A, S, D,** and **W** KEYS (or arrow keys), and the mouse, to navigate through the game level. Listen for the ocean background near the water, and the control room backgrounds in the control room at the top of the stairs.

3. Press COMMAND+P (Mac) or CTRL+ P (Windows) to exit the game.

Working with Music

In this lesson, you arrange an interactive score that follows the action. The lesson introduces you to basic game music concepts and techniques for creating an interactive score.

Media Used: Pro Tools Session: PTGA_Walkthrough_06.ptt
Unity Project: PTGA_Walkthroughs

Duration: 90 Minutes

GOALS

- Understand game music
- Acquire game music assets
- Edit your game music
- Master the use of music in games
- Export music
- Implement music

Understanding Game Music

At first glance, it may seem that scoring for games is similar to scoring for film or television (see Figure 6.1). However, some distinct differences apply to music for games. A film or television composer usually knows the specific duration of a cue and can adapt her compositional approach accordingly. On the other hand, a game composer never knows the specific length of time that the player will be hearing a cue (except when scoring a cinematic). This variability can make game composition, and especially the editing process, much more complex.

Figure 6.1
A musical score

Game Music Terminology

A number of terms are important to understand when working with game music. Familiarity with these terms will allow you to more easily communicate with an experienced game composer or game music editor. In addition, when you've been hired to write the game music, you'll want to sound like you know what you're talking about!

- **Score**—Music that has been composed specifically for a game.

- **Cue**—A section of the score that coincides with a particular level or cinematic in the game.

- **Song**—Generally, a self-contained composition with a featured vocalist. In many games, current popular songs are licensed as a co-marketing effort between the game development company and the record label.

- **Soundtrack**—The combination of the game score and related songs, used in reference to the album, CD, or electronic download that can be purchased by the public.

- **Temp**—An existing piece of music that has temporarily been implemented in the game. Temp music can help the composer understand the musical direction that the game producer desires. (On the other hand, many composers loathe temp music because they are often pressured to imitate the temp music in their scores.)

- **Diegetic**—Music that can be "heard" by the characters in the game. Environmental music is by definition diegetic.

- **Non-diegetic/extra-diegetic**—Music that cannot be "heard" by the characters in the game. The score is typically extra-diegetic, which means that it is intended for the ears of the player and not the characters in the game. (Note: The term non-diegetic is typically used in industry despite being incorrect. The technically correct term is extra-diegetic.)

- **Transition**—A part of a cue that is used to transition from one theme to another.

- **Motif**—A musical theme that is used to create a game identity, or to reinforce the presence of a particular character in the game.

- **Hit point**—A timecode location where the musical content must be synchronized closely to a particular onscreen action. In game music, hit points only occur in cinematics.

Assessing Music Requirements

Typically, deciding on a style of music for a game is the easiest part of the compositional process. In many games, an appropriate musical style is obvious based on the genre, location, era, and/or subject matter. For other games, just about any musical style can work, and the producer can choose arbitrarily.

Cinematic Cues

Cinematics are scored in exactly the same fashion as a film or television program. The composer usually knows the rough duration of the scene. Ideally, the composer will also know of any particular hit points that need to be incorporated into the composition.

Gameplay Cues

A big issue facing game composers and game music editors is knowing how many cue sections to write for a particular cue. This can be best determined by playing the game level while paying particular attention to the number of different gameplay situations (or "states") that are presented. For example, a typical action adventure game includes several gameplay states:

- **Intro**—An introductory section of the game level before any action begins. The intro state is also commonly called idle.

- **Combat**—A state in which the player is engaging enemy combatants.

- **Near Death**—A state in which the player has taken a significant amount of damage and is close to death.

- **Death**—The state in which the player is dead.

- **Victory**—The state in which the player has completed the game level objectives.

These are just some examples of gameplay states that can trigger different sections of a music cue. The game engine technology and available programming resources are big factors in determining just how many cue sections can be implemented. This is certainly a determination that is best made before the composer writes any cues!

Creating Interactive Arrangements

Ideally, each of the different cue sections should be able to transition into one another. This is one of the biggest differences between scoring for games and scoring for film and television. Game composers use two primary methods for creating interactive arrangements: layering and splicing. Usually, the choice of arrangement method is based on the preference of the composer, but in some cases the game engine may be limited to one arrangement technology or the other.

Layering

In a game score, a *layer* is an audio file that contains a single track or a bounced collection of tracks. The arrangement is created by muting and un-muting layers or by fading layers in and out (See Figure 6.2). The game engine controls the playback of the layers based on the gameplay state as described previously.

Note: The Intro loop plays all the time, whereas the other layers turn on and off depending on the gameplay state.

Splicing

With a splicing (or *jump cut*) approach to arranging, there are no layers. All of the tracks of a cue section are bounced to a single audio file (sometimes called a *chunk* or *sub cue*). Only one audio file will play in the game at any particular time.

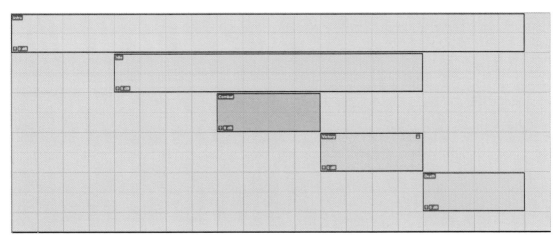

Figure 6.2
An example of layering

The game engine creates the arrangement by "jumping" from the end of one file to the beginning of the next. Because some cue sections must be able to transition into several other cue sections, multiple transitions may be necessary. Each of these transitions must be composed and bounced to a separate file (see Figure 6.3).

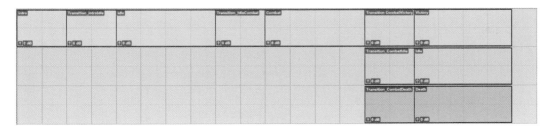

Figure 6.3
An example of splicing

Note: The Combat section has three possible transitions: Victory, Idle, and Death.

Acquiring Game Music Assets

Game music elements can be gathered using one of two methods: by scoring original compositions and by selecting from production music libraries.

- **Scoring**—Composing a unique musical score for the game.
- **Browsing music libraries**—Obtaining pre-recorded music or loops from commercial music libraries.

In this lesson, you're going to learn to use the second method, browsing a music library for elements to create your music cues.

Browsing Music Libraries

Like sound effects and backgrounds, game music can be arranged from elements that are transferred from production music libraries. Pro Tools includes an assortment of royalty free music elements from Big Fish Audio that you can use to create a score. In addition, dozens of other high-quality libraries are available on the market.

DigiBase for Music

Browsing and searching for music elements in DigiBase is identical to browsing and searching for sound effects. The Workspace browser navigation and search functions operate in the exact same manner. However, the Workspace browser provides an additional function that can make auditioning music elements easier: auditioning at the session tempo.

Auditioning Music at the Session Tempo

A DigiBase function that is unique to music workflow is the ability to audition files at the session tempo. This feature makes use of the Elastic Audio functionality in Pro Tools. Later in this lesson, you'll learn how to set your session tempo, and use some more advanced Elastic Audio functionality, but for now you'll focus on the benefits of using Elastic Audio to audition files. You'll begin with a brief look at the available Elastic Audio plug-ins, then you'll check out the auditioning workflow.

The available Elastic Audio plug-in types include the following:

- **Polyphonic**—Best suited for complex loops and multi-instrument mixes

- **Rhythmic**—Best suited for material with clear attack transients like drums, percussion, piano, or bass guitar

- **Monophonic**—Best suited for monophonic material where formant preservation is a concern, such as vocals

- **Varispeed**—Creates tape-like speed changes and is not well suited for auditioning

To audition music files at the session tempo:

1. Enable the AUDIO FILES CONFORM TO SESSION TEMPO (METRONOME) button in the browser toolbar (see Figure 6.4).

Figure 6.4
Audio Files Conform To Session Tempo button

2. Select an **ELASTIC AUDIO** plug-in from the Elastic Audio plug-in selector in the browser toolbar (see Figure 6.5).

Figure 6.5
Elastic Audio plug-in selector

3. Place the insertion point in the session at the location containing the tempo you want to preview. (If the session has no tempo changes, this step is not necessary.)

4. Audition the file using any of the methods discussed in the previous lessons. The files will audition at the session tempo automatically.

In the Avid Learning Series   Complete elastic audio functionality is covered in the "Pro Tools 101" book by Avid.

Walkthrough: Acquiring Game Music

In this walkthrough you learn how to use the splicing method to create interactive cue sections.

Her are the music cue sections you need:

■ Idle

■ Combat

■ Victory

Her are some suggested music elements:

■ **Idle**—Simple percussion or solo instrument groove or drone

■ **Combat**—Large drum or multi-instrument groove

■ **Victory**—An additional variation on the drum or multi-instrument groove

To prepare the session:

1. Open the PTGA_Walkthrough_06.ptt session file.

2. Keep the default session parameters.

3. Click **OK.**

4. Save a copy of the session with your initials added to the filename.

5. Prepare the session with the following settings:
   - **Edit Mode:** Absolute Grid
   - **Grid Value:** One bar
   - **Loop Playback:** Enabled
   - **Tempo Rulers:** Enabled (Conductor Icon in Transport window)
   - **Main Timebase:** Bars|Beats
   - **Tempo Ruler:** Showing

Browsing and Searching Music Elements

Often, the music arranging process begins by browsing or searching production music libraries. For this part of the walkthrough, you'll use DigiBase to search for useful elements and audition them at the session tempo.

To search music elements using DigiBase:

1. Press OPTION+; (Mac) or ALT+; (Windows) to open the Workspace browser.

2. Enable the AUDIO FILES CONFORM TO SESSION TEMPO button in the browser toolbar and choose the RHYTHMIC ELASTIC AUDIO plug-in from the Elastic Audio plug-in selector.

3. Click the FIND button (magnifying glass) in the Workspace, or press COMMAND+F (Mac) or CTRL+F (Windows) to initiate a search.

Tip: Set the Kind field to Audio File to get faster search results.

4. Select the volumes you want to search by clicking the checkboxes.

5. Select AUDIO FILE from the Kind pop-up menu.

6. Type a search term like "percussion" or "drums" into the search field. Press RETURN or ENTER or just click the SEARCH button to execute the search. After a few moments, the assets that match your search will appear.

7. Browse through the found assets.

8. Click the SPEAKER icon or the waveform to audition the files. The files will play back at the session tempo.

Importing Music Elements into Pro Tools

Once you've found a variety of compatible elements for the needed cue sections, import them into the session.

To import the sound elements to the Clip List:

1. Disable AUDIO FILES CONFORM TO SESSION TEMPO.

2. Click the SPEAKER icon or the waveform for each found asset to audition the files.

3. Identify sound elements that will work for each of the game cues: Idle, Combat, and Victory.

4. Select the desired element(s) in the Workspace browser.

5. Drag and drop the elements into the Clip List.

Caution: If Pro Tools asks, do *not* import the tempo with the music elements.

Editing Music

In the "Understanding Game Music" section, you looked at the different ways of arranging cue sections for playback. In this section, you'll discover the tools and techniques for creating the cue sections that you need.

Using Identify Beat

When music loops are imported into Pro Tools, the tempo of one of the loops is often used to set the session tempo. The remaining loops can then be conformed to this new session tempo when arranging the composition so that all loops play back with matching tempos. Identify Beat is the quickest way to determine the tempo of an imported music loop. It also conforms the Edit Grid to the loop's tempo, paving the way for tempo matching additional loops.

To use Identify Beat to calculate the tempo of a loop:

1. Set the MAIN TIME scale to Bars|Beats.

2. Position the loop at the beginning of the first bar in the session (1|1|000) (see Figure 6.6).

Figure 6.6
Grid before using Identify Beat

3. Using the Smart Tool as the Grabber tool, select the clip.

4. Choose **EVENT > IDENTIFY BEAT**, or press **COMMAND+I** (Mac) or **CTRL+I** (Windows). The Add Bar|Beat Markers dialog box will appear (see Figure 6.7).

Figure 6.7
Add Bar/Beat Markers dialog box

5. Make sure that the Start Location is set to 1|1|000 and that the Start Time Signature reflects the meter of the selected loop.

6. Adjust the End Location to the correct Bar|Beat location based on the playback length of the loop. For example, for a two-bar loop you would set the end location to 3|1|000, and for a four-bar loop you would set the end location to 5|1|000.

7. Click **OK**. Pro Tools will automatically calculate the tempo of the loop and conform the Edit Grid to the new tempo (see Figure 6.8).

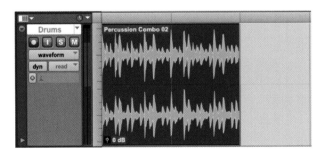

Figure 6.8
Grid is now conformed to the tempo of the clip

Using Elastic Audio for Tempo Matching

Once a tempo has been established for your session, you have several ways to conform additional loops to the new tempo, including using Time Compression/Expansion and Beat Detective. However, the most powerful way is to use Elastic

Audio along with the TCE Trimmer. When Elastic Audio is enabled for a track, the functionality of the TCE Trimmer is modified. Instead of using the TCE plug-in algorithm specified in the Pro Tools preferences, the TCE Trimmer invokes the Elastic Audio plug-in that has been selected on the track. The result is a clip that is quickly conformed to the session tempo, while simultaneously taking full advantage of the flexible modes and superior quality of the Elastic Audio technology.

Real-Time Processing vs. Rendered Processing

Two processing types are available when using Elastic Audio: real-time processing and rendered processing.

- **Real-time**—Changes take place immediately, but an additional load is placed on system resources. This processing type is used most often.

- **Rendered**—Changes must be rendered, and clips appear offline during this time. Once the rendering is complete, no additional load is placed on system resources. This processing type is rarely used unless system performance errors arise while using real-time processing.

Elastic Audio and the TCE Trimmer

As mentioned previously, TCE Trimmer takes on a different functionality when used on a track with Elastic Audio enabled.

To enable Elastic Audio on a track:

1. Click the track's **ELASTIC AUDIO PLUG-IN** selector (see Figure 6.9) and select the appropriate Elastic Audio plug-in. (See the previous section titled "Auditioning Music at the Session Tempo" for a description of the Elastic Audio plug-in types.) The clips on the track may temporarily go offline while Elastic Audio analysis is performed. The waveforms will appear grayed out while the files are offline.

Figure 6.9
The Elastic Audio button

2. Click the track's **ELASTIC AUDIO PLUG-IN** selector again and select **REAL-TIME PROCESSING** or **RENDERED PROCESSING** from the bottom of the pop-up menu (see Figure 6.10).

Figure 6.10

Elastic Audio plug-in selector

To use the TCE Trimmer with Elastic Audio:

1. Enable the **GRID EDIT** mode.

2. Set the **GRID VALUE** to one bar (1|0|000) (see Figure 6.11). This setting is ideal for conforming audio to the nearest bar.

Figure 6.11

Grid Value set to one bar

3. Click and hold the **TRIMMER** tool in the toolbar. The Trimmer tool mode selector will open (see Figure 6.12).

Figure 6.12

Trimmer tool pop-up menu

4. Select the **TCE** mode for the Trimmer tool.

5. Verify that the clip you want to conform begins at the beginning of a bar. The Edit Selection indicators are the best way to know for sure (see Figure 6.13).

Figure 6.13

Edit Selection indicators in the Edit window toolbar

6. Click with the Smart Tool as the TCE Trimmer tool near the end of the clip and drag the clip end point to the desired bar and beat location. The TCE Trimmer will invoke the selected Elastic Audio plug-in to shorten or lengthen the clip (see Figure 6.14).

Figure 6.14
Clip before (left) and after (right) using the TCE Trimmer

For more information on Elastic Audio, see "Working with Elastic Audio" in the "Pro Tools 101: An Introduction to Pro Tools 10" book by Avid.

In the Avid Learning Series

Using Clip Groups

A *clip group* is a collection of any combination of audio and MIDI clips that looks and acts like a single clip. Clip groups are indispensable when trying out different arrangements of cue sections. They allow all of the clips on all of the tracks of a cue section to be non-destructively grouped into a single clip. The clip groups can then be arranged to test transitions.

Clip groups can be ungrouped at anytime, allowing you to access the individual underlying clips for editing. After you've performed an edit to the underlying clips, you can regroup the clips, returning them to their grouped state.

To create a clip group:

1. Using the Smart Tool as the Selector tool, select the clips to be grouped. You can select multiple clips on a track as well as clips on multiple tracks (see Figure 6.15).

2. Choose **CLIP > GROUP** or press **OPTION+COMMAND+G** (Mac) or **CTRL+ALT+G** (Windows). The selected clips will be combined into a solid block, as shown in Figure 6.16.

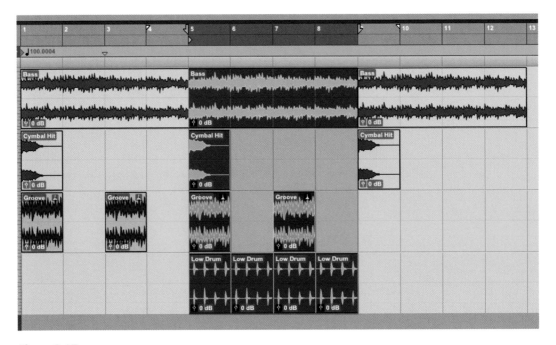

Figure 6.15
Selection of clips on multiple tracks

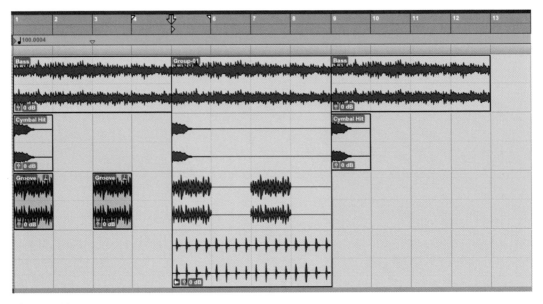

Figure 6.16
Selected clips have been combined into a clip group

To ungroup clips:

1. Using the Smart Tool as the Grabber tool, select the clip group.

2. Choose **CLIP > UNGROUP** or press **OPTION+COMMAND+U** (Mac) or **CTRL+ALT+U** (Windows). The clips will return to their ungrouped state.

To regroup clips:

1. Using the Smart Tool as the Grabber tool, select any clip from the ungrouped clip group.

2. Choose **CLIP > REGROUP** or press **OPTION+COMMAND+R** (Mac) or **CTRL+ALT+R** (Windows). The previous clip group will be recreated.

In the Avid Learning Series   For more information on clip groups, see "Clip Groups" in the Pro Tools 101 book.

Coloring Clip Groups

One particularly good use for the Pro Tools color palette is assigning colors to clip groups. Assigning a unique color to each clip group can assist in identification, especially when you have many clip groups in the session.

When working with music cues, assigning a unique color to each cue section will help you quickly identify each one, making it easier to try out different arrangements and audition transitions (as discussed later).

To assign a unique color to a clip group:

1. Using the Smart Tool as the Grabber tool, select a clip group (see Figure 6.17).

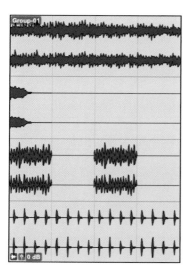

Figure 6.17
Clip group with its default color

2. Choose **WINDOW > COLOR PALETTE**. The Color Palette window will open. The currently assigned color of the clip group will be highlighted, and the Apply to Selected selector will be set to Clips In Tracks (see Figure 6.18).

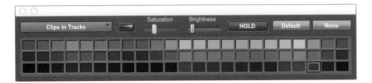

Figure 6.18
Color Palette window with the original color highlighted

3. Select and click a new color in the Color Palette window (see Figure 6.19).

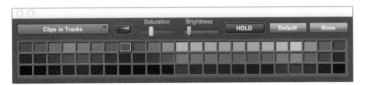

Figure 6.19
Color Palette window with the new color highlighted

The selected clip group will display the newly assigned color (see Figure 6.20).

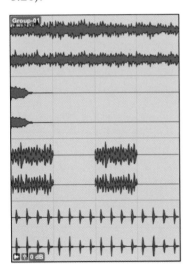

Figure 6.20
Clip group changes to show the new color

Using Shuffle Mode

Once the cue sections have been made into clip groups and color coded, it's easy to audition the transitions using the Shuffle Edit mode.

To arrange clip groups using Shuffle mode:

1. Enable **SHUFFLE EDIT** mode.

2. Arrange each of your clip groups so that they are lined up back to back.

3. Set the **GRID VALUE** to one bar (1|0|000).

4. Play back the session to audition the arrangement and the transitions between each of the music cues.

5. Using the Smart Tool as the Grabber tool, click and drag the clips to try out different arrangements (see Figures 6.21-6.23). Pay special attention to transitions between cue sections that will occur back to back during gameplay. (For example, ensure smooth transitions from Intro to Idle, Idle to Combat, Combat to Idle, and Combat to Victory; Idle to Victory may be less important, if it won't occur during gameplay.)

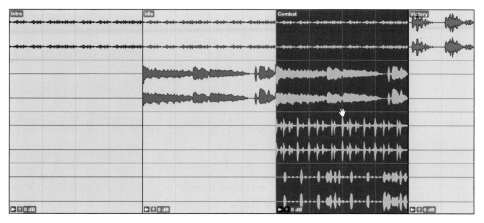

Figure 6.21
The Combat clip is clicked with the Grabber

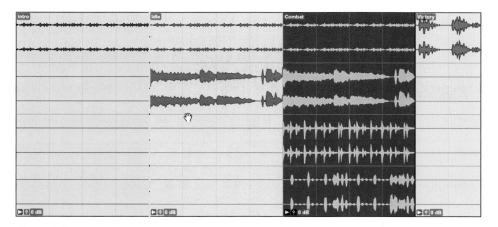

Figure 6.22
The Combat clip is dragged to the beginning of the Idle clip (the mouse button is still held down); a highlight appears at the beginning of the Idle clip

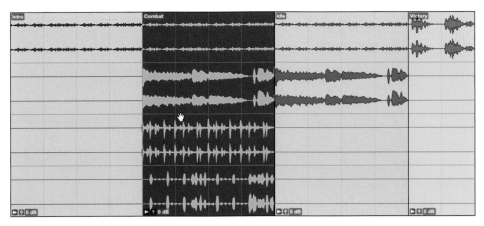

Figure 6.23
After the mouse button is released the Combat clip moves to the highlighted position; the Idle clip shuffles to the right

Walkthrough: Editing Music

In this walkthrough you learn how to create a cue with three different sections. Then you test the transitions to make sure they work well.

To build the Idle section of the cue:

1. Option-click (Mac) or Alt-click (Windows) on the clips you imported into the Clip List to audition them.

2. Select a clip to begin the composition and drag it onto the Tracks list. Pro Tools will automatically create a new track and place the clip at the beginning of the session.

3. The track will automatically be named based upon the dropped clip name. Change the track name to something meaningful, such as **drums** or **synth**.

To use Identify Beat to set the session tempo:

1. Using the Smart Tool as the Grabber tool, select the clip.

2. Choose EVENT > IDENTIFY BEAT or press COMMAND+I (Mac) or CTRL+I (Windows).

3. Adjust the End Location to the correct Bar|Beat location based on the number of bars in the clip.

4. Click **OK.** Pro Tools will automatically calculate the tempo of the loop and conform the Edit Grid to the new tempo.

5. With the first clip selected, press **COMMAND+D** (Mac) or **CTRL+D** (Windows) or select **EDIT > DUPLICATE** to duplicate the clip. You'll reuse the first clip in the combat theme.

To build a Combat section of the cue, you'll add another element:

1. Audition some additional music elements in the Clip List.

2. Verify that the **GRID EDIT** mode is enabled and that the Grid Value is set to one bar.

3. Select a clip that works well with the first clip, and drag it onto the empty space at the bottom of the Edit window. Pay attention to where the purple clip start and end locators appear in the Timebase rulers. Drop the clip at an appropriate location to begin the Combat section. Pro Tools will automatically create another new track and place the clip at the location where you dropped it.

4. Rename the track to give it a meaningful name.

To use Elastic Audio and the TCE Trimmer to conform the clip to the session tempo:

1. Resize the new track as needed to show the Elastic Audio plug-in selector (try a track height of medium).

2. Click the **ELASTIC AUDIO PLUG-IN** selector on the new track and select the appropriate Elastic Audio plug-in.

3. Click the **TRIMMER TOOL** button in the toolbar and enable the TCE Trimmer.

4. Click with the Smart Tool as the TCE Trimmer tool near the end of the clip and drag the clip end point to the desired bar and beat location.

To break it back down for the Victory section of the cue:

1. Audition some additional music elements in the Clip List.

2. Select a clip that works well with the first two clips, and drag it onto the empty space at the bottom of the Edit window. Drop it in an appropriate location to begin the Victory section. Pro Tools will automatically create another new track and place the clip at the location where you dropped it.

3. Rename the track to something meaningful.

4. Enable **ELASTIC AUDIO** on the track, and use the **TCE TRIMMER** to conform the clip to the session tempo.

These minimal cue sections are just a starting point. Feel free to add additional elements to these sections or, if you're familiar with using MIDI and Instrument tracks, try adding some virtual instruments to augment them. Move on to the next section once you are happy with all of your music cue sections.

To use clip groups to isolate the cue sections:

1. Verify that the **GRID EDIT** mode is still enabled and that the Grid Value is still set to one bar.

2. Click and drag in the Bars|Beats ruler with the Smart Tool, and select across the first cue section. By clicking in the ruler, you automatically select across all tracks.

3. Press **COMMAND+OPTION+G** (Mac) or **CTRL+ALT+G** (Windows) or select **CLIPS > CREATE CLIP GROUP** to create a clip group from your selection.

4. Rename the clip group **Idle**.

5. Repeat Steps 2-4 to create clip groups for the Combat and Victory sections.

To assign a unique color to each clip group:

1. Using the Smart Tool as the Grabber tool, select the first clip group.

2. Choose **WINDOW > COLOR PALETTE**. The Color Palette window will open. The currently assigned color of the clip group will be highlighted, and the Apply to Selected selector will be set to Clips In Tracks.

3. Click on a new color from the Color Palette window to assign it to the selected clip group.

4. Repeat Steps 1-3 for each of the other clip groups.

To use Shuffle mode to try different arrangements:

1. Enable **SHUFFLE EDIT** mode.

2. Using the Smart Tool as the Grabber tool, rearrange the clips to test all of the possible transitions:

   - Idle to Combat
   - Combat to Idle
   - Combat to Victory

If any of the transitions don't work, you may need to modify one of the music cue sections. In a real-world game music situation, you might also compose a special transition for any trouble spots. Then you would need to implement the transitions into the game (or request assistance from a programmer).

Walkthrough: Mastering Music

In a typical game music project, music can be exported using either a Bounce To Tracks or Bounce To Disk workflow. Because you have so few cue sections, it will be faster to use Bounce To Disk.

Tip: In a larger project with many cues, the cues are typically bounced to tracks, exported, imported into a dedicated mastering session, and then bounced to disk.

In this walkthrough you learn how to maximize the levels before exporting. You also insert a quality dither plug-in to take the files from 24-bit to 16-bit before you bounce.

To add an ultra-maximizer to the master fader:

1. Create a stereo master fader (see Figure 6.24).

Figure 6.24
New Tracks dialog box

2. Use the Edit Window View selector or the View menu to display the INSERTS **A-E** column in the Edit window.

3. Insert a MAXIM plug-in on the first insert of the master fader (see Figure 6.25).

Figure 6.25
Maxim inserted on the master fader

4. Select the MIXING LIMITER preset (see Figure 6.26).

5. Select the first clip group in your session.

6. Press PLAY to hear the cue section played through Maxim.

7. Experiment with the Threshold setting to get a consistently loud signal.

8. Be sure that the Dither switch is disabled. You'll insert a better dither plug-in after Maxim.

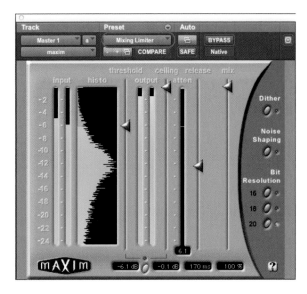

Figure 6.26
Mixing Limiter preset

To add dither to the master fader:

1. Insert a **POWR DITHER** plug-in on the last insert of the master fader (see Figure 6.27).

Figure 6.27
POWr Dither inserted on the master fader

2. Adjust the plug-in parameters as follows:
   - **Bit Depth:** 16-bit
   - **Algorithm:** Noise Shaping Type 1

Figure 6.28
POWr Dither plug-in interface

Walkthrough: Exporting Music Using Bounce To Disk

Your music clip groups are now ready to be exported using Bounce To Disk. In this walkthrough you learn how to do just that.

To export your music clips:

1. Select the first clip group.

2. Select FILE > BOUNCE TO > DISK or press OPTION+COMMAND+B (Mac) or CTRL+ALT+B (Windows). The Bounce dialog box will appear.

3. Set the BOUNCE settings as follows:

   - **Bounce Source:** Mix (Stereo)
   - **File Type:** WAV
   - **Format:** Stereo (Interleaved)
   - **Bit Depth:** 16-bit
   - **Sample Rate:** 48kHz
   - **Conversion Options:** Convert After Bounce

4. Click the BOUNCE button. A Save dialog box will appear.

5. Name the bounced file **MX_Idle.01**.

6. Create a folder named **PTGA_Walkthrough_06_MUS** to store all of the music files.

7. Click SAVE to bounce the clip to disk.

8. Once the bounce finishes, repeat Steps 1-7 to bounce each of the remaining clip groups. Name the remaining bounced files as follows:

   - **MX_Combat.01**
   - **MX_Victory.01**

Walkthrough: Implementing Music in Unity

Now that you've exported your music from Pro Tools, you're ready to implement it in Unity.

To prepare the Unity project:

1. Open the PTGA_Walkthroughs Unity project.

2. Select the Walkthrough_05 scene that you created in Lesson 5.

3. Duplicate the scene by choosing **EDIT > DUPLICATE** or pressing **COMMAND+D** (Mac) or **CTRL+D** (Windows).

4. Name the duplicated scene **Walkthrough_06** and add your initials.

5. Double-click the duplicated level to make it active.

To import the audio files:

1. Navigate to the folder where you bounced your music clips.

2. Drag the folder onto the Unity Project window. The folder and all of its contents will automatically be imported into the project.

To assign the music in the Inspector:

1. Click the **AUDIO_MANAGER** item in the Hierarchy window.

2. Assign the sounds to specific triggers in the Inspector window as follows:
   - **Music_Idle:** MX_Idle.01
   - **Music_Combat:** MX_Combat.01
   - **Music_Victory:** MX_Victory.01

3. **ASSIGN** the following **SETTINGS**:
   - **Music_Idle_Volume:** 0.35
   - **Music_Combat_Volume:** 0.35
   - **Music_Victory_Volume:** 0.35

To test the music:

1. Select **EDIT > PLAY** or press **COMMAND+P** (Mac) or **CTRL+P** (Windows) to launch the game.

2. Listen for the Idle cue to begin immediately. Then cast a spell by pressing the mouse button to trigger the Combat cue. You'll have to complete the mission objectives to hear the Victory cue. Complete the mission objectives by walking over to the NPC character, crossing the bridge and killing all of the spiders, and then returning to the NPC character.

3. Press **COMMAND+P** (Mac) or **CTRL+P** (Windows) to exit the game.

Summary

In this lesson you learned how to add music to the game. You should now be able to:

- Understand game music terminology and the two methods for arranging an interactive score.

- Use Pro Tools features to edit, master, and export game music.

- Implement game music in Unity.

Review/Discussion Questions

1. What is the difference between a score and a cue? (See "Understanding Game Music" on page 174.)

2. How are cinematic cues different from gameplay cues? (See "Gameplay Cues" on page 175.)

3. What are the two methods for creating interactive arrangements of a cue? How are they different? (See "Creating Interactive Arrangements" on page 176.)

4. Which Elastic Audio plug-ins are typically used for auditioning music elements? (See "Acquiring Game Music Assets" on page 177.)

5. How is the functionality of the TCE Trimmer different when trimming a clip on a track with Elastic Audio enabled than without Elastic Audio enabled? (See "Elastic Audio and the TCE Trimmer" on page 183.)

6. What is the key command for creating a clip group? How are clip groups useful for auditioning music transitions? (See "Using Clip Groups" on page 185.)

Adding Music to the Game

In this exercise, you learn how to arrange an interactive score that follows the action. To complete this exercise, you create several music loops that change based on game actions.

Media Used:
Pro Tools: PTGA_Exercise_06
Unity: PTGA_Exercises

Duration:
60 Minutes

Acquiring Game Music Assets

In this exercise, you use the splicing method to create interactive cue sections.

Music cue sections needed:

- Idle
- Combat
- Victory

Suggested music elements:

- **Idle**: Simple percussion or solo instrument groove
- **Combat**: Large drum or multi-instrument groove
- **Victory**: An additional variation on the drum or multi-instrument groove

To prepare the session, follow these steps:

1. Open the PTGA_Exercise_06.ptt session file.
2. Keep the default session settings.
3. Click **OK**.
4. Save a copy of the session with your initials added to the filename.
5. Prepare the session with the following settings:
   - **Edit Mode:** Absolute Grid
   - **Grid Value:** One bar
   - **Loop Playback:** Enabled

Browsing and Searching Music Elements

For this part of the exercise, you use the Workspace browser to search for music elements and audition them at the session tempo. You'll use these elements to compose a single-layer 2- to 4-bar loop for the Idle section, a multiple-layer Combat section (with the Idle loop as a base), and a separate single- or multiple-layer 2- to 4-bar loop for the Victory section.

To use DigiBase to search for music elements, follow these steps:

1. Press **OPTION+;** (Mac) or **ALT+;** (Windows) or select **WINDOW > WORKSPACE** to open the Workspace browser.
2. Enable the **AUDIO FILES CONFORM TO SESSION TEMPO** button in the browser toolbar and choose the appropriate **ELASTIC AUDIO** plug-in (such as Rhythmic) from the Elastic Audio plug-in selector.

3. Click the FIND button (magnifying glass) in the Workspace, or press COMMAND+F (Mac) or CTRL+F (Windows) to initiate a search.

Tip: Set the Kind field to Audio File to get faster search results.

4. Select the volumes you want to search by clicking the checkboxes.

5. Type a search term like **rock** into the search field. Press RETURN or ENTER or just click the SEARCH button to execute the search. After a few moments, the assets that match "rock" will appear.

6. Browse through the found assets.

7. Click the SPEAKER icon or the waveform to audition each file at the session tempo. Identify appropriate music elements for each cue section: Idle, Combat, and Victory.

Importing Music Elements into Pro Tools

Once you've found a variety of compatible elements for the needed cue sections, you're ready to import them into the session.

To import the sound elements to the Clip List, follow these steps:

1. Disable AUDIO FILES CONFORM TO SESSION TEMPO.

2. Select the desired element(s) in the Workspace browser.

3. Drag and drop the elements into the Clip List.

Caution: If Pro Tools asks, do *not* import the tempo with the music elements.

Editing Game Music

Now that you've imported some music loops, you can use them to create a cue with three different sections. Then you need to test the transitions to make sure they work well.

To build the Idle section of the cue, follow these steps:

1. Option-click (Mac) or Alt-click (Windows) on the clips you imported in the Clip List to audition them.

2. Select the clip you want to use for the Idle section and drag it onto the Track List. Pro Tools will automatically create a new track and place the clip at the beginning of the session.

3. The track will automatically be named based upon the dropped clip name. Change the track name to something meaningful like "drums" or "synth."

To set the Session Tempo using Identify Beat, follow these steps:

1. Using the Smart Tool as the Grabber tool, select the clip.

2. Choose **EVENT > IDENTIFY BEAT** or press **COMMAND+I** (Mac) or **CTRL+I** (Windows).

3. Adjust the end location to the correct Bar|Beat location based on the number of musical bars in the selected clip.

4. Click **OK.** Pro Tools will calculate the tempo of the loop and conform the Edit Grid to the new tempo.

5. With the first clip selected, press **COMMAND+D** (Mac) or **CTRL+D** (Windows) or select **EDIT > DUPLICATE** to duplicate the clip. You'll reuse this first element for the Combat theme.

To build a Combat section of the cue by adding another element, follow these steps:

1. Verify that the **GRID EDIT** mode is enabled and that the Grid value is set to one bar.

2. Audition some additional music elements in the Clip List.

3. Select a clip that works well with the first clip to use as the second layer for the Combat section. Drag the clip onto the empty space at the bottom of the Edit window. Pay attention to where the purple clip start and end locators appear in the Timebase rulers as you drag.

4. Drop the clip at an appropriate location to begin the Combat section, where it will overlap with the duplicated Idle clip. Pro Tools will automatically create another new track and place the clip at location where you dropped it.

5. Rename the track using a meaningful name.

To conform the clip to the session tempo using Elastic Audio and the TCE Trimmer tool, follow these steps:

1. Click the **ELASTIC AUDIO PLUG-IN** selector on the new track and select the appropriate Elastic Audio plug-in.

2. Click on the **TRIMMER** tool in the toolbar and enable the TCE Trimmer.

3. Click with the Smart Tool as the TCE Trimmer tool near the end of the clip and drag the clip end point to the desired bar and beat location.

To break it back down for the Victory section of the cue, follow these steps:

1. Audition some additional music elements in the Clip List.

2. Select a clip that works well with the first two clips, and drag it onto the empty space at the bottom of the edit window.

3. Drop the clip in an appropriate location to begin the Victory section (where it does not overlap with the Idle and Combat sections). Pro Tools will automatically create another new track and place the clip at the location where you dropped it.

4. Rename the track using a meaningful name.

5. Enable ELASTIC AUDIO on the track and use the TCE Trimmer to conform the clip to the session tempo.

6. These minimal cue sections are just a starting point. Feel free to add elements to these sections or, if you're familiar with using MIDI and instrument tracks, try adding some virtual instruments to augment them. Move on to the next section once you are happy with all of your music cue sections.

To isolate the cue sections using clip groups, follow these steps:

1. Verify that the GRID EDIT mode is still enabled and that the Grid Value is still set to one bar.

2. Click in the BARS|BEATS RULER with the Smart Tool, and drag to select across the first cue section. By clicking and dragging in the ruler, you will automatically select across all tracks.

3. Press OPTION+COMMAND+G (Mac) or CTRL+ALT+G (Windows) or select CLIPS > CREATE CLIP GROUP to create the first clip group.

4. Rename the CLIP GROUP **Idle**.

5. Repeat Steps 2-4 for the Combat and Victory sections.

To assign a unique color to each clip group, follow these steps:

1. Using the Smart Tool as the Grabber tool, select the first clip group.

2. Choose WINDOW > COLOR PALETTE. The Color Palette window will open. The currently assigned color of the clip group will be highlighted, and the Apply to Selected selector will be set to Clips In Tracks.

3. Click on a new color from the Color Palette to apply it to the Idle clip group.

Tip: You'll want to use distinctly different colors for each of the clip groups, so that they are easy to identify visually. Try using yellow for the Idle section, red for the Combat section, and blue for the Victory section.

4. Repeat Steps 1-3 for the other clips.

To try different arrangements using shuffle mode, follow these steps:

1. Enable the SHUFFLE EDIT mode.

2. Using the Smart Tool as the Grabber tool, rearrange the clips to test all of the possible transitions:

   • Idle to Combat (Yellow to Red)
   • Idle to Victory (Yellow to Blue)
   • Combat to Idle (Red to Yellow)
   • Combat to Victory (Red to Blue)

If any of the transitions don't work, you may need to modify one or more of the music cue sections.

Mastering Game Music

Now that you've edited and tested your music cue, it's time to maximize the levels before exporting. You also need to insert a quality dither plug-in for converting from 24-bit to 16-bit during the bounce.

To add an ultra-maximizer to the master fader, follow these steps:

1. Create a stereo master fader.

2. Insert a MAXIM plug-in on the first insert of the master fader.

3. Select the MIXING LIMITER preset.

4. Select the first clip group.

5. Press PLAY to hear the cue section played through Maxim.

6. Experiment with the THRESHOLD setting to get a consistently loud signal.

7. Be sure that the DITHER switch is disabled, as you will add a better dither plug-in after Maxim.

To add dither to the master fader, follow these steps:

1. Insert a POWR DITHER plug-in on the last insert of the master fader.

2. Adjust the plug-in parameters as follows:
    - **Bit Depth:** 16-bit
    - **Algorithm:** Noise Shaping Type 1

Exporting Game Music

With the Maxim and Dither plug-ins set, the music clip groups are now ready to be exported. You will repeat the following process for each of the clip groups.

To export the music clips, follow these steps:

1. Select the first clip group.

2. Select FILE > BOUNCE TO > DISK or press OPTION+COMMAND+B (Mac) or CTRL+ALT+B (Windows). The Bounce dialog box will appear.

3. Set the bounce settings as follows:
    - **Bounce Source:** Stereo Mix
    - **File Type:** WAV
    - **Format:** Stereo
    - **Bit Depth:** 16-bit
    - **Sample Rate:** 48kHz
    - **Conversion Options:** Convert After Bounce

4. Click BOUNCE. The Save dialog box will appear.

5. Name the bounced file **MX_Idle.01** (first clip group bounce).

6. Create a folder named **PTGA_Exercise_06_MUS** to store all of the music files.

7. Click SAVE to bounce the clip to disk.

8. Once the bounce finishes, repeat the appropriate steps to bounce the remaining clip groups. Note that you may also need to adjust the Maxim Threshold setting for each of the remaining clip groups. Name the remaining bounced files as follows:
    - **MX_Combat.01** (second clip group bounce)
    - **MX_Victoy.01** (third clip group bounce)

Implementing Music

Now that you have exported the clips from Pro Tools for each of your cue sections, you need to implement them in Unity.

To prepare the Unity project, follow these steps:

1. Open the PTGA_Exercises Unity project.

2. Select the Exercise _05 scene that you created in Exercise 5.

3. Duplicate the file by choosing EDIT > DUPLICATE or pressing COMMAND+D (Mac) or CTRL+D (Windows).

4. Name the duplicated scene **Exercise_06** and add your initials.

5. Double-click the duplicated level to make it active.

To import the audio files, follow these steps:

1. Navigate to the folder where you bounced your music clips.

2. Drag the folder onto the Unity Project window. The folder and all of its contents will automatically be imported into the project.

To assign the audio files in the Inspector, follow these steps:

1. Click the **AUDIO_MANAGER** item in the Hierarchy window.

2. Assign the sounds to specific triggers in the Inspector window as follows:

   - **Music_Idle:** MX_Idle.01
   - **Music_Combat:** MX_Combat.01
   - **Music_Victory:** MX_Victory.01

3. Assign the following settings:

   - **Music_Volume:** 0.3

To test the music, follow these steps:

1. Select EDIT > PLAY or press COMMAND+P (Mac) or CTRL+P (Windows) to launch the game.

2. Listen for the Idle cue to begin immediately. Fire a weapon by pressing the mouse button to trigger the Combat cue. You'll have to kill all of the robots to hear the Victory cue.

3. Press COMMAND+P (Mac) or CTRL+P (Windows) to exit the game.

Working with Vehicle Sounds

Vehicle sounds aren't just for car racing games anymore. It's now common for games of all genres to include a vehicle component. In this lesson, you look at techniques for recording, editing, and implementing convincing vehicle sounds.

Media Used: Pro Tools Session: PTGA_Walkthrough_07.ptt
Unity Project: PTGA_Vehicle_Walkthrough

Duration: 90 Minutes

GOALS

- Understand vehicle sounds
- Acquire vehicle sounds
- Edit vehicle sounds
- Master vehicle sounds
- Export vehicle sounds
- Implement vehicle sounds

Understanding Vehicle Sounds

Vehicle sounds have been a part of video games for many years. We've witnessed the progression of vehicle sounds from the gritty, low fidelity sounds of Atari's classic *Pole Position,* to the modern, ultra realistic engine simulations of Microsoft's *Forza Motorsport* and SCEA's *Gran Turismo.* And, while driving games are the most obvious application for vehicle sound design, it's not uncommon for a first person shooter or action adventure game to have a vehicle component. Therefore, it's important to have a solid understanding of what it takes to make vehicles sound good during gameplay (see Figure 7.1).

Figure 7.1
A typical vehicle recording session

Assessing Vehicle Sound Requirements

As with other aspects of game audio, it's important to understand the game development software's capabilities before beginning the audio design process. The importance of the vehicle to the overall game usually determines the sophistication of the vehicle sound implementation and the resources that the development team is willing to contribute. Engines are the most complex part of dealing with vehicles and, therefore, display the greatest variation in terms of required sound elements and commitment of processing resources. There are three basic levels of vehicle engine complexity: the vehicle simulator, the standard vehicle, and the minimal vehicle.

- **Vehicle simulator**—The most realistic and resource-intensive model.

- **Standard vehicle**—A less complex model that works well for most game genres.

- **Minimal vehicle**—A simple model that requires minimal resources.

Vehicle Simulator

The vehicle simulator (or "sim") is easily the most complex and resource-intensive vehicle model. A typical driving sim will model the engines of many high-performance vehicles. These vehicles may have complex intakes and multiple exhausts that must be recorded and blended to create a realistic simulation. In addition, discrete engine loops are recorded at very close RPM intervals, such as 500 RPM spacings (for example, 500, 1,000, 1,500, and so on). This interval is applied from idle to redline for the vehicle. This can result in a dozen or more discrete engine loops, which are then pitched and crossfaded to create a single engine simulation (see Figure 7.2).

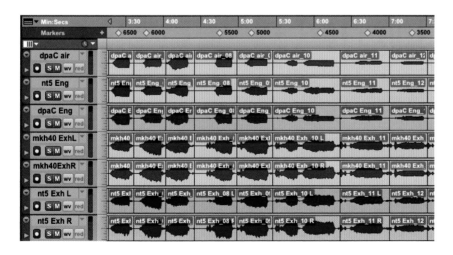

Figure 7.2
Typical Pro Tools session for a vehicle simulator engine recording

Perhaps the most difficult aspect of recording for a driving sim is that vehicles must be recorded under load. *Load* is when the vehicle engine is actually working under stress, like it would be during real driving. Obviously, recording the engine while driving is not really possible due to wind noise, road noise, traffic laws, and other factors. So how is it done? A device called a *chassis dynamometer* (or *dyno*) is used. The vehicle is actually parked on the dyno, which includes a roller or set of rollers; you can sort of see the dyno being used in Figure 7.1. Then the vehicle is "driven" while its wheels turn the rollers in a simulation of road load. The dyno allows the engine to be safely recorded under load, without wind or road noise.

Standard Vehicle

So, what do you do if you don't have access to a Ferrari and a dyno? Most games don't have access to these resources either. Thus the need for the standard vehicle. In a typical game where the vehicles are not the exclusive focus, a more simplified approach is employed. For this vehicle, the discrete engine loops are recorded at wider RPM intervals such as 2,000 RPMs. (For example, 1,000, 3,000, 5,000, and so on.) This approach results in three or four discrete loops that are then pitched and crossfaded to create a single engine simulation, as shown in Figure 7.3.

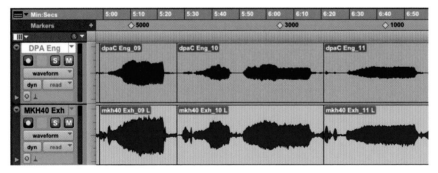

Figure 7.3
A typical Pro Tools session for a standard vehicle engine recording

The major difference between a vehicle sim model and the standard vehicle model is that the standard vehicle engine is not recorded under load. It is much more practical for the vehicle to be recorded while parked. This means that no specialized automotive equipment is required to record the vehicle. It also means that the vehicle will never sound quite as realistic as a vehicle in a driving sim, but that's not the focus of this type of game.

Of course, if you don't mind using library recordings, the standard vehicle model can benefit immensely from using high-quality loops that were recorded under load. These types of files are readily available from several manufacturers.

Minimal Vehicle

When designing an engine simulation for a portable device (such as the Sony PSP or Nintendo DS) or a phone (like the iPhone) the primary concern is often minimizing system resources. This usually means using a small number of engine loops to keep processing overhead and file sizes to an absolute minimum, making the minimal vehicle model. Generally, a single engine loop is used for this purpose (see Figure 7.4).

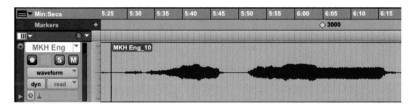

Figure 7.4
A typical Pro Tools session for a minimal vehicle recording session

With a single loop, it's a great idea to use a loop that was recorded somewhere in the middle range for the particular vehicle. For example, if the pitch range for the engine simulation will be 1,000 to 5,000 RPMs, the ideal engine loop will be recorded at 3,000 RPMs. Of course, specific vehicles may have specific RPMs that sound spectacular for that vehicle, so don't be afraid to bend the rules a little.

Acquiring Vehicle Sounds

As with other sounds and effects you've learned about, you have two primary ways to gather vehicle sounds for a game: recording the sounds yourself and selecting sounds from sound libraries.

- **Recording sounds**—This will involve field recording the vehicle sounds.

- **Browsing sound libraries**—This will typically involve purchasing vehicle sounds from proprietary and commercial sound libraries.

Recording Vehicle Sounds

There are a lot of issues to think about when recording vehicles. First, you have to find the right vehicle. Then you have to find a good location for recording. And don't forget about the audio gear you'll need! Here are some tips for recording vehicles in the field.

Location Scouting

It is difficult (if not impossible) for vehicles to be recorded in a controlled studio environment. However, it's still a good idea to scout out the quietest possible location for making your vehicle recordings. Keep in mind that you'll be placing microphones very close to the vehicle, so a small amount of noise from wind or other sources shouldn't be a problem. On the other hand, you'll definitely want to find a location where other vehicles won't drive past in the middle of your recording.

Microphone Selection

Your first instinct when taking microphones into the field may be to use dynamic microphones. Dynamic mics are inexpensive and practically indestructible. Unfortunately, a typical dynamic mic doesn't work well for vehicle recording. The dynamic mic simply doesn't perform well in situations where high sound pressure levels are combined with fine sonic details. A good condenser microphone, although expensive and relatively fragile, is a much better choice.

Microphone Placement

You'll want to record with at least two microphones, if possible. The standard technique is to place one mic near the exhaust and the other near the engine. If you have additional mics, you can put multiple mics at each location (see Figure 7.5).

Figure 7.5
Microphones at the engine and exhaust

You will save yourself a lot of time (and headaches) to do these simultaneously. Otherwise, you'll have two separately recorded clips that will almost never match in pitch. (Keep in mind that someone will need to sit in the car holding the accelerator steady with his foot. This is not a very precise process.) If the engine and exhaust are not recorded simultaneously, you may need to pitch-shift one of the recordings in Pro Tools to match the other, *which you want to avoid if at all possible.* It's hard enough to get all of the loops pitched properly in the game development software!

Naming Channels

Many field recorders allow you to name the record channels. If this is supported on your device, it is a great idea to name the channels based on the mic type and mic placement used during the recording session. For example, a Sennheiser MKH40 near the exhaust could be labeled MKH40 EXH. Or a DPA 4011 near the engine could be labeled 4011 ENG. This information will be copied to the audio file metadata and can later be accessed in Pro Tools.

Obviously, if you are recording directly into a Pro Tools rig using a laptop, you can use these same naming conventions to name the tracks.

Slate

As with dialogue and background recording, it is a very good idea to slate each of your field recorded takes. Simply stating the vehicle type, RPM level, and take number can save a lot of headaches when you start editing the material. This can be accomplished with a minimum of effort by simply speaking into the one of the field recording mics.

Recording Duration

For vehicle recording, your goal should be to get at least 10 seconds of steady material at each RPM level. So you'll want to allow the engine to completely transition from one RPM level to the next before counting to 10. Those transitions are often the most interesting part of the sound, but they are your worst enemy when it comes to creating loops.

Walkthrough:
Recording Vehicle Sounds (Optional)

In this walkthrough you learn how to record vehicle sounds. Creating vehicle sounds can be one of the most satisfying aspects of game sound design. However, it's important to understand your game engine technology before beginning the recording process. You'll be working from your standard vehicle model, which is optimized for the following engine loops:

- 1,000 RPMs

- 3,000 RPMs

- 5,000 RPMs

To record a vehicle sound:

1. Position the microphone(s).

2. If possible, name the channels on the recorder using the microphone type and position.

3. Record-arm the recorder.

4. Check the levels to make sure they're loud enough without clipping. Be sure to keep the headphones at a reasonable volume and use the recorder's meters to set the levels! (The best way to check levels is to run the vehicle through the full RPM range.)

Note: If your field recorder has a Confidence Monitor capability, you should enable it now.

5. Begin recording.

6. Slate the recording with the vehicle type, RPM level, and take. For example, Toyota Tacoma, 5000 RPMs, Take 3.

Tip: If you're recording with a single microphone, be sure to state the mic position as part of the slate!

7. Have an assistant hold the vehicle accelerator steady at the desired RPM level.

Tip: Most sound recordists begin with the highest RPM level first to avoid overheating the vehicle.

8. Once the vehicle has stabilized at the desired RPM level, record for at least 10 seconds.

9. When you've completed the take, pause the recorder. Most recorders will automatically create a discrete audio file each time you pause.

10. Repeat Steps 5-9 for each additional RPM level.

Tip: Don't forget to name the files with descriptive terms on the recorder (if possible) or after you've copied them to your Pro Tools computer.

To copy files:

1. Connect your device or removable media to your computer.

2. Copy the files over to your computer's audio drive.

Walkthrough: Acquiring Vehicle Elements

In this walkthrough, you prepare the vehicle session for editing.

To prepare the Pro Tools session:

1. Open the PTGA_Walkthrough_07.ptt session file.

2. Keep the default session settings.

3. Click **OK.**

4. Save a copy of the session with your initials added to the filename.

5. Prepare the session with the following settings:
   - **Edit Mode:** Slip
   - **Loop Playback:** Enabled

To import vehicle sounds into Pro Tools:

If you were able to field record a vehicle, import those recorded assets into the session. Otherwise, you will skip these steps and work with the clips that are already included in the session.

1. Select the desired element(s) in the Workspace browser.

2. Drag and drop the elements onto the Clip List.

Editing Vehicle Sounds

Although editing vehicle sounds combines many of the techniques you've used for editing backgrounds and sound effects, Pro Tools provides several additional features that you'll use for this process.

Edit Groups

You've already looked at clip groups as a way to combine several clips into one. Unfortunately, creating clip groups for many clips on a collection of tracks can require many steps. In some cases, Edit Groups can do the job much more quickly.

Edit Groups group all of the clips on two or more tracks so that they can be selected, moved, and edited together. With just a couple of steps, an Edit Group can be created from an unlimited number of tracks.

To create an Edit Group:

1. Select the **ENGINE** and **EXHAUST** tracks in the session.

2. Click the **GROUP LIST POP-UP** selector and select **NEW GROUP** or press **COMMAND+G** (Mac) or **CTRL+G** (Windows). The Create Group dialog box will appear (see Figure 7.6).

Figure 7.6
Create Group dialog box

3. Set the Group Type to Edit.

4. Click **OK.** The new group will appear in the Groups list (see Figure 7.7).

Figure 7.7
Groups list

To enable or disable a group:

■ Click the **GROUP NAME** in the Group list. When enabled, the Group Name will be highlighted.

To suspend all groups:

■ Click the **GROUPS LIST POP-UP** selector (see Figure 7.8) and select **SUSPEND ALL GROUPS** or press **COMMAND+SHIFT+G** (Mac) or **CTRL+SHIFT+G** (Windows).

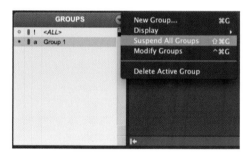

Figure 7.8
Groups list pop-up menu

Mixing Engine Source Elements

Once you have your vehicle engine recordings imported into the session, you'll need to separate the channels onto discrete tracks. With a Vehicle Sim model, you might need a half-dozen tracks (or more), including multiple intake, engine, and exhaust tracks. For the standard vehicle model used in this lesson, you'll only need a track for the engine loop and a track for the exhaust (see Figure 7.9).

Once the engine and exhaust channels have been split onto separate tracks, you can begin the process of mixing the source elements. This is accomplished by adjusting the volume of the two tracks to find the best mix. Often, a different balance of the two channels will sound better at each of the RPM levels. For example, the exhaust will probably have the most character at the low RPM levels, whereas the engine might sound better at the higher RPM levels.

Tip: It's a good idea to automate these levels so that they can be recalled at a later date.

Figure 7.9
Overview of the Pro Tools vehicle recording session

Output Windows

Output windows can be quite helpful when setting levels on a laptop or single display desktop computer.

To open an Output window in the Edit window:

1. Enable the I/O view in the Edit Window View selector (see Figure 7.10).

2. In the Edit window, click the **OUTPUT WINDOW** button in the track's I/O view (see Figure 7.11).

   A floating Output window will open (see Figure 7.12).

Figure 7.10
Edit Window View selector

Figure 7.11
Output Window button in the Edit window

To open an Output window from the Mix window:

■ In the Mix window, click the **OUTPUT WINDOW** button on the track's I/O view (see Figure 7.13).

Figure 7.12
Floating Output window

Figure 7.13
Output Window button on a channel strip in the Mix window

To open an additional Output window, do one of the following:

■ Disable the **OUTPUT WINDOW TARGET** button on the currently open Output window. Then click the **OUTPUT WINDOW** button on another desired track.

■ Hold the **SHIFT KEY** and click the **OUTPUT WINDOW** button on another desired track (see Figure 7.14).

Figure 7.14
Output Window Target button

Writing Static Automation

Aside from cinematics, game audio doesn't tend to require a whole lot of automation. This is because the game audio workflow typically involves working on individual sound effects rather than large mixes. However, as you witnessed in Lesson 4,
"Working with Sound Effects," there are still some great opportunities to use
automation during the sound design process.

One of the best uses for automation is to write a static automation setting that
persists throughout a given clip. This is especially useful when you have multiple
clips on a track that require different automation settings (see Figure 7.15).

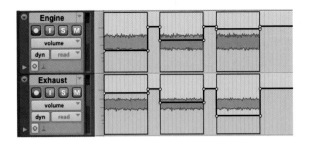

Figure 7.15
Both tracks contain static
volume automation

Trimming Automation Playlists

To make manual adjustments to the automation playlists, you can use the Trimmer
tool. This allows you to make a change over a selected area.

To set static volume automation using the Trimmer tool:

1. Using the Smart Tool as the Grabber tool, select the clip (see Figure 7.16).

Figure 7.16
Two tracks with their clips selected

2. On the track where the clip is located, set the Track view to Volume (see Figure 7.17).

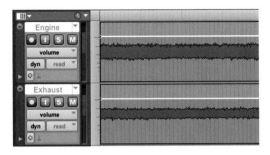

Figure 7.17
Tracks changed to Volume view

Shortcut: With Commands Keyboard Focus (A-Z) enabled, you can also press the Minus (–) alphanumeric key to toggle between the Waveform and Volume Track views.

3. Position the Smart Tool in the upper third of the clip. The tool will automatically switch to show a variation of the Trimmer tool.

4. Click and drag to trim the volume automation up and down. A small indicator will appear in the upper-left corner to show the current volume level and the "delta" between the current level and the previous level (see Figure 7.18).

Shortcut: You can hold the Command (Mac) or Ctrl (Windows) key to trim with a finer resolution.

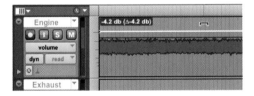

Figure 7.18
Trimming volume automation with the Trimmer tool

Note: If you've created Edit Groups, trimming the volume automation of one clip may trim the volume of additional clips. It may be necessary to disable the Edit Group by clicking the group name in the Group list before trimming.

5. Release the mouse button. The new volume setting will be written for the duration of the selection.

Write to Current

A faster and more intuitive way to write static volume settings is to use the Write to Current command. This command is only available on Pro Tools|HD systems or Pro Tools software with Complete Production Toolkit 2.

To set static volume automation using Write to Current:

1. Make sure that automation is *not* suspended and Volume automation (VOL) is enabled in the Automation window by choosing **WINDOW > AUTOMATION** or pressing **COMMAND+4** (Mac) or **CTRL+4** (Windows) on the numeric keypad. (The Suspend button should be gray and the VOL enable button should be red.) (See Figure 7.19.)

Figure 7.19
Automation window

2. Using the Smart Tool as the Grabber tool, select the clip.

3. On the track where the clip is located, set the Track view to Volume.

4. Set the volume of the track to the desired level using the Channel Fader (or a control surface).

5. Select **EDIT > AUTOMATION > WRITE TO CURRENT** or press **COMMAND+/** (Mac) or **CTRL+/** (Windows). The current volume level will be written for the duration of the selection.

Note: Write to Current works only on the visible automation playlist.

Walkthrough: Editing Vehicle Sounds

In this walkthrough you learn how to create a mix of the vehicle engine elements.

To drag the clips to tracks:

1. Drag the 1,000 RPM engine clip from the Clip List to the Engine track.

2. Using the Smart Tool as the Grabber tool, select the clip.

3. While holding **Control** (Mac) or **Start** (Windows), drag the 1,000 RPM exhaust clip from the Clip List to the Exhaust track. The start of the Exhaust clip will automatically align to the start of the Engine clip.

4. Repeat Steps 1-3 for the 3,000 and 5,000 RPM clips. Be sure to leave some time between the clips.

To select the tracks and create an Edit Group:

1. Select the **Engine** track by clicking the track name.

2. While holding **Shift**, select the **Exhaust** track.

3. Click the **Group List** pop-up and select **New Group** or press **Command+G** (Mac) or **Ctrl+G** (Windows). The Create Group dialog box will appear.

4. Name the group **Engines**, set the **Group Type** to Edit, and click **OK**. A new Edit Group will be created.

To create a mix from the vehicle elements:

1. Set the Track view for both the Engine and Exhaust tracks to Volume.

2. Choose **Window > Automation** to open the Automation window.

3. In the Automation window, click the **Suspend** button to suspend automation playback.

4. Open the Output windows for the Engine and Exhaust tracks. Position them so that they are visible on top of the Edit window.

5. Using the Smart Tool as the selector, double-click to select either of the 1,000 RPM clips. Because they are part of an Edit Group, both clips will automatically be selected.

6. Press **Play** to audition the clips together.

7. Using the faders on the Output windows, adjust the mix levels for the Engine and Exhaust clips.

8. When you're happy with the levels, choose **Edit > Automation > Write To Current** or press **Command+/** (Mac) or **Ctrl+/** (Windows) to execute the Write to Current command. This will write the current volume levels to the selected clips.

9. Stop playback.

10. Repeat Steps 4-9 for the 3,000 and 5,000 RPM clips.

11. In the Automation window, click the **Suspend** button again to enable automation playback.

Bounce the Mixed Elements

Now that you've created a mix of the vehicle elements, you'll use Bounce To Tracks to create mixed clips.

To use the Bounce To Tracks technique to create mixed clips:

1. Set the Track view for both the Engine and Exhaust tracks back to Waveform.

2. Set the Engine and Exhaust track outputs to the Bounce bus.

3. Record-enable the **BOUNCE** track.

4. Using the Smart Tool as the Grabber tool, select one of the 1,000 RPM clips on either the Engine or Exhaust tracks.

5. Press **RECORD** then **PLAY** in the Transport window or on the Edit window toolbar to begin recording.

6. Repeat Steps 3 and 4 for the 3,000 RPM and 5,000 RPM clips.

7. Record-disable the **BOUNCE** track.

8. Rename the resulting clips **EngineMix_1000**, **EngineMix_3000**, and **EngineMix_5000**.

Loop the Bounced Clips

Now that you've got your engine elements bounced, you can edit them into loops.

To edit the engine loops:

1. Enable **SLIP EDIT** mode. Dismiss the warning about losing automation data, if it appears.

2. Using the Smart Tool as the selector, double-click to select the EngineMix_1000 clip.

3. Enable **ZOOM TOGGLE**.

4. Press **PLAY** to audition the clip.

5. Listen to the clip and try to find a steady section of about 1-2 seconds in duration.

6. Using the Smart Tool as the Selector tool, select the steady section.

7. Play the new selection. Listen to see if the selection sounds steady enough to make a good loop.

8. If the loop sounds okay, press **COMMAND+T** (Mac) or **CTRL+T** (Windows) or select **EDIT > TRIM CLIP > TO SELECTION**. This will trim the clip down to the selection.

9. Disable **ZOOM TOGGLE**.

To trim the clip start and end points to zero crossings:

1. If necessary, use the Smart Tool as the Grabber tool to select the trimmed clip.

2. Press the **LEFT ARROW KEY** to center the beginning of the selected clip.

3. Recall the fifth Zoom preset. This should zoom you in to the sample level if the preset hasn't been changed.

4. Using the Smart Tool as the Trimmer tool, trim the clip start to a zero crossing.

5. Press the **RIGHT ARROW KEY** to center the end of the selected clip.

6. Using the Smart Tool as the Trimmer tool, trim the clip end to a zero crossing.

7. Audition the loop.

8. Zoom back out until you can see the other clips.

Repeat the "Loop the Bounced Clips" section for the EngineMix_3000 and EngineMix_5000 clips.

Walkthrough: Mastering Vehicle Sounds Using AudioSuite Normalize

Now that you've edited your vehicle sounds, you'll need to maximize the levels before exporting. Because you're not running any real time plug-ins, you can use AudioSuite Normalize to increase the maximum level of your engine loops while maintaining the relative levels.

In this walkthrough you learn how to run an AudioSuite Normalize on the vehicle sounds.

To normalize the clips:

1. Select all of the mixed engine clips.

2. Select **AUDIOSUITE > OTHER > NORMALIZE**.

3. Adjust the plug-in parameters as follows:

- **Level:** Create Individual Files
- **Selection Reference:** Playlist
- **Use In Playlist:** Enabled
- **Playlist Mode:** Clip by Clip
- **Chan/Track Process Mode:** Level On Each Chan/Track
- **Level:** 0.1 dBFS

4. Press the PROCESS button to apply the effect to the selected clips.

5. Name the normalized clips **VEH_1000.01**, **VEH_3000.01**, and **VEH_5000.01**.

Walkthrough: Exporting Vehicle Sounds Using Export Clips as Files

Next, you'll need to prepare your finished vehicle sounds for export. Because you're not using plug-ins, you can use Export Clips as Files for a faster than real-time export.

In this walkthrough you learn how to export the vehicle sounds using Export Clips as Files.

To export the vehicle sounds:

1. Select all of the clips.

2. Select EXPORT CLIPS AS FILES from the Clip List pop-up menu, or press COMMAND+SHIFT+K (Mac) or CTRL+SHIFT+K (Windows). The Export Selected dialog box will appear.

3. Set the export settings as follows:

- **File Type:** WAV
- **Format:** (Multiple) Mono
- **Bit Depth:** 16-bit
- **Sample Rate:** 48kHz

4. Click the CHOOSE button and create a folder named **PTGA_Walkthrough_07_VEH** to store all of the vehicle clips. Select it.

5. Back in the Export Selected dialog box, click EXPORT.

Walkthrough: Implementing Vehicle Sounds in Unity

Once you've exported your vehicle sounds from Pro Tools, you're ready to implement them in Unity. In this walkthrough you learn how to implement the vehicle sounds in Unity.

To prepare the Unity project:

1. Open the PTGA_Vehicle_Walkthrough Unity project.

2. Select the Level_01 scene in the Project window.

3. Duplicate the file by choosing **Edit > Duplicate** or pressing **Command+D** (Mac) or **Ctrl+D** (Windows).

4. Add your initials to the name of the duplicated level.

5. Double-click the duplicated level to make it active.

To import the audio files:

1. Navigate to the folder where you bounced your vehicle sounds.

2. Drag the folder onto the Unity Project window. The folder and all of its contents will automatically be imported into the project.

To assign the vehicle sounds in the Inspector:

1. Click the **AUDIO_MANAGER** item in the Hierarchy window.

2. Assign the sounds to specific triggers in the Inspector window as follows:

   - **Clip_Motor_Low:** VEH_1000.01
   - **Clip_Motor_Medium:** VEH_3000.01
   - **Clip_Motor_High:** VEH_5000.01

To test the vehicle:

1. Select **Edit > Play** or press **Command+P** (Mac) or **Ctrl+P** (Windows) to launch the game.

2. Use the **Up** and **Down Arrow keys** to accelerate and brake. Use the **Left** and **Right Arrow keys** to steer. Listen for the engine loops.

3. Press **Command+P** (Mac) or **Ctrl+P** (Windows) to exit the game.

Summary

In this chapter you learned about working with vehicle sounds. You should now be able to:

- Work with different vehicle engine models.

- Use Pro Tools to edit, master, and export vehicle sounds.

- Implement vehicle sounds in Unity.

Review/Discussion Questions

1. What are the three classifications of vehicle engine models? How are they different? (See "Understanding Vehicle Sounds" on page 208.)

2. If only two parts of a vehicle are being recorded, what should they be? (See "Microphone Placement" on page 212.)

3. How are Edit Groups useful when editing vehicle sounds? (See "Edit Groups" on page 216.)

4. Which automation playlist is modified by the "Write to Current" command? (See "Write to Current" on page 222.)

5. Why is normalize a good choice for mastering vehicle sounds? (See "Mastering Vehicle Sounds" on page 225.)

Adding Vehicle Sounds to the Game

In this exercise you learn how to create realistic vehicle sounds. For this exercise, you create engine sounds for an off-road Baja truck.

Note: This exercise makes use of a different Unity project than the other exercises in this book.

Media Used:

Pro Tools: PTGA_Exercise_07
Unity: PTGA_Vehicle_Exercise

Duration:

60 Minutes

Acquiring Vehicle Sounds

In this section, you acquire vehicle sounds for the Baja truck. You need the following engine loops—1,000 RPM, 3,000 RPM, and 5,000 RPM. For the engine loops, you can choose either to record the sounds or to use the sounds included in the session.

Recording Vehicle Sounds (Optional)

Creating vehicle sounds can be one of the most satisfying aspects of game sound design. However, it's important to understand your game engine technology before beginning the recording process.

The Standard Vehicle model is used in this exercise, which is optimized for the following engine loops:

- 1,000 RPMs

- 3,000 RPMs

- 5,000 RPMs

To record vehicle sounds:

1. Position the microphone(s). For best results, use good-quality condenser microphones, and record both at the engine position and at the exhaust position simultaneously.

2. If possible, name the channels on the recorder to reflect the microphone type and position.

3. Record-arm the recorder.

4. Check the levels to make sure they're loud enough without clipping. Be sure to keep the headphones at a reasonable volume and use the recorder's meters to set the levels! (The best way to check levels is to run the vehicle through the full RPM range.)

Note: If your field recorder has a **Confidence Monitor** capability, you should enable it now.

5. Begin recording.

6. Slate the recording with the vehicle type, RPM level, and take. For example, Toyota Tacoma, 5000 RPMs, Take 1.

Tip: If you're recording with a single microphone, be sure to state the mic position as part of the slate!

7. Have an assistant hold the vehicle accelerator steady at the desired RPM level. Most sound recordists begin with the highest RPM level first to avoid overheating the vehicle.

8. Once the vehicle has stabilized at the desired RPM level, record for at least 10 seconds.

9. When you've completed the take, pause the recorder. Most recorders will automatically create a discrete audio file each time you pause.

10. Repeat Steps 5-9 for each additional RPM level.

Tip: Don't forget to name the files with descriptive terms on the recorder (if possible) or after you've copied them to your Pro Tools computer.

To copy the files to your computer:

1. Connect your device or removable media to your computer.

2. Copy the files over to your computer's audio drive.

Preparing the Pro Tools Session

Vehicle sounds needed:

■ Engine Loops

Before beginning the sound editing process, you'll need to prepare the session:

1. Open the PTGA_Exercise_07.ptt session file.

2. Keep the default session parameters.

3. Click **OK.**

4. Save a copy of the session with your initials added to the filename.

5. Prepare the session with the following settings:
   - **Edit Mode:** Slip
   - **Loop Playback:** Enabled

Importing Vehicle Sounds into Pro Tools

If you were able to field record a vehicle, import those recorded assets into the session. Otherwise, you'll work with the clips that are already included in the session.

To import the sounds to the Clip List:

1. Select the desired element(s) in the Workspace browser.

2. Drag and drop the elements onto the Clip List.

Editing Vehicle Sounds

Once you've imported the necessary vehicle sounds, you'll need to create a mix of the elements.

To drag the clips to tracks:

1. Drag the **1,000 RPM ENGINE** clip from the Clip List to the Engine track.

2. Using the Smart Tool as the Grabber tool, select the clip.

3. While holding **CONTROL** (Mac) or **START** (Windows), drag the **1,000 RPM EXHAUST** clip from the Clip List to the **EXHAUST** track. The start of the exhaust clip will automatically align to the start of the engine clip.

4. Repeat Steps 1-3 for the 3,000 and 5,000 RPM clips. Be sure to leave some time between the clips.

To select the tracks and create an Edit Group:

1. Select the Engine track by clicking the track name.

2. While holding Shift, select the Exhaust track.

3. Click the **GROUP LIST POP-UP** selector and select **NEW GROUP** or press **COMMAND+G** (Mac) or **CTRL+G** (Windows). The Create Group dialog box will appear.

4. Name the group **Engines**, set the **GROUP TYPE** to Edit, and click **OK**. A new Edit Group will be created.

To create a mix from the vehicle elements:

1. Set the Track view for both the Engine and Exhaust tracks to Volume.

2. Choose **WINDOW > AUTOMATION** to open the Automation window.

3. In the Automation window, click the **SUSPEND** button to suspend automation playback.

4. Open the Output windows for the Engine and Exhaust tracks. Position them so that they are visible on top of the Edit window.

5. Using the Smart Tool as the Selector tool, double-click either of the 1,000 RPM clips. Because they are part of an Edit Group, both the Engine and the Exhaust clips will automatically be selected.

6. Press **PLAY** to audition the clips together.

7. Using the faders on the Output windows, adjust the mix levels for the Engine and Exhaust clips.

8. When you're happy with the levels, choose **EDIT > AUTOMATION > WRITE TO CURRENT** or press **COMMAND+/** (Mac) or **CTRL+/** (Windows) to execute the Write to Current command. This will write the current volume levels to the selected clips.

Note: If Write to Current is not available on your Pro Tools system, simply use the Trimmer tool to set the levels for the Engine and Exhaust clips.

9. Stop playback.

10. Repeat Steps 4-9 for the 3,000 and 5,000 RPM clips.

11. In the Automation window, click the **SUSPEND** button again to enable automation playback.

Bouncing the Mixed Elements

Once you've created a mix you like for each of the vehicle elements, you can use the Bounce To Tracks technique to create mixed clips.

To create mixed clips using the Bounce To Tracks technique, follow these steps:

1. Set the Track view for both the Engine and Exhaust tracks back to Waveform.

2. Set the Engine and Exhaust track outputs to the Bounce bus.

3. Record-enable the **BOUNCE** track.

4. Using the Smart Tool as the Grabber tool, select the 1,000 RPM clip on either the Engine or Exhaust track.

5. Press **RECORD** then **PLAY** in the Transport window or on the Edit Window toolbar to begin recording.

6. Repeat Steps 3 and 4 for the 3,000 RPM and 5,000 RPM clips.

7. Record-disable the **BOUNCE** track.

8. Rename the resulting clips **EngineMix_1000**, **EngineMix_3000**, and **EngineMix_5000**.

Looping the Bounced Clips

Now that you've bounced your engine elements, you need to edit them into loops.
Follow these steps to do so:

1. Enable the **SLIP EDIT** mode.

2. Using the Smart Tool as the Grabber tool, select the EngineMix_1000
   clip.

3. Enable the **ZOOM TOGGLE**.

4. Press **PLAY** to audition the clip.

5. Listen to the clip to identify a steady section of about 1-2 seconds in duration.

6. Using the Smart Tool as the Selector tool, select the steady section.

7. Play the new selection. Listen to see if the selection sounds steady enough
   to make a good loop.

8. If the loop sounds okay, press **COMMAND+T** (Mac) or **CTRL+T** (Windows)
   or select **EDIT > TRIM CLIP > TO SELECTION** to trim off portions of the clip
   outside of the selection. Otherwise, repeat the process using a different
   selection.

9. When finished, disable **ZOOM TOGGLE**.

To trim the clip start and end points to zero crossings, follow these steps:

1. If necessary, use the Smart Tool as the Grabber tool to select the trimmed
   clip.

2. Press the **LEFT ARROW KEY** to center the beginning of the selected clip.

3. Recall **ZOOM PRESET 5.** This should zoom you in to the sample level
   (provided that the preset hasn't been changed).

4. Using the Smart Tool as the Trimmer tool, trim the clip start to a zero
   crossing.

5. Press the **RIGHT ARROW KEY** to center the end of the selected clip.

6. Using the Smart Tool as the Trimmer tool, trim the clip end to a zero
   crossing.

7. Audition the loop.

8. Zoom back out until you can see the other clips in the session.

Repeat the previous two sections for the EngineMix_3000 and EngineMix_5000
clips.

Mastering Vehicle Sounds

Once you've edited your vehicle sounds, you'll need to maximize the levels before exporting. Because you are not running any real-time plug-ins, you can use AudioSuite Normalize to increase the maximum level for the engine loops and crashes.

To run an AudioSuite Normalize on the sounds, follow these steps:

1. Select all of the mixed engine clips and your final crash clips.

2. Select AudioSuite > Other > Normalize.

3. Adjust the plug-in parameters as follows:
   - **Level:** Create Individual Files
   - **Selection Reference:** Playlist
   - **Use In Playlist:** Enabled
   - **Playlist Mode:** Clip by Clip
   - **Chan/Track Process Mode:** Level On Each Chan/Track
   - **Level:** –0.1dBFS

4. Press the Process button to apply the effect to the selected clips.

5. Name the normalized clips **VEH_1000_01**, **VEH_3000_01**, **VEH_5000_01**.

Exporting Vehicle Sounds

In this section of the exercise, you prepare your finished vehicle sounds for export. Because you have not used real-time plug-ins, you can use the Export Clips as Files command for a faster than real-time export.

To export the vehicle sounds, follow these steps:

1. Select all of the clips.

2. Select Export Clips As Files from the Clip List pop-up menu, or press Command+Shift+K (Mac) or Ctrl+Shift+K (Windows). The Export Selected dialog box will appear.

3. Set the export settings as follows:
   - **File Type:** WAV
   - **Format:** (Multiple) Mono
   - **Bit Depth:** 16-bit
   - **Sample Rate:** 48kHz

4. Click the **CHOOSE** button and create a folder named **PTGA_Exercise_07_ VEH** to store all of the vehicle clips. Select the folder.

5. Back in the Export Selected dialog box, click **EXPORT**.

Implementing Vehicle Sounds

After you've exported your vehicle sounds from Pro Tools, you're ready to implement them in Unity.

To prepare the Unity project, follow these steps:

1. Open the PTGA_Vehicle_Exercise Unity project.

2. Select the Level_01 scene in the Project window.

3. Duplicate the file by choosing **EDIT > DUPLICATE** or pressing **COMMAND+D** (Mac) or **CTRL+D** (Windows).

4. Add your initials to the end of the duplicated scene.

5. Double-click the duplicated scene to make it active.

To import the audio files, follow these steps:

1. Navigate to the folder where you bounced your vehicle sounds.

2. Drag the folder onto the Unity Project window. The folder and all of its contents will automatically be imported into the project.

To assign the vehicle sounds in the Inspector, follow these steps:

1. Click the **AUDIO_MANAGER** item in the Hierarchy window.

2. Assign the sounds to specific triggers in the Inspector window as follows:

   - **Clip_Motor_Low:** VEH_1000_01
   - **Clip_Motor_Medium:** VEH_3000_01
   - **Clip_Motor_High:** VEH_5000_01

To test the vehicle, follow these steps:

1. Select **EDIT > PLAY** or press **COMMAND+P** (Mac) or **CTRL+P** (Windows) to launch the game.

2. Use the **UP** and **DOWN ARROW KEYS** to accelerate and brake. Use the **LEFT** and **RIGHT ARROW KEYS** to steer. Listen for the engine loops.

3. Press **COMMAND+P** (Mac) or **CTRL+P** (Windows) to exit the game.

Working with Cinematics

Cinematics bring all of the sound elements together. In this lesson, you'll look at cinematic post-production techniques, including advanced editing and mixing.

Media Used: Pro Tools Session: PTGA_Walkthrough_08.ptt
Unity Project: PTGA_Walkthroughs

Duration: 90 Minutes

GOALS

■ Understand cinematics

■ Acquire cinematic elements

■ Edit cinematic audio

■ Mix cinematic audio

■ Master cinematic audio

■ Export cinematic mixes

■ Implement cinematics

Understanding Cinematics

Cinematics are essentially in-game movies, such as those that play when you launch a game or transition between levels (see Figure 8.1). In recent games, the cinematic has evolved to a level that is on par with the best that Hollywood has to offer. The introductory cinematic can make or break a game at the point of sale, both in a traditional brick and mortar store and an online store. If done well, every die-hard gamer on the planet will want to see how the gameplay delivers on the promise of the cinematic. If done poorly, even decent gameplay may not be able to save the title from obscurity.

Figure 8.1
Cinematics are essentially in-game movies

And nothing shows off a brilliant design concept or cutting edge technology like a great cinematic. Incredible visual effects, realistic motion capture, and blockbuster sound design are all on display in cinematics.

The "Food" Groups

Like traditional film and television sound design, sound for cinematics is often broken down into groups. You'll sometimes hear the term food groups applied to these families of sounds.

Here is a list of the sound design food groups, along with commonly used abbreviations:

- Dialogue (DX, DIA)
- Music (MX)
- Effects (FX, SFX)

In film post-production, most of these groups are broken down further. For example, the dialogue group will almost certainly include sub-groups for production dialogue, ADR, and voiceover. For game cinematics, the dialogue and music groups don't normally need to be broken down further, but the effects group is often broken down in the following manner:

- Foley (FLY, FOL)
- Sound effects (FX, SFX)
- Backgrounds (BG)

By now, these terms should all look pretty familiar!

Note: These sound effects sub-groups can be broken down even further depending on the complexity of the project.

Assessing Cinematic Requirements

The cinematic post-production process usually begins with something called a *spotting session.* During the spotting session, the sound designer will watch each of the cinematics to determine where sound editing needs to occur. In feature film post-production, this information will often be added to a spreadsheet or cataloged using spotting software. This is especially important when tasks are being delegated to multiple sound editors.

In game audio, most cinematic post-production is performed by a single person or a small group of two or three editors. Therefore, elaborate spotting methods are not normally used. Most sound designers will simply use Memory Locations in Pro Tools to build a list of markers where sound design is needed.

Memory Locations

You may already be familiar with the use of Memory Locations in Pro Tools. In particular, the marker is very popular among Pro Tools users. In cinematic post-production, the marker can be used during spotting to mark locations where sound design or sound editing is needed. Furthermore, the Memory Locations window can function as a sort of "to do" list to help track progress. Pro Tools permits up to 999 Memory Locations in each session, so there's no need to worry about conserving Memory Locations while spotting.

After creating the markers for your session, you can use the Memory Locations window to view and recall your markers.

To create a marker:

1. Choose VIEW > RULERS > MARKERS to display the Marker Ruler.

2. Place the cursor at the desired location in the session.

3. Click the ADD MARKER/MEMORY LOCATION button (+) at the start of the Marker Ruler, or press ENTER on the numeric keypad. The New Memory Location dialog box will open (see Figure 8.2).

Figure 8.2
New Memory Location dialog box

4. In the Time Properties section of the dialog box, select MARKER.

5. Give the Memory Location a meaningful name to help you remember its purpose.

6. Click OK. The marker will appear on the Marker Ruler (see Figure 8.3).

Figure 8.3
Marker Ruler

To view the Memory Locations window:

■ Choose **Window > Memory Locations** or press **Command+5** (Mac) or **Ctrl+5** (Windows) on the numeric keypad (see Figure 8.4).

Figure 8.4
Memory Locations window

To recall a marker from the Memory Locations window:

■ Click on a marker name in the Memory Locations window. The marker location will be recalled instantly, and the playback cursor will move to that location.

Acquiring Cinematic Elements

When working with cinematics, you will want to use the existing game assets for the cinematic sound design. This repurposing of existing sound elements is crucial to maintaining cohesion between the cinematics and the gameplay. Cinematics may make use of dialogue, Foley, sound effects, backgrounds, music, and vehicle sounds. Therefore, an efficient cinematic post-production workflow is dependent upon a solid system of organization during the rest of the game sound design process. Having the ability to quickly locate existing assets will save a lot of time and headaches. The methods for acquiring cinematic elements include browsing sound libraries and using existing game assets.

In this lesson, you'll use DigiBase to locate existing game assets and browse libraries.

Using Catalogs in DigiBase

With third-party sound librarians like NetMix and SoundMiner, proprietary assets can be added back into the sound effects database. This database can then be browsed and searched during cinematic post-production to locate appropriate sound assets. You can achieve a similar result by using catalogs in DigiBase.

Catalogs are a great way to organize frequently used assets, regardless of where they are stored. A catalog is essentially a folder full of aliases or shortcuts. Placing a file in a catalog does not physically move the file, but creates an alias that links back to the original.

To create a catalog of an existing folder:

1. Open the Workspace browser by choosing **WINDOW > WORKSPACE** or pressing **OPTION+;** (Mac) or **ALT+;** (Windows) (see Figure 8.5).

Figure 8.5
Workspace browser with a folder of sound assets

2. Drag and drop a single folder onto the Catalog icon in the Workspace browser. Pro Tools will automatically create a fully indexed catalog with the same name as the dropped folder (see Figure 8.6).

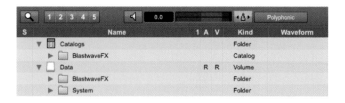

Figure 8.6
Catalog has been created from the folder

Working with Digital Video

In previous lessons, you have worked exclusively with audio assets. Working with cinematics will require a new type of media: digital video. Fortunately, working with digital video in Pro Tools is simple and intuitive.

1. To import digital video into Pro Tools, do one of the following:

   - Choose **FILE > IMPORT > VIDEO** or press **OPTION+COMMAND+SHIFT+I** (Mac) or **CTRL+ALT+SHIFT+I** (Windows) and locate the desired video file. Then click **OPEN**.

   - Drag and drop the desired digital video file from a DigiBase browser or the Mac Finder or Windows Explorer into the Edit window.

   The Video Import Options dialog box will appear (see Figure 8.7).

Figure 8.7
Video Import Options dialog box

2. In the dialog box, select an import destination and location (see Figure 8.8).

Figure 8.8
Destination pop-up menu

3. Set the other import options if necessary.

4. Click **OK.** Pro Tools will import the selected file.

Walkthrough: Acquiring Cinematic Elements

In this walkthrough you learn how to acquire the cinematic elements necessary for the game. You learn to import your digital video and conduct a spotting session. Then you'll organize your existing sound assets into catalogs to aid in finding and importing useful elements. All files you need to complete this walkthrough can be found on the DVD.

You need the following cinematic sounds:

- **Backgrounds**—Ocean and Wind

- **Sound effects**—Airship

- **Music**—Previously created cue sections

- **Dialogue**—Previously created DIA_Player_07 audio file

Recommended search terms:

- **Backgrounds**—Ocean, Wind, and Water
- **Sound effects**—Airplane, Engine, and Balloon

To prepare the session:

1. Open the PTGA_Walkthrough_08.ptt session file.

Shortcut: **If a Missing Files dialog box appears, select Skip All and click OK to dismiss the message.**

2. Keep the default session settings.

3. Click **OK.**

4. Save a copy of the session with your initials added to the filename.

5. Prepare the session with the following settings:
   - **Edit Mode:** Slip
   - **Main Counter:** Time Code
   - **Nudge Value:** One frame

To import the digital video:

1. Open the Workspace browser.

2. Click the **FIND** button (magnifying glass) to enter search mode.

3. Set the Kind field to Video File.

4. Enter the term **PTGA_Walkthrough_08** into the Name field.

5. Click the **SEARCH** button. The results will appear in the bottom half of the window.

6. Drag and drop the PTGA_Walkthrough_08 QuickTime movie file into the Edit window. The Video Import Options dialog box will appear.

7. Set the Destination to New Track.

8. Set the Location to Session Start.

9. Click the **OK** button. Pro Tools will automatically import the QuickTime movie and place it on a new movie track at the session start.

To conduct a spotting session:

1. If necessary, open the Video window by choosing **WINDOW > VIDEO** or pressing **COMMAND+9** (Mac) or **CTRL+9** (Windows) on the numeric keypad.

2. Resize the Video window by clicking and dragging on any of the window borders, or by right-clicking on the window itself and choosing a new size from the pop-up menu.

3. Open the Memory Locations window by choosing WINDOW > MEMORY LOCATIONS or pressing COMMAND+5 (Mac) or CTRL+5 (Windows) on the numeric keypad.

4. Play through the movie and look for any events or transitions that require sound design or editing. Mark the events by pressing the Enter key on the numeric keypad, or by clicking the ADD MARKER/MEMORY LOCATION button (+) at the start of the Marker Ruler. The New Memory Location dialog box will open.

5. In the New Memory Location dialog box, enter a description of the event in the Name field, set the Time Property to Marker, and click OK. A new memory location will appear in the Marker Ruler and in the Memory Locations window.

6. Play through the end of the movie and add markers as necessary. Suggested events to address include the following:

    ● Locations where the airship flies past the camera (try to find the peak of the flyby). Name this marker **Airship**.

    ● Location where narration should start. The narration will state, "I'd been lost for three days when I spotted an island in the distance" and should begin at the scene change where the camera cuts to the spaceship approaching over the Palm trees. Name this marker **Dialogue Start**.

    ● Scene transitions (for editing backgrounds). These are locations where you will want to add ocean, wind, water, and other ambience to set the atmosphere for the scene. A good place for ambience sounds is in the final section as the spaceship comes in for a landing over the mountains. Name these markers **Ambience1**, **Ambience2**, and so on.

    ● Locations where music should start or end. Use your own judgment to determine where music should play in the scene.

To create catalogs from existing folders:

1. Return to the Workspace browser.

2. Enter SEARCH mode.

3. Use the checkboxes to limit your search to the volume where your audio assets have been saved.

4. Set the Kind field to Folder.

5. Enter the term **PTGA_Walkthrough** into the Name field.

6. Click the **SEARCH** button. The folders containing audio file exports from the previous lessons will appear.

7. In the Workspace browser, click and drag each of your export folders onto the Catalogs icon. Pro Tools will automatically create a catalog for each of the folders.

Tip: **You may want to create a catalog from the BlastwaveFX folder as well.**

To import audio assets:

1. Using the Memory Locations window as your "to do" list, locate relevant files by searching and browsing in DigiBase. Be sure to use your newly created catalogs to quickly locate existing assets.

   Assets to import include the following:

   ● DIA_Player_07 audio file to use for beginning narration

   ● Airship sounds

   ● Ambience

   ● Music (search for "music" or "MX")

2. Once you've located a useful asset, import it to the Clip List.

Editing Cinematic Audio

You've already discussed many of the editing techniques that will be used for cinematic post-production editing. However, a couple of additional organizational features in Pro Tools can be extremely helpful when dealing with cinematics within a large session.

Showing and Hiding Tracks

When working with large numbers of tracks, it can be a bit overwhelming to keep a session organized. Showing and hiding tracks can reduce the number of visible tracks and make a large session more manageable.

To show or hide a track, do one of the following:

■ Click the **TRACK SHOW/HIDE** icon to the left of the track name in the Track list (see Figure 8.9).

■ Right-click the Track name in the Track list or in the Edit or Mix windows and select **HIDE** from the pop-up menu (see Figure 8.10).

Figure 8.9
The Track list

Figure 8.10
Select Hide from the
Track pop-up menu

To show all tracks:

■ Click the **TRACK LIST** menu and select **SHOW ALL TRACKS** (see Figure 8.11).

Figure 8.11
Select Show All Tracks from the Track list pop-up menu

To hide all tracks:

■ Click the **TRACK LIST** menu and select **HIDE ALL TRACKS**.

Deactivating Tracks

Another useful option when working with a large session is to deactivate tracks that you aren't currently using. When a track is inactive, all of the its plug-ins, sends, voices, and automation are disabled. This frees computer and DSP resources for other purposes.

Deactivated tracks can be made active again anytime you need to work with them. When a deactivated track is again made active, all of its settings are restored to their previous state (see Figure 8.12).

Tip: You can recognize an inactive track because its channel strip will appear grayed out.

To toggle a track inactive/active:

■ Control+Command-click (Mac) or Ctrl+Start-click (Windows) on the Track Type indicator in the Mix window (see Figure 8.13).

Figure 8.12
Active and inactive track

Figure 8.13
Track Type indicator

To make one or more tracks inactive or active, do one of the following:

■ Select the track(s) and choose **TRACK > MAKE INACTIVE/ACTIVE**.

■ Right-click the Track Name in the Track list or in the Mix or Edit window and choose **MAKE INACTIVE/ACTIVE** (see Figure 8.14).

Figure 8.14
Select Make Inactive from the Track pop-up menu

Editing with Playlists

When you create a new track in Pro Tools, it contains a single empty Edit playlist. As you edit clips on the track, you are actually adding them to this playlist. One of the most powerful editing features in Pro Tools is the ability to create multiple Edit playlists. Creating additional playlists allows you to experiment with different ideas, with the assurance that you can return to the original playlist at any time.

To select an edit playlist on a track:

- Click the **PLAYLIST SELECTOR** on the track and select the desired playlist from the pop-up menu (see Figure 8.15).

Figure 8.15
Playlist pop-up menu

To create a new empty edit playlist on a track:

- Click the **PLAYLIST SELECTOR** on the track and select **NEW**.

To duplicate the currently selected edit playlist on a track:

- Click the **PLAYLIST SELECTOR** on the track and select **DUPLICATE**.

Walkthrough: Editing Cinematic Audio

In this walkthrough you learn how to begin the post-production editing process.

To edit the dialogue:

1. Use the **SHOW/HIDE** controls to show only the DX_01 track.

2. Drag the **DIALOGUE** clip from the Clip List and drop it on the DX_01 track.

3. Recall the **DIALOGUE START** marker. Then Control-click (Mac) or Start-click (Windows) on the **DIALOGUE** clip with the Grabber tool to align the clip start with the marker location.

4. Nudge the clip to position it where you think it sounds best.

5. Using the Smart Tool, trim the dialogue and add fades.

To edit the sound effects:

1. Use the **SHOW/HIDE** controls to show only the FX_01 track.

2. Drag a spaceship flyby clip from the Clip List and drop it on the FX_01 track.

3. Add a sync point into the clip where the sound peaks, by pressing **COMMAND+,** (Mac) or **CTRL+,** (Windows).

4. Recall the airship marker that you positioned earlier. Then Control+Shift-click (Mac) or Start+Shift-click (Windows) on the clip to align the sync point of the clip to the marker location.

5. Create a new playlist on the track and repeat Steps 2-4 using a different spaceship flyby clip to create an alternate flyby.

6. Display **INSERTS F-J** using the Edit Window View selector.

7. Insert the **AIR FLANGER** plug-in on the last insert of the FX_01 track.

8. Select the **05 SOFT FLANGER** preset.

9. Enable **AUTOMATION** for the **MIX** parameter by holding **CONTROL+OPTION+COMMAND** (Mac) or **CTRL+START+ALT** (Windows) and clicking on the control in the plug-in window.

10. Return to the FX_01 track in the Edit window and change the Track view to display the **AIR FLANGER > MIX** parameter.

11. Use the **PENCIL** tool to draw some automation for the Mix parameter. Generally, you'll want to increase the Mix percentage as the sound trails off.

12. Audition the two playlists on the track and decide which one you like best.

To edit the backgrounds:

1. Use the **SHOW/HIDE** controls to show only the BG track.

2. Drag the **AMBIENCE BACKGROUND** element from the Clip List to the BG_01 track.

3. Using the ambience markers that you positioned earlier, use the Smart Tool to trim and fade the Ambience clip. Be sure to let it extend past the transition points by a few frames.

4. Repeat Steps 2 and 3 for the remaining backgrounds.

To edit the music:

1. Use the **SHOW/HIDE** controls to show only the MX_01 track.

2. Using the markers that you positioned earlier, drag an intro music clip to the MX_01 track.

3. Use the other music clips to create a score for the cinematic.

4. When you are finished, duplicate the EDIT playlist on the MX_01 track and create an alternate score.

Mixing Cinematic Audio

Because your previous lessons dealt primarily with individual sound elements, complex mixes were not required. However, when working with cinematics, multiple sound elements must be mixed into a single stereo mix.

Post-Production Signal Flow

One of the most important concepts in post-production mixing is signal flow. You might be familiar with a basic music mixing signal flow, which routes signals from audio tracks directly to a stereo bus or master fader. A post-production mixing signal flow is somewhat more complex because of something called stems.

Game audio borrows the term stem from the film-mixing world. A *stem* is simply a mix of sound elements from the same food group. Even in a simple post-production mix, the mixer is expected to deliver dialogue, music, and sound effects stems along with the final stereo or multichannel mix. The reason for this is that the stems can be repurposed to create alternate final mixes. For example, if the producer feels that the dialogue is mixed a little too loud, only the stems would be required to make a new mix with the dialogue level reduced. Neither the original sound elements nor the original Pro Tools session would be required to make such a change. In fact, this new mix could be created using video-editing software or a different digital audio workstation.

There is another reason why stems have become popular for cinematic post-production. In game audio, unlike film and television, the stems may actually be used for the final playback from the game software sound engine. Modern game consoles are so powerful that playing back three 5.1 stems (dialogue, music, and sound effects) requires very little of their available processing power. Another advantage to this approach is that the stem volume levels can be adjusted directly from the console.

I/O Setup

Before the correct bussing can be assigned in Pro Tools, the necessary busses must be created in the I/O setup. In this example, you have three stereo busses for summing dialogue, music, and effects tracks. Then you have three additional stereo busses for recording dialogue, music, and effects stems. The final bus is for the stereo mix stem (see Figure 8.16).

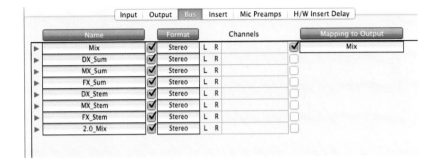

Figure 8.16
I/O Setup window showing the required busses

Track Setup

In Table 8.1, you can see the correct routing for the tracks. The audio track outputs are each assigned to the appropriate summing bus for their food group. These summing busses then feed a trio of Aux inputs. The outputs of the Aux inputs are assigned to the stem busses for their food group. The stem busses feed a trio of Audio tracks that will eventually record the stems. Finally, the outputs of the stem Audio tracks are assigned to the stereo mix bus. This final bus feeds an additional audio track, which will be used to record the stereo mix. Table 8.1 and Figure 8.17 help to explain the signal flow.

Table 8.1   Signal Flow

Track Type	Input Assignment	Output Assignment
Source tracks	N/A	Summing busses
Summing tracks	Summing busses	Stem busses
Stem tracks	Stem busses	Mix bus
Mix track	Mix bus	Hardware output

Note: The summing tracks are currently assigned to the hardware output for monitoring purposes. You won't be making the final Stem and Mix bus assignments until the "Mastering" section, later in this lesson.

Using Sends for Plug-In Processing

In previous lessons, you used AudioSuite and TDM/RTAS plug-ins to perform many different types of signal processing. For the most part, the plug-in was applied to a single clip or inserted directly onto a track containing sound elements.

Figure 8.17
I/O setup for the cinematic session

But, what if you want to apply a single effect to multiple tracks in the session? This is a common situation, especially with time-based effects like reverb and delay. However, inserting a reverb or delay onto each track in a large session is a guaranteed way to run out of processing power!

The solution is to insert the plug-in on an Aux input, and then use Sends to route tracks to the Aux. This way, any or all tracks can make use of the plug-in with virtually no increase in processing requirements.

To create a send to a new track for plug-in processing (Pro Tools 9.0 or later):

1. On an existing track, click the **SEND** selector and select **NEW TRACK** from the pop-up menu (see Figure 8.18).

Figure 8.18
Send Assign pop-up menu

2. In the resulting New Track dialog box, modify the settings to create a new aux input (see Figure 8.19).

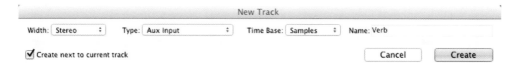

Figure 8.19
New Track dialog box resulting from Send assignment

3. Click **OK.** Pro Tools will automatically create a new aux input and new internal mix bus, and assign the bus as both the send output and the input to the new aux. In addition, both the aux input and bus will receive the name that was specified. (Reverb, Delay, and so on)

4. Assign a plug-in (such as D-Verb, shown in Figure 8.20) on an insert of the new aux input.

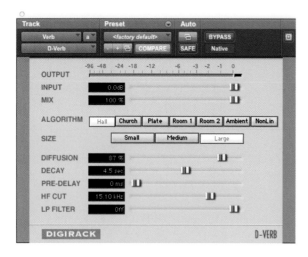

Figure 8.20
The D-Verb plug-in interface

5. Turn up the volume fader on the aux input. (Unity gain is a good starting point.)

6. Turn up the send level on the source track until you achieve the desired amount of reverb.

Basic Dynamic Automation

In Lesson 4, "Working with Sound Effects," and Lesson 7, "Working with Vehicle Sounds," you looked at creating basic plug-in and volume automation, respectively. These methods of automating parameters are also useful for cinematic mixing. However, dynamic volume and pan automation is probably the most important type of automation when mixing cinematics (or any large session).

Automation Modes

Pro Tools provides five basic modes of automation:

- **Off**—Automation cannot be played or recorded.

- **Read**—Automation is played but not recorded.

- **Touch**—Automation is recorded only when a control is being touched.

- **Latch**—Automation starts recording when a control is touched and continues recording until the transport is stopped.

- **Write**—Automation is recorded anytime the transport is in motion.

Using Touch Mode

For the purposes of this course, the previous simplistic explanations of each automation mode will suffice. Although each of the modes is important, you'll be focusing on the most useful mode when working without a control surface: Touch mode.

To record automation in Touch mode:

1. Open the Automation window by choosing **WINDOW > AUTOMATION** or pressing **COMMAND+4** (Mac) or **CTRL+4** (Windows) on the numeric keypad.

2. Verify that automation is *not* suspended and that all of the automation types are enabled. (The Suspend button should be gray and all of the automation enable buttons should be red, as shown in Figure 8.21.)

Figure 8.21
Automation window

3. Enable **TOUCH** mode by selecting Touch from the Automation Mode selector on the track (see Figure 8.22).

4. Begin playback. Move the volume and pan controls as needed. Pro Tools will automatically record all of the control adjustments.

5. When you're finished, stop playback. Pro Tools will add the automation data to the appropriate automation playlist.

Figure 8.22
Automation Mode buttons in the Mix and Edit windows, and the Automation Mode pop-up menu

6. You can then view and edit this automation by changing the Track view (see Figures 8.23 and 8.24).

Click this drop-down

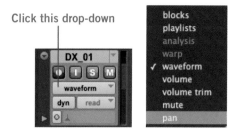

Figure 8.23
Track View button in the Edit window, and the Track View pop-up menu

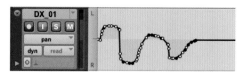

Figure 8.24
Viewing the Pan automation playlist

In the Avid Learning Series   For more information about automation, see "Basic Automation" in the "Pro Tools 101: An Introduction to Pro Tools 10" book by Avid.

Loudness Calibration

Calibrating your Pro Tools monitoring chain is an essential part of mixing game cinematics. While a complete explanation of calibration exceeds the scope of this course, a few basic concepts can get you started down the right path. Let's begin with a conceptual overview and some basic calibration terminology.

The purpose behind calibrating your Pro Tools system is to establish a known relationship between the loudness levels displayed in your Pro Tools meters and the loudness levels reaching your ears. Digital systems such as Pro Tools measure loudness in decibels (dB) relative to a maximum available peak level, or full scale. This measurement scale is referred to as "decibels relative to full scale," or dBFS. The maximum possible level in this scale (before clipping) is therefore 0dBFS, and peak measurements are shown as negative values below this maximum (for example, 6dBFS).

The perceived loudness of a signal reaching your ears can be measured using sound pressure level meters, or SPL meters, which apply weighting filters to approximate the sensitivities of the human ear to various frequency ranges. A commonly used weighting for audio reproduction and broadcast applications is C weighting. Loudness measurements made using this weighting are denoted as "decibels, C weighted," or dBC. These measurements are made relative to a 0dB reference level representing the threshold of human perception, and peak measurements are therefore shown as positive values above this minimum (for example, 85dBC).

When you calibrate your system, you establish a relationship between the dBFS levels shown in Pro Tools and the measured dBC levels that a listener (or game player) hears.

Reference Levels

If you are familiar with post-production work for film and television, you may be aware that film mixing typically uses 20dBFS = 85dBC SPL as a reference level for calibration, while TV mixing typically uses 20dBFS = 79dBC SPL. However, both of these reference levels are far too loud for mixing game cinematics! This is because with film and television mixes, average program levels usually fall somewhere between 20dBFS and 10dBFS, only occasionally exceeding 10dBFS. By contrast, game cinematic program levels can average well over 10dBFS for the duration of the cinematic.

Believe it or not, there is actually sound logic behind this increased volume level. The real issue here is that cinematic levels must compete with gameplay levels that are consistently above the 10dBFS threshold, and may even hover in the range of full scale (0dBFS). If the cinematic were mixed to film or television standards, players would experience a significant change in volume when transitioning from gameplay to cinematics and vice versa.

So what does all this mean? It means that ideal game cinematic mixes should range from 10dBFS to near full-scale levels (0dBFS). There is no standard reference level for game cinematic mixing. Some game cinematic mixers calibrate as low as 20dBFS = 65dBC SPL. The best strategy is to find a level that is comfortable for listening to during an all day mixing session. Then be sure to use that calibration reference for the duration of a project. And calibrate each day before you start mixing!

Simplified Calibration in Pro Tools

Before attempting to calibrate, you'll need some kind of basic SPL meter. One of the most popular is an inexpensive model from Radio Shack that costs about $50 USD (see Figure 8.25).

Figure 8.25
A basic SPL meter

Although not particularly accurate by ANSI standards, such a meter is certainly accurate enough to perform some basic calibration. Software options are also available for computers and smartphones. Whatever method you use, a couple of basic functions are required for the SPL meter or software:

- C weighting

- Slow response

To perform basic stereo loudness calibration in Pro Tools:

1. Open an existing session or create a new session in Pro Tools.

2. Create a stereo master fader. Assign the master fader to the interface output that connects to your studio speakers.

3. Insert a MULTI-MONO SIGNAL GENERATOR plug-in on the master fader (see Figure 8.26). (There is no multi-channel version of Signal Generator.)

Caution: The signal generator will begin generating a test tone right away so be
           sure your monitor levels are not too high!

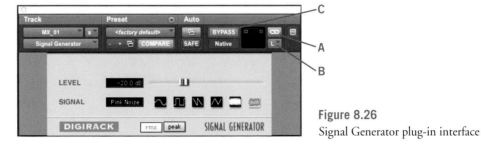

Figure 8.26
Signal Generator plug-in interface

4. Set the plug-in level to 20.0dB.

5. Set the Signal to Pink Noise (the right-most button).

6. Set the Signal type to RMS.

7. Unlink the left and right channels of the plug-in by clicking the MASTER
    LINK button (see Figure 8.26A).

8. Choose the left channel from the Channel Selector pop-up menu (see
    Figure 8.26B).

9. With the left channel selected, click the MASTER BYPASS button (see
    Figure 8.26C). This will only bypass the left channel of the plug-in; the
    right channel will continue to generate the test tone. You can now calibrate
    the level of your right speaker.

10. Set the SPL meter to C Weighting and Slow Response.

11. With the meter position at your listening position, adjust the monitor
    level of your right speaker until the meter reads 65dBC SPL.

12. When finished, click the BYPASS button again to un-bypass the left channel.

13. Repeat Steps 8-11 for the left channel/speaker by choosing the right channel
    from the Channel Selector pop-up menu instead.

Tip: When you finish calibrating, make the Signal Generator inactive and leave
       it inserted on the master fader. That way, you'll be able to quickly calibrate
       again upon returning to the session at a later date.

Multiple Monitoring Systems

Television and music mixers will almost always check their mixes on at least one
alternate pair of monitors. The primary idea here is to listen to the mix on a physically smaller speaker system that represents the typical consumer listening setup.

The same alternate monitoring technique can be quite helpful when mixing game cinematics. In game audio, you have two inexpensive options when it comes to alternate monitors: small multimedia speakers or television speakers.

Small multimedia speakers (such as those from M-Audio or Logitech seen in Figure 8.27) can be used with or without a subwoofer. You should definitely test both ways if you can. These speakers represent a typical computer based gaming system. Television speakers are a great choice and don't require any additional investment aside from some adapters to connect to your mixer or Pro Tools interface. These speakers represent a low-end console gaming system. If it sounds good on these, it should sound good on anything!

Figure 8.27
Small multimedia speakers from M-Audio

Either way, be sure to calibrate your alternate monitors so that you'll be mixing at consistent levels for the duration of any project.

Walkthrough: Mixing Cinematic Audio

In this walkthrough you learn how to perform post-production mixing. Before you write any automation, you'll want to create some reverb sends and get rough levels. Next you'll enhance the sound design with some additional automation. Then you'll polish the mix with adjustments to the summing busses.

To create a reverb send on the sound effects tracks:

1. Select the first FX_01 track.

2. Shift-click on the BG_01 track. All of the sound effects tracks (FX_01, FL_01, BG_01) should be selected.

3. Use the Edit window view selector to show Sends A-E.

4. Hold **Option+Shift** (Mac) or **Alt+Shift** (Windows) and click a **Send output** selector on any of the selected tracks. This will create the same Send assignment across all of the selected tracks.

5. In the resulting New Track dialog box, modify the settings to create a new stereo aux input and name it **Reverb**.

6. Click **OK.** Pro Tools will automatically create a new stereo aux input named **Reverb**, a new internal mix bus named **Reverb**, and assign the bus as both the send output and the input to the new aux.

7. Set the output assignment of the reverb aux input to FX_Sum bus.

8. Assign a **D-VERB** plug-in on an insert of the Reverb aux input.

9. Turn up the volume fader on the Reverb aux input to unity gain.

10. Raise the send levels on each track as needed to add reverb to the mix.

To create a rough mix:

1. Begin playback and listen to the current cinematic mix. There will be some obvious problems with volume levels.

2. With all of the tracks still in Read automation mode, adjust the volume and pan settings to get a basic mix. Do not adjust the levels on the summing tracks or the stem tracks.

To enable tracks to record dynamic automation:

1. Put the FX_01 track into Touch automation mode.

2. Put all of the Submix tracks (DX_Sum, MX_Sum, FX_Sum) into Touch mode as well.

To record volume and pan automation on the FX_01 track:

1. Play from the beginning of the session.

2. Record a gentle rise and fall in the volume of the FX_01 track as the airship approaches the screen and passes.

3. Continue to play the cinematic until you're happy with the volume automation.

4. Repeat Steps 1-3, but this time record a left to right sweep with the pan knob as the airship approaches and passes. Be careful not to touch the volume fader!

To record volume automation on the summing tracks:

1. Play from the beginning of the session.

2. Adjust the volume of the music and sound effects summing busses down so that the dialogue can be heard clearly, and then bring them back up after the dialogue finishes. If you're mixing with the mouse, you may need to make multiple passes.

3. Increase the volume of the sound effects summing bus (FX_Sub) after the music ends.

To automate the reverb send on the FX_01 track:

1. Click on the REVERB send on the FX_01 track to open the Send window.

2. Play from the beginning of the session.

3. Record a gentle rise in the send level as the airship flies away from the camera.

4. Continue to play the cinematic and adjust the automation until you're happy.

Mastering Cinematic Audio

When working with cinematics, mastering refers to creating the various stems and mixes that are needed before exporting. You'll be using an advanced variation on Bounce To Tracks to record your stems and stereo mix simultaneously. You won't be using an ultra-maximizer here because you want to preserve the full dynamic range of the mix.

Walkthrough: Mastering Cinematic Audio

In this walkthrough you learn how to record your stems and your final stereo mix.

To route the stem busses and print stems:

1. Switch the display to the Mix window by pressing **COMMAND+=** (Mac) or **CTRL+=** (Windows).

2. Set the output assignments for the following tracks as shown in Figure 8.28:
   - **DX_Sub track output:** DX_Stem
   - **MX_Sub track output:** MX_Stem
   - **FX_Sub track output:** FX_Stem
   - **DX_Stem, MX_Stem, and FX_Stem track outputs:** 2.0_Mix bus

Figure 8.28
Output assignments

3. Switch the display to the Edit window by pressing **COMMAND+=** (Mac) or **CTRL+=** (Windows).

4. Record-enable the DX_Stem, MX_Stem, FX_Stem, and 2.0_Mix tracks.

5. Enable **SLIP EDIT** mode.

6. Using the Smart Tool as the Grabber tool, select the QuickTime movie. This will ensure that your stem and final mix clips will exactly match the duration of the movie.

7. Press **RECORD** then **PLAY** in the Transport window or on the Edit window toolbar to begin recording. All of the stems as well as the stereo mix will be recorded simultaneously.

8. Listen to be sure that the mix sounds correct.

9. Disable recording on all of the tracks.

Walkthrough: Exporting Cinematic Mixes

Now that you've printed your stems and final mix, you're ready to export your clips. Normally, you would use a simple Export Clips as Files to export the clips to be implemented by a producer or programmer. Because you're handling the implementation yourself, however, you're going to use a hybrid approach. You'll use Export Clips as Files to create clips for the stems and final mix, but you're also going to use Bounce To QuickTime Movie to create a new movie with your mix embedded into the file. You'll use the new QuickTime movie for implementation in the Unity.

Note: Because Bounce To QuickTime Movie doesn't apply dither, you'll create a master fader and insert a dither plug-in before the bounce.

In this walkthrough you learn how to export the Cinematics to a QuickTime movie.

To export the stems and stereo mix:

1. Select all of the final bounced clips on the stem tracks or in the Clip List.

2. Select EXPORT CLIPS AS FILES from the Clip List pop-up menu, or press COMMAND+SHIFT+K (Mac) or CTRL+SHIFT+K (Windows). The Export Selected dialog box will appear.

3. Set the export settings as follows:
   - **File Type:** WAV
   - **Format:** Stereo
   - **Bit Depth:** 16-bit
   - **Sample Rate:** 48kHz

4. Create a folder named **PTGA_Walkthrough_08_MOV** to store all of the Lesson 8 clips.

5. Click EXPORT.

To bounce the stereo mix to a QuickTime movie:

1. Create a stereo master fader and verify that it is assigned to your stereo mix bus.

2. Insert a **POWr DITHER** plug-in on the last insert of the master fader. The default settings should be 16-bit and Type 1.

3. Select FILE > BOUNCE TO > QUICKTIME MOVIE. The Bounce dialog box will appear.

4. Set the bounce settings as follows:
   - **Bounce Source:** Mix (Stereo)
   - **File Type:** QuickTime
   - **Format:** Stereo Interleaved
   - **Bit Depth:** 16-bit

- **Sample Rate:** 48kHz
- **Conversion Options:** Convert After Bounce

5. Click the **Bounce** button. The Save dialog box will appear.

6. Name the bounced file **PTGA_Walkthrough_08_ST_MIX**.

7. Make sure that the destination is set to your PTGA_Walkthrough_08_MOV folder.

8. Click **Save** to bounce the clip to a new QuickTime movie.

Walkthrough: Implementing Cinematics

Now that you've bounced your mix to a QuickTime movie from Pro Tools, you're ready to implement the cinematic in Unity, which is what you'll do in this walkthrough.

Note: The free version of Unity does not permit importing of QuickTime movies. For this reason, a copy of the QuickTime movie has already been imported into the Unity project. You can simply import your stereo mix into Unity and synchronize it with the existing movie.

To prepare the Unity project:

1. Open the PTGA_Walkthroughs Unity project.

2. Select the Walkthrough_06 scene in the Project window.

3. Duplicate the file by choosing **Edit > Duplicate** or pressing **Command+D** (Mac) or **Ctrl+D** (Windows).

4. Rename the file **Walkthrough_08** and add your initials to the name of the duplicated scene.

5. Double-click the duplicated level to make it active.

To import the audio files:

1. Navigate to the folder where you bounced your cinematic.

2. Drag and drop the QuickTime movie onto the Unity Project window. Unity will automatically convert the QuickTime into separate video and audio assets.

Note: If you are using the free version of Unity, you will not be able to import the QuickTime movie. Import your stereo mix file instead.

To assign the cinematic files in the Inspector:

1. Click the **AUDIO_MANAGER** item in the Hierarchy window.

2. Assign the cinematic to a specific trigger in the Inspector window as follows:
   - **Cinematic Clip:** PTGA_Walkthrough_08
   - **Cinematic Audio:** PTGA_Walkthrough_08_ST_Mix

To test the cinematic:

1. Select **EDIT > PLAY** or press **COMMAND+P** (Mac) or **CTRL+P** (Windows) to launch the game. The cinematic will play automatically at the beginning of the level.

2. Press **COMMAND+P** (Mac) or **CTRL+P** (Windows) to exit the game.

Summary

In this lesson you learned how to work with cinematics. You should now understand:

- The sound design "food groups" and conducting a spotting session.

- Techniques for working with DigiBase catalogs and importing digital video.

- How to use Pro Tools features for editing, mixing, mastering, and exporting cinematic audio, including working with tracks, using I/O setup, using sends, and recording automation.

- How to implement cinematics in Unity.

Review/Discussion Questions

1. What are the three sound design "food groups?"
   (See "The Food Groups" on page 238.)

2. Which type of Memory Location is used when conducting a spotting session? (See "Conduct a Spotting Session" on page 244.)

3. How are DigiBase catalogs useful for cinematic sound design?
   (See "Using Catalogs in DigiBase" on page 241.)

4. Describe two methods that can be used to show or hide a track.
   (See "Showing and Hiding Tracks" on page 245.)

5. When might a new playlist be useful for cinematic sound editing?
   (See "Editing Cinematic Audio" on page 246.)

6. What type of track is used for summing in a post-production mixing workflow? What type is used to record stems? (See "Mixing Cinematic Audio" on page 251.)

7. Why is it important to calibrate your monitoring signal chain when mixing cinematics? (See "Mixing Cinematic Audio" on page 251.)

Adding Cinematics to the Game

In this exercise you learn how to bring all of the elements together to create audio for a cinematic.

Media Used:

Pro Tools: PTGA_Exercise_08
Unity: PTGA_Exercises

Duration:

60 Minutes

Acquiring Cinematic Elements

To get started, you need to import the digital video for the cinematic and conduct a spotting session. Then you will organize your existing sound assets into catalogs to aid in finding and importing useful elements.

Cinematic sounds needed:

- **Backgrounds:** Ocean
- **Sound effects:** Spaceship Flyby, Landing, and Power Down
- **Music:** New Loops or previously created cue sections
- **Foley:** Spaceship landing gear
- **Dialogue:** Previously created DIA_Player_05 audio file

Recommended search terms:

- **Backgrounds:** Ocean, Wind, Water
- **Sound effects:** Spaceship, Descend, Impact, Sci Fi
- **Foley:** Servo, Robot

Before beginning the sound acquisition process, you'll need to prepare the session:

1. Open the PTGA_Exercise_08.ptt session file.
2. Keep the default session settings.
3. Click **OK.**
4. Save a copy of the session with your initials added to the filename.
5. Prepare the session with the following settings:
   - **Edit Mode:** Slip
   - **Main Counter:** Time Code
   - **Nudge Value:** One frame

To import the digital video, follow these steps:

1. Open the Workspace browser.
2. Click the **FIND** button (magnifying glass) to enter search mode.
3. Set the Kind field to Video File.
4. Enter the term **PTGA_Exercise_08** into the Name field.
5. Click the **SEARCH** button. The results will appear in the bottom half of the window.

6. Drag and drop the PTGA_Exercise_08 QuickTime movie into the Edit window. The Video Import Options dialog box will appear.

7. Set the Destination to New Track.

8. Set the Location to Session Start.

9. Click the **OK** button. Pro Tools will automatically import the QuickTime movie and place it on a new movie track at the session start.

To conduct a spotting session, follow these steps:

1. If necessary, open the Video window by choosing **WINDOW > VIDEO** or pressing **COMMAND+9** (Mac) or **CTRL+9** (Windows) on the numeric keypad.

2. Resize the Video window by clicking and dragging on any of the window borders, or by right-clicking on the window itself and choosing a new size from the pop-up menu.

3. Open the Memory Locations window by choosing **WINDOW > MEMORY LOCATIONS** or pressing **COMMAND+5** (Mac) or **CTRL+5** (Windows) on the numeric keypad.

4. Play through the movie and look for any events or transitions that require sound design or editing. Mark the events by pressing the Enter key on the numeric keypad, or by clicking the **ADD MARKER/MEMORY LOCATION** button (+) at the start of the Marker Ruler. The New Memory Location dialog box will open.

5. In the New Memory Location dialog box, enter a description of the event in the Name field, set the **TIME** property to Marker, and click **OK**. A new memory location will appear in the Marker Ruler and in the Memory Locations window.

6. Play through the end of the movie and add markers as necessary. Be sure to address the following events:

   - Location where narration should start
   - Locations where the spaceship flies past the camera (try to find the peak of the flyby)
   - Scene transitions (for editing backgrounds)
   - Locations where music should start or end

To create catalogs from existing folders, follow these steps:

1. Return to the Workspace browser.

2. Click the **FIND** button (magnifying glass) to enter Search mode.

3. Set the Kind field to Folder.

4. Enter the term **PTGA_Exercise** into the Name field.

5. Click the **SEARCH** button. The folders containing audio file exports from the previous lessons will appear.

6. In the Workspace browser, click and drag each of the folders onto the Catalogs icon. Pro Tools will automatically create a catalog for each of the folders.

Tip: You may want to create a catalog from the BlastwaveFX folder as well.

To import audio assets, follow these steps:

1. Using the Memory Locations window as your "To Do" list, locate relevant files by searching and browsing in DigiBase. Be sure to use your newly created catalogs to quickly locate existing assets.

   Assets to import include the following:

   • DIA_Player_05 audio file to use for beginning narration
   • Spaceship sounds
   • Ambience
   • Music (search for music or MX)

2. Once you've located a useful asset, import it to the Clip List.

Editing Cinematic Audio

Once you've imported the digital video and sound assets, you can begin the post-production editing process.

To edit dialogue, follow these steps:

1. Use the **SHOW/HIDE** controls to show only the DX_01 track.

2. Drag the **DIALOGUE** clip from the Clip List and drop it on the DX_01 track.

3. Right-click the clip and select **SPOT**. Spot the start of the dialogue to 01:00:03:00.

4. Nudge the clip to position it where you think it sounds best.

5. Using the Smart Tool, trim the dialogue and add fades.

To edit Foley, follow these steps:

1. Use the **SHOW/HIDE** controls to show only the FL_01 track.

2. Drag the landing gear elements from the Clip List onto the FL_01 track.

3. Use **TAB TO TRANSIENTS** to locate the primary transient of each landing gear element, and then add a sync point at that location in the clip.

4. Using the markers that you positioned earlier, align the sync point of each landing gear element to a marker location.

To edit sound effects, follow these steps:

1. Use the **SHOW/HIDE** controls to show only the FX_01 track.

2. Drag your favorite spaceship flyby clip from the Clip List onto the FX_01 track.

3. Add a sync point into the clip where the sound peaks.

4. Using the Spaceship marker that you positioned earlier, align the **SYNC POINT** of the Spaceship clip to the marker location.

5. Insert an **AIR FLANGER** plug-in on the last insert of the FX_01 track.

6. Select the 05 Soft Flanger preset.

7. Enable automation for the **MIX** parameter by holding **CONTROL+OPTION+COMMAND** (Mac) or **CTRL+START+ALT** (Windows) and clicking on the control in the plug-in window.

8. Return to the FX_01 track in the Edit window and change the Track view to display the **AIR FLANGER > MIX** parameter.

9. Use the **PENCIL** tool to draw some automation for the **MIX** parameter. Generally, you'll want to increase the mix percentage as the sound trails off.

To edit backgrounds, follow these steps:

1. Use the **SHOW/HIDE** controls to show only the BG track.

2. Drag the **OCEAN BACKGROUND** element from the Clip List to the BG_01 track.

3. Using the scene transition markers that you positioned earlier, trim and fade the Ocean clip with the Smart Tool. Be sure to let it extend past the starting transition points by a few frames.

To edit music, follow these steps:

1. Use the **Show/Hide** controls to show only the music track, MX_01.

2. Using the markers that you positioned earlier, drag an intro music clip to the MX_01 track.

3. Use the other music clips to create a score for the cinematic.

Mixing Cinematic Audio

After completing the sound editorial process, you can start mixing. In this section, you will create a reverb send and return and mix your session using automation.

To create a reverb send on the sound effects tracks, follow these steps:

1. Select the first sound effects track (FL_01).

2. Shift-click on the last sound effects track (BG_01). All of the sound effects tracks (FL_01 FX_01, BG_01) should be selected.

3. Hold **Option+Shift** (Mac) or **Alt+Shift** (Windows) while assigning a reverb Send on any one of the sound effects tracks. This will create the same Send on all of the selected tracks.

To create a rough mix, follow these steps:

1. Begin playback and listen to the current cinematic mix. Note any problems with volume levels.

2. With all of the tracks still in Read Automation mode, adjust the volume and pan settings to get a basic mix. Do not adjust the levels on the summing tracks or the stem tracks.

To enable tracks to record dynamic automation, follow these steps:

1. Put the FX_01 track into Touch Automation mode.

2. Put all of the submix tracks (DX_Sub, MX_Sub, FX_Sub) into Touch Automation mode as well.

To record volume and pan automation on the FX_01 track, follow these steps:

1. Play from the beginning of the session.

2. Record a gentle rise and fall in the volume of the FX_01 track as the spaceship approaches the screen and passes.

3. Continue to play the cinematic until you're happy with the volume automation.

4. Repeat Steps 1-3, but this time, record a left-to-center sweep with the pan knob as the spaceship approaches and passes. Be careful not to touch the volume fader!

To automate the reverb send on the FX_01 track, follow these steps.

1. Click on the REVERB send on the FX_01 track to open the Send window.

2. Play from the beginning of the session.

3. Record a gentle rise in the Send level as the spaceship flies away from the camera.

4. Continue to play the cinematic and adjust the automation until you're happy.

To record volume automation on the summing tracks, follow these steps:

1. Play from the beginning of the session.

2. Adjust the volume of the music and sound effects summing busses down so that the dialogue can be heard clearly, and then bring them back up after the dialogue finishes. If you're mixing with the mouse, you may need to complete multiple passes.

3. Increase the volume of the sound effects summing bus after the music ends.

To check your mix, follow these steps:

1. If possible, listen to the mix through an alternate set of speakers (or headphones).

2. Adjust the mix as needed to ensure that it translates to the other monitoring system.

Post-Production Mastering

Now that you've created a mix, you need to record your stems and your final stereo mix.

To route the stem busses and print stems, follow these steps:

1. Set the following output assignments:
   - **DX_Sub track output:** DX_Stem
   - **MX_Sub track output:** MX_Stem
   - **FX_Sub track output:** FX_Stem
   - **DX_Stem, MX_Stem, and FX_Stem track outputs:** 2.0_Mix bus

2. Record-enable the DX_Stem, MX_Stem, FX_Stem, and 2.0_Mix tracks.

3. Enable SLIP EDIT mode.

4. Using the Smart Tool as the Grabber tool, select the QuickTime movie on the Video track. This will ensure that the stem and final mix clips you record exactly match the duration of the movie.

5. Press RECORD then PLAY in the Transport window or on the Edit Window toolbar to begin recording. All of the stems as well as the stereo mix will be recorded simultaneously.

6. Listen to be sure that the mix sounds correct.

7. When finished, disable recording on all of the tracks.

Exporting Cinematic Mixes

Next, you need to export the stem and final mix clips you recorded so that you can implement them into the game engine.

To export the stems and stereo mix, follow these steps:

1. Select all of the final bounced clips on the stem tracks or in the Clip List.

2. Select EXPORT CLIPS AS FILES from the Clip List pop-up menu, or press COMMAND+SHIFT+K (Mac) or CTRL+SHIFT+K (Windows). The Export Selected dialog box will appear.

3. Set the export settings as follows:

    *   **File Type:** WAV
    *   **Format:** Stereo
    *   **Bit Depth:** 16-bit
    *   **Sample Rate:** 48kHz

4. Click the CHOOSE button and create a folder named **PTGA_Exercise_08_ MOV** to store all of the Exercise 8 clips. Click CHOOSE again to select this folder.

5. Click the EXPORT button at the bottom of the Export Selected dialog box to complete the export.

To bounce the stereo mix to a QuickTime movie, follow these steps:

1. Create a stereo master fader.

2. Insert a POWR DITHER plug-in on the last insert of the Master fader. The default settings should be 16-bit and Type 1.

3. Select **FILE > BOUNCE TO > QUICKTIME MOVIE**. The Bounce dialog box will appear.

4. Set the bounce settings as follows:

   - **Bounce Source:** Mix (Stereo)
   - **File Type:** QuickTime
   - **Format:** Stereo Interleaved
   - **Bit Depth:** 16-bit
   - **Sample Rate:** 48kHz
   - **Conversion Options:** Convert After Bounce

5. Click **BOUNCE**. The Save dialog box will appear.

6. Name the bounced file **PTGA_Exercise_08_ST_MIX**.

7. Make sure that the destination is set to your PTGA_Exercise_08_MOV folder.

8. Click **SAVE** to bounce the clip to a new QuickTime movie.

Implementing Cinematics

After you've bounced your mix to a QuickTime Movie from Pro Tools, you're ready to implement the cinematic in Unity.

Note: The free version of Unity does not permit importing of QuickTime movies. For this reason, a copy of the QuickTime movie has already been imported into the Unity project. You can simply import your stereo mix into Unity and synchronize it with the existing movie.

To prepare the Unity project, follow these steps:

1. Open the PTGA_Exercises Unity project.

2. Select the Exercise_06 scene that you created in Exercise 6.

3. Duplicate the file by choosing **EDIT > DUPLICATE** or pressing **COMMAND+D** (Mac) or **CTRL+D** (Windows).

4. Name the duplicated scene **Exercise_08** and add your initials.

5. Double-click the duplicated level to make it active.

To import the movie file, or the stereo mix, follow these steps:

1. Navigate to the folder where you bounced your QuickTime movie.

2. Drag the folder onto the Unity Project window. The folder and all of its contents will automatically be imported into the project.

Note: If you are using the free version of Unity, you will not be able to import the QuickTime movie. Import your stereo mix file instead, following the same instructions described here.

To assign the audio files in the Inspector, follow these steps:

1. Click the **AUDIO_MANAGER** item in the Hierarchy window.

2. Assign the sounds to specific triggers in the Inspector window as follows:

   - **Intro Cinematic:** PTGA_Exercise_08_ST_MIX
   - **Intro Cinematic Clip:** PTGA_Exercise_08_ST_MIX

To test the cinematic, follow these steps:

1. Select **EDIT > PLAY** or press **COMMAND+P** (Mac) or **CTRL+P** (Windows) to launch the game. The cinematic will play automatically at the beginning of the level.

2. Press **COMMAND+P** (Mac) or **CTRL+P** (Windows) to exit the game.

INDEX

Avid Learning Series

License Agreement/Notice of Limited Warranty

By opening the sealed disc container in this book, you agree to the following terms and conditions. If, upon reading the following license agreement and notice of limited warranty, you cannot agree to the terms and conditions set forth, return the unused book with unopened disc to the place where you purchased it for a refund.

License:

The enclosed software is copyrighted by the copyright holder(s) indicated on the software disc. You are licensed to copy the software onto a single computer for use by a single user and to a backup disc. You may not reproduce, make copies, or distribute copies or rent or lease the software in whole or in part, except with written permission of the copyright holder(s). You may transfer the enclosed disc only together with this license, and only if you destroy all other copies of the software and the transferee agrees to the terms of the license. You may not decompile, reverse assemble, or reverse engineer the software.

Notice of Limited Warranty:

The enclosed disc is warranted by Course Technology to be free of physical defects in materials and workmanship for a period of sixty (60) days from end user's purchase of the book/disc combination. During the sixty-day term of the limited warranty, Course Technology will provide a replacement disc upon the return of a defective disc.

Limited Liability:

THE SOLE REMEDY FOR BREACH OF THIS LIMITED WARRANTY SHALL CONSIST ENTIRELY OF REPLACEMENT OF THE DEFECTIVE DISC. IN NO EVENT SHALL COURSE TECHNOLOGY OR THE AUTHOR BE LIABLE FOR ANY OTHER DAMAGES, INCLUDING LOSS OR CORRUPTION OF DATA, CHANGES IN THE FUNCTIONAL CHARACTERISTICS OF THE HARDWARE OR OPERATING SYSTEM, DELETERIOUS INTERACTION WITH OTHER SOFTWARE, OR ANY OTHER SPECIAL, INCIDENTAL, OR CONSEQUENTIAL DAMAGES THAT MAY ARISE, EVEN IF COURSE TECHNOLOGY AND/OR THE AUTHOR HAS PREVIOUSLY BEEN NOTIFIED THAT THE POSSIBILITY OF SUCH DAMAGES EXISTS.

Disclaimer of Warranties:

COURSE TECHNOLOGY AND THE AUTHOR SPECIFICALLY DISCLAIM ANY AND ALL OTHER WARRANTIES, EITHER EXPRESS OR IMPLIED, INCLUDING WARRANTIES OF MERCHANTABILITY, SUITABILITY TO A PARTICULAR TASK OR PURPOSE, OR FREEDOM FROM ERRORS. SOME STATES DO NOT ALLOW FOR EXCLUSION OF IMPLIED WARRANTIES OR LIMITATION OF INCIDENTAL OR CONSEQUENTIAL DAMAGES, SO THESE LIMITATIONS MIGHT NOT APPLY TO YOU.

Other:

This Agreement is governed by the laws of the State of Massachusetts without regard to choice of law principles. The United Convention of Contracts for the International Sale of Goods is specifically disclaimed. This Agreement constitutes the entire agreement between you and Course Technology regarding use of the software.